IN COMMEMORATION OF THE WORK OF
THE EIGHT THOUSAND YALE MEN
WHO TOOK PART IN THE WORLD WAR
1914-1918

HOW AMERICA WENT TO WAR

. .

THE GIANT HAND
THE ROAD TO FRANCE I.
THE ROAD TO FRANCE II.
THE ARMIES OF INDUSTRY I.
THE ARMIES OF INDUSTRY II.
DEMOBILIZATION

HOW AMERICA WENT TO WAR

AN ACCOUNT FROM OFFICIAL SOURCES OF THE NATION'S WAR ACTIVITIES 1917-1920

DEMOBILIZATION

OUR INDUSTRIAL AND MILITARY DEMOBILIZATION AFTER THE ARMISTICE
1918-1920

BY BENEDICT CROWELL
THE ASSISTANT SECRETARY OF WAR AND
DIRECTOR OF MUNITIONS 1917-1920

AND ROBERT FORREST WILSON
FORMERLY CAPTAIN, UNITED STATES ARMY

ILLUSTRATED WITH PHOTOGRAPHS FROM THE COLLECTIONS OF THE WAR AND NAVY DEPARTMENTS

NEW HAVEN
YALE UNIVERSITY PRESS
LONDON · HUMPHREY MILFORD · OXFORD UNIVERSITY PRESS
MDCCCCXXI

CONTENTS

ILLUSTRATIONS

ILLUSTRATIONS

ACKNOWLEDGMENT

The authors acknowledge their [illegible] to Major Robert H. Fletcher, Jr., General Staff, who [illegible] from the various war department bureaus [illegible] of the material on which this book is based. Also their thanks are due to the numerous former and present officials of the War Department and officers of the Army who read the manuscript and criticized it constructively.

B. C. & R. F. W.

Washington, D. C.,
[illegible]

ACKNOWLEDGMENT

THE authors acknowledge their indebtedness to Major Robert H. Fletcher, Jr., General Staff, who collected from the various war department bureaus concerned most of the material on which this book is based. Also their thanks are due to the numerous former and present officials of the War Department and officers of the Army who read the manuscript and criticized it constructively.

B. C. & R. F. W.

Washington, D. C.,
September, 1921.

ACKNOWLEDGMENT

The authors acknowledge their indebtedness to Major Robert H. Fletcher, Jr., General Staff, who collected from the various war department bureaus concerned most of the material on which this book is based. Also their thanks are due to the numerous former and present officials of the War Department and officers of the Army who read the manuscript and criticized it constructively.

B. C. R. F. W.

Washington, D. C.
September, 1921

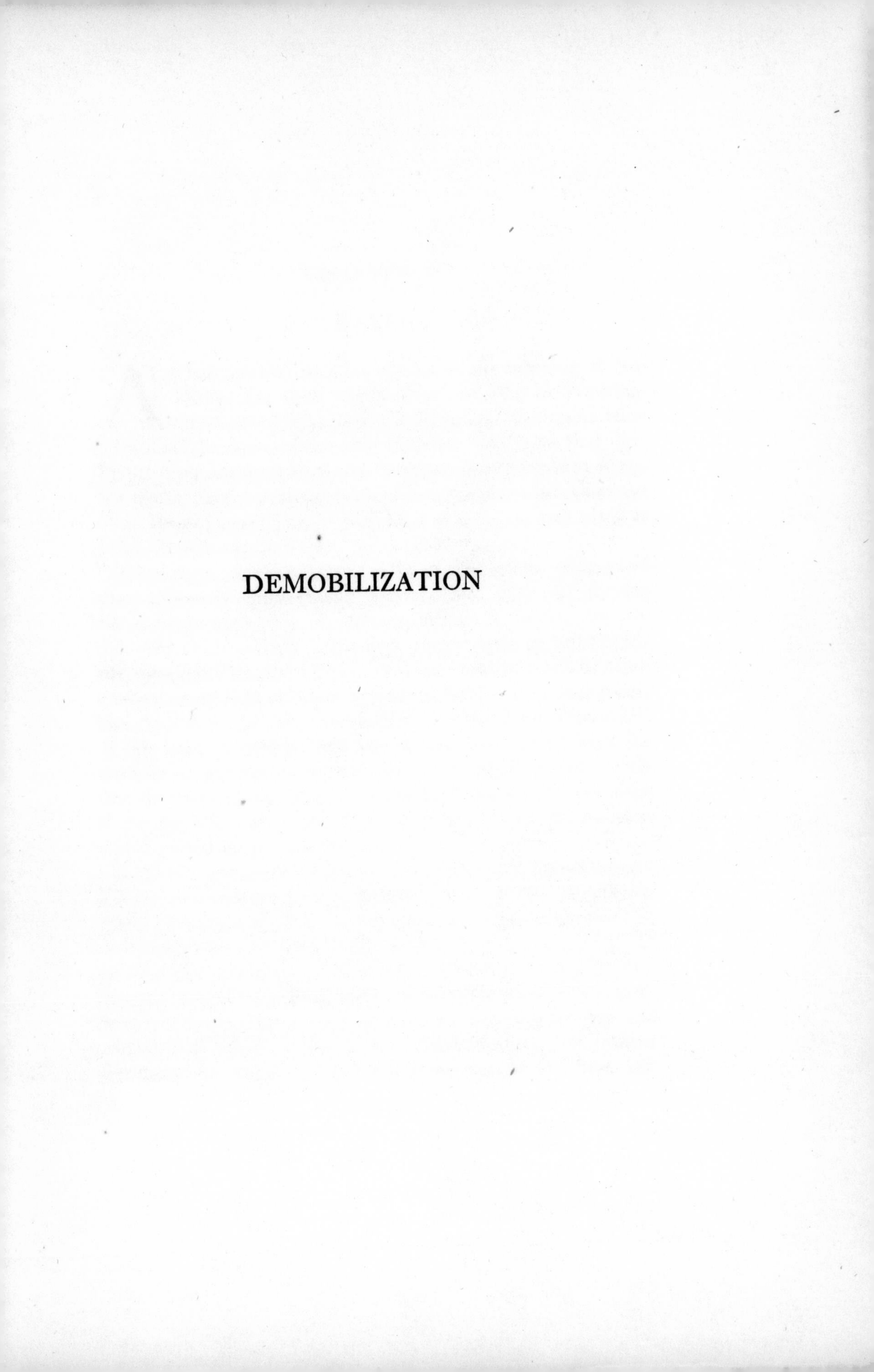

DEMOBILIZATION

CHAPTER I

HALT!

AT a few minutes past ten o'clock of the morning of November 11, 1918, the Secretary of War in Washington received from General Pershing a communication informing the Government that eleven o'clock a.m. that day, French time, an armistice with Germany had gone into effect. No message more momentous had ever come to the American War Department. The World War was at an end. It was peace. It was victory.

Over there on that American front which had penetrated the supposedly impregnable Argonne and now commanded the enemy's main line of communications at Sedan, boys in our own khaki wriggled, charged, fought, plunged ahead all the morning, like the players of some mighty football team gaining every inch of advance possible before an intermission; and finally, as the whistles shrilled and the great silence fell at last upon a theatre that had shaken and roared with the thunder of war for more than four years, they set their heels into the turf of a line that was to be held as a starting-off place if the armistice, too, should prove to be only an intermission and a period of recuperation.

Behind these outpost men were the American Expeditionary Forces, two million strong. Behind the A. E. F. in America was a training and maintenance army nearly as numerous.

Behind the uniformed and organized Army as it existed on the eleventh day of November was another force of a quarter of a million men, technically under arms. These were Selective Service men, drafted men, entraining that day and adding themselves to the human flood sweeping on toward Germany. In number this force alone was larger than any ever previously enrolled at one time in the American military service, except the forces called to the colors during the Civil War; yet so expanded had become our values that they attracted only passing attention in the midst of larger war activities. These inductives were one more increment—that was all.

And behind the Army itself were twenty-five million American men between the ages of eighteen and forty-five, registered, classified, and numbered in the order in which they too in turn should join the current that led, if necessary, to the supreme sacrifice.

The foundation on which rested this human edifice was industrial. Nothing less than the whole of America's material resources had been pledged to the end of victory. The whole of America's resources! How inadequately could pigmy man realize their might before he took them all and formed and molded them into one single-purpose machine! That machine was born in travail that broke men's bodies and reputations, that threw down the mighty from their seats and exalted those of low degree, that moved inexorably but surely. And when the machine was built it released forces terrifying even to men accustomed to administering the greatest of human activities, forces well-nigh ungovernable.

It took seven million workers, men and women, to operate the war industrial machine—seven million Americans delving in the earth for ores, chemicals, and fuels, felling the forests, quarrying the rocks, carrying the raw materials to the mills, tending the fires and the furnaces, operating the cranes, guiding the finishing machinery with a precision never before demanded, slaughtering the beeves, curing the meat, packing the vegetables, weaving the fabrics, fashioning the garments, transporting all, and accomplishing the million separate tasks necessary to the munitioning of the Army.

And as a background to all this, behind both the military and the industrial armies, was another force, perhaps the greatest force of all—the will of the people themselves, of one hundred million Americans who, without the coercion and duress of law and as a purely voluntary act, denied their appetites, their pleasures, and their vanities, contributed their utmost to the war finances, made war gardens to add to the food supply, produced millions of articles for the comfort of the soldiers both well and wounded, and in one way or another put forth effort that did not flag until victory came.

Such was America in a war that truly threatened her existence—America invincible.

The armistice put an end to all this enterprise and effort. It did more—the armistice was a command to the Government to scrap the war machine and restore its parts to the peaceful order in which they had been found. In military law, an armistice denotes the temporary cessation of hostilities; but the armistice of 1918 was a finality. Its terms destroyed the German military power. Those in authority, aware that the armistice was to be no period of waiting with collected forces for the outcome of negotiations, did not pause even to survey the magnitude of the thing they had built: they turned immediately to the task of dismantling it. Some of the processes of demobilization began before the guns ceased to fire. Five days before the armistice the A. E. F. canceled many of the foreign orders for important supplies. On November 1 we stopped sending combatant troops to France. In late October the Ordnance Department created an organization for demobilizing war industry.

However, before the machine could be knocked down and its parts distributed, it had to be stopped. There are two ways of stopping the limited express. One is to throw a switch ahead of it—effective, but disastrous to the train. The other way is to put on the brakes.

The war-industry machine had attained a momentum almost beyond mundane comparisons. Slow in gaining headway, like any other great mass, as thousands added their brains and their muscles to its progress it gathered speed until, at the first day of the armistice, it was nearing the point at which it could consume the material resources and turn them out as finished war products up to the capacity of American mechanical skill and machinery to handle them. It had not quite reached that point. Many of the vital but easily manufactured supplies had long since reached the pinnacles of their production curves, but some of the more difficult ones were not yet in full manufacture. On Armistice Day, however, the industry was not more than six months away from the planned limit of its fecundity.

For the administration of the industrial enterprise the task ahead was first to bring that momentum to a halt and then to break up the machine. The easiest way was to throw a switch ahead of it—in other words, to issue a blanket stop-order on all military manufacturing projects. But to have done that would have been to court consequences as disastrous as those of war itself. Business and industry would have fallen into chaos and the country would have been filled with jobless men. The other way, the way chosen, was to apply the brakes to the thousands of wheels.

The magnitude of the task ahead was appalling. The liquidation of the war industry was seen to be a matter as complex, as intricate, as full of the possibilities of error and failure as the mobilization itself. In only one respect did demobilization begin with an advantage: there was at hand an organization, the organization which had administered the creation of the Army and the manufacture of its supplies, ready to be turned into a wrecking crew.

Balanced against this situation was the countering fact that the men of this organization were war weary. Ahead of them were none of the conspicuous rewards that follow conspicuous war service. The nation does not award medals and other honors to those who restore the conditions of peace. The people themselves were satiated with war and desired nothing so much as a space in which they could forget battles and campaigns. At best, demobilization was to be a thankless job. Moreover, many of the executives, particularly those in the industrial organization, were men of large personal affairs, serving their country at a sacrifice. For the most part they were disheartened men, denied the satisfaction of seeing the full fruition of their plans have its effect against a hateful enemy.

Photo by Signal Corps

THE LAST SHOT

Photo by Signal Corps

THE ARMISTICE AT A MUNITIONS FACTORY

Photo by Howard E. Coffin

VICTORY
WAR TROPHIES IN PLACE DE LA CONCORDE, PARIS

Photo by Howard E. Coffin

RECONSTRUCTION
BRITISH SOLDIER'S GRAVE IN FIELD NEAR MEAUX

Every interest of personal gain called to them after the armistice to desert their official posts and return to the satisfactions of private endeavor, and only the righteous sense of their duty to the nation held them in the organization.

It was necessary for the organization not only to remain intact, but to speed the activities of demobilization as it had sped those of mobilization. The pre-armistice spirit had in some way to be maintained. On November 11 the war was costing the United States about $50,000,000 a day. Every day of indecision in adopting the plan of demobilization and every day's delay in carrying out the plan added tremendously to the burden of taxation that would rest upon the nation for generations to come.

Demobilization meant, first of all, the disbanding of the American Army. Whatever economic considerations might graduate the termination of war industry, no such considerations were to be permitted to retard the homeward progress of the troops. Four million American homes demanded their men at once; and whether the immediate return of the troops meant unemployment and distress or not, the Government was determined to comply with the demand.

The creation of the Army and its movement toward France had involved the rail transportation of about 8,000,000 soldiers in special cars and trains. The home movement would require an operation almost as great. Of the 2,000,000 men of the American Expeditionary Forces, more than half had crossed the ocean in foreign ships, all of which, of course, were withdrawn from our service immediately after the armistice. The unbroken eastward transatlantic procession of troopships had continued for about fourteen months. On the first day of the armistice the transatlantic ferrying capacity of the American-flag troopships was not much in excess of 100,000 men a month. Moreover, practically all our troop transports had reached the point of having to be laid up for reconditioning. Assuming, however, that they could be kept in continuous operation, they could not bring back to America more than two-thirds of the troops in the time it had taken the whole

A. E. F. to cross to France. Yet the problem of demobilization was to repatriate the A. E. F. in that time at most.

Demobilization involved a final cash settlement with every one of the four million men under arms; computations of back pay, complicated as they were with allotments and payments for government war bonds and the war risk insurance; and, finally, the payment to each soldier of the sixty-dollar bonus voted by the Congress. Demobilization also included the care of the wounded for many months after the fighting ceased, their physical and mental reconstruction, and their reëducation to enable them to take useful places in the world.

On the industrial side demobilization was the liquidation of a business whose commitments had reached the staggering total of $35,000,000,000. Demobilization meant taking practically the entire industrial structure of the United States, which had become one vast munitions plant, and converting it again into an instrumentality for producing the commodities of peaceful commerce. This without stopping an essential wheel, and also in the briefest possible time, for the world was in sore need of these products. Efficient demobilization, it follows, would permit the 7,000,000 industrial war workers to turn without a break in employment from the production of war supplies to that of peace supplies.

At the base of modern business stability lies the inviolability of contracts. He who breaches a contract must expect to pay indemnity, and the Government cannot except itself from this rule. Demobilization meant the suspension and termination of war contracts running into billions in value, many of them without a scrap of paper to show as a written instrument; it meant termination without laying the Government open to the payment of damages, and therefore it implied the honorable adjustment of the claims of the contractors.

One of the conditions on which complete demobilization depended was the adoption of a future military policy for the United States. But this was in the hands, not of the military organization, but of Congress. The whole program, therefore, could not be put through until Congress had acted. After the policy was defined, then it became the duty of the demobilization forces to choose and store safely the reserve equipment for the permanent establishment and for the field use of a possible future combatant force until another war industry could be brought into existence.

When that had been done there would remain a surplus of military property. It thereupon became the function of demobilization to dispose of this property through a sales organization that would have in its stocks goods of a greater variety and value than those at the disposal of any private sales agency in the United States. This branch of the work also included the sale of great quantities of A. E. F. supplies in Europe, which was already glutted with the surpluses of its own armies. The sales at home must include the sale of hundreds of buildings put up for the war establishment.

Paradoxically, demobilization included the acquirement of large quantities of real estate—for the storage of reserve supplies and the creation of a physical plant for the permanent military establishment.

Finally, demobilization meant the delicate business of striking a cash balance that would terminate our relations with the Allies, meeting their claims against us for the supply of materials and for the use and destruction of private property abroad, and pressing our own claims against them for materials sold to them.

The astonishing thing was the swiftness with which this great program was carried through. Within a year after the last gun was fired America had returned to the normal. The whole A. E. F. had been brought back in American vessels in ten months. In that time practically the entire Army had been paid off, disbanded, and transported to its homes. War businesses were braked to a standstill in an average time of three months, without a single industrial disturbance of any consequence. At the end of the year the greater part of the manufacturers' claims had been satisfied with compromises fair both to the contractors and to the Government. The savings in contract terminations and adjustments had run into billions of dollars. A blanket settlement had been made with the Allies, thus virtually closing up our business in Europe. A permanent military policy had been written into law. The storage buildings and spaces were filled with reserve materials inventoried, catalogued, and protected against deterioration. Packed away compactly were the tools and machinery of an embryonic war industry ready to be expanded at will in the event of another war. Materials, largely of special war value and therefore normally to be regarded as scrap and junk, had been sold to the tune of billions, the exercise of ingenuity in the sales department producing a recovery that was remarkably large, averaging 64 per cent of the war cost.

Such was our war demobilization. No other single business enterprise in all human history compared with it in magnitude; yet, in the midst of the peace negotiations and amid the economic crises fretting the earth, it attracted scant notice. To-day, only the continuing sale of surplus war materials and the adjudication of the last and most difficult of the industrial claims give evidence of the enterprise which engaged the efforts of the whole nation so short a time ago.

CHAPTER II

THE A. E. F. EMBARKS

THE American Expeditionary Forces, on November 11, 1918, were ill prepared to conduct the manifold activities leading to their demobilization. Up to that day the expedition had been too busy going ahead to think much about how it was to get home. But now had come the armistice, the end. The great adventure was over. The *guerre* was *fini*.

At once a great wave of homesickness spread over the A. E. F. That song of careless valor, "Where do we go from here?" to the swinging beat of which a million men had marched forward over the French roads, became a querulous "When do we go home?" When indeed? It had taken nearly a year and a half to transport the A. E. F. to France. Disregarding the fact that the Army overseas had at its disposal less than half as many troopships as had supported it up to November 11, before the men could start home in great numbers there had first to be created in France an embarkation system with a capacious equipment of camps and port buildings, if the expedition were to return in good order and not as a disorganized mob.

Never was a daily journal scanned with such emotion as was the *Stars and Stripes* by its readers during this period of waiting. The *Stars and Stripes* was the official newspaper of the enlisted men of the A. E. F. After the armistice anything pertaining to the return of the troops to America was the most important news which the publication could possibly print. The *Stars and Stripes* published the monthly schedules of transport sailings, told of the extraordinary expansion of the

Yankee transport fleet, noted the continual improvement in the shipping efficiency of that fleet, rejoiced in black-face type when some ocean flyer broke the record for the turn-around, as the round trip to America and back was called, and in general kept the *personnel* of the expedition informed of the movement homeward. But, although the return of the A. E. F. was a transportation feat actually more astonishing than that which had placed the forces in Europe, yet to the hundreds of thousands of homesick boys who watched the brown fields of France turn green in the spring of 1919, the pace of the snail and the turtle seemed speed itself in comparison to the progress made by the demobilization machine.

The A. E. F. in November, 1918, possessed no port equipment capable of quick conversion into a plant for embarking the expedition. There had been no need of large port installations in France for the use of debarking troops. The A. E. F. had crossed to France under a scheme of identification that was a marvel of system and organization. Once the system was perfected, every military unit bore as part of its name a so-called item number that told the debarkation officers (by reference to the shipping schedules) exactly where each unit should go upon arrival. So it was with individuals and small detachments traveling as casuals. Their item numbers placed them instantly in the great structure of the A. E. F. No need for vast port rest camps in which thousands must wait until G. H. Q. disposed of them. They were placed before they sailed from America. Expense and confusion saved by the art of management!

The armistice changed all about. Our military ports in France had to become ports for the embarkation of troops with an equipment vastly expanded. America had sent to France an Army perfectly clothed and accoutered. For the sake of uniformity the home ports of embarkation had prepared the 2,000,000 troops for the voyage, and this meant issuing smaller or larger quantities of clothing and other personal articles to practically every man who sailed. The A. E. F. proposed to return its men to their homes well dressed, clean, and self-respecting, and it was logical, too, to accomplish this purpose in France in the process of embarking the troops. To carry out the plan, however, required an extensive plant, something not to be materialized by a wave of the hand. France after the armistice was to witness an extensive military construction carried on by the Americans at their ports.

Brest, Bordeaux, and St. Nazaire had been the three principal landing places for our troops sent to France directly from the United States. Brest, near the northeasternmost extremity of France, possessed a harbor with water that could accommodate the largest ships afloat, but the water near shore was too shallow for docks at which large ships could berth. Consequently the troops rode in lighters between ships and shore. This was Brest's chief disadvantage as a military port, but it was not a serious disadvantage.

Next southward came St. Nazaire, on the Loire River a few miles inland. The first of the expeditionary troops landed at St. Nazaire, in July, 1917. The port boasted of docks with berths for troopships, but the waters of the river were too shallow for the largest transports.

Still farther south was Bordeaux, fifty-two miles from the ocean on the Gironde River. What few troops landed at Bordeaux were incidental, for the port construction at Bordeaux and other great developments at Bassens and Pauillac nearer the mouth of the river were conducted by the A. E. F. with the view of making the Gironde the chief ocean terminal for the reception of army supplies shipped from the United States. Troopships could tie up to the docks at Bordeaux, but the Gironde was so narrow and its tidal currents were so swift that the military administration of the port had to manage the stream on a schedule as it might operate a single-track railroad. There were several places in the river where vessels could not pass each other.

After November 11 followed a few days of indecision and bewilderment in the A. E. F. No one in Europe knew precisely what the armistice meant or what the victorious armies could expect. Quickly, however, it transpired that the armistice was permanent; it was peace itself for all practical purposes, and the only forces we should need to maintain in France would be those chosen to conduct the measured advance into Germany and to garrison the occupied territory. Within a week General Pershing designated the troops for the Army of Occupation and released the rest of the American Expeditionary Forces (more than half its total numerical strength) for return to the United States as soon as transportation facilities were available. He charged the Chief Quartermaster of the expedition with the duty of embarking the returning forces.*

The Chief Quartermaster of the A. E. F. at once designated Brest, St. Nazaire, and Bordeaux as the ports of embarkation. The early plan was to send 20 per cent of the expedition home *via* Bordeaux and the rest in equal numbers through St. Nazaire and Brest. As it worked out, practically all the overseas soldiers returned through these three ports, although a few sailed from Marseilles, Le Havre, and La Pallice. The division of work, however, did not materialize as planned. Bordeaux handled less than its fifth of the forces, and the embarkations at St. Nazaire were not much larger than those at Bordeaux. The great mass of the A. E. F. came back *via* Brest, and at Brest was set up the largest installation for the embarkation of passengers the world had ever seen.

The troops of the A. E. F. were of two general sorts—those of the line organized by divisions, corps, and armies, also known as combat troops, and those of supply, who conducted the thousand and one enterprises necessary to the maintenance of a force as large as the A. E. F. three thousand miles away from home. The two sorts of troops were not evenly balanced in number, the combat troops being considerably the more

* In this the system differed from that in use in the United States. Not the Quartermaster Corps but the Embarkation Service in the United States prepared the overseas troops for the voyage and embarked them on the transports. The Embarkation Service also operated many of the transports. After the armistice the Embarkation Service, now merged into the Transportation Service, continued to manage the Army's ocean shipping facilities, and it also attended to the details of debarking troops at the ports in this country; but its jurisdiction over those troops began only after they had boarded the ships in France.

Photo by Signal Corps

CAMP STREET IN LE MANS AREA

Photo by Signal Corps

BATH HOUSE AT BREST

Photo by Howard E. Coffin

IN CAMP PONTANEZEN

Photo by Signal Corps

COMPANY STREET IN PONTANEZEN

numerous. It was evident that their embarkation offered separate problems.

With the combat troops mass travel could be conducted at its greatest efficiency. The divisional troops were homogeneous, their transportation needs were essentially alike, and a single order could control the movements of tens of thousands of them at once. The supply troops, on the other hand, were heterogeneous. They were organized in thousands of units of varying sizes and kinds. Many of them, particularly officers, were serving in the organization as individuals attached to no particular units. The travel problems of these various elements differed widely. Therefore it was decided to handle the embarkation of divisional troops and supply troops separately. The general demobilization plan adopted about the middle of December, 1918, provided for the establishment of a great embarkation center for the divisional troops—an area which should be convenient to all three ports of embarkation, in which area the combat troops in their large units could be prepared for the overseas voyage, and from which they could go directly to the ships without pausing in the embarkation cities. The installations at the ports themselves were to be used especially in the embarkation of supply troops.

At Le Mans, a spot about midway between Paris and the Biscay coast, the A. E. F. possessed a plant that might be expanded quickly to serve as the divisional embarkation center. When the great flood of American troops began debouching upon French soil in the early summer of 1918 it became evident to the command of the expedition that it needed an area in which the incoming divisions might assemble as their units debarked from the transports and where they might rest while their ranks were being built up to prescribed strength by the addition of replacements. By this time, too, the system of supplying replacement troops to the A. E. F. had become automatic. The replacements were the only American soldiers who crossed to France without definite objective. They were to be used in France as the A. E. F. needed them to fill up its divisional ranks. It was necessary, therefore, to provide a reservoir upon which the depleted combat divisions could draw for replacements. Le Mans was selected as the site of this reservoir and also as the assembling point for the debarking organized divisions. The Le Mans area before the armistice was known as the A. E. F.'s classification and replacement camp.

The reasons which brought about the selection of Le Mans as the site for the replacement and divisional depot served also to make the place the ideal location for the expedition's embarkation center. Le Mans was at the junction of trunk-line railroads leading to Brest, St. Nazaire, and Bordeaux. It also possessed good railroad connections with Paris and with the front, which in the summer of 1918 had been advanced by the Germans until it was close to the metropolitan limits of Paris and was therefore not far from Le Mans. The depot was established in July, 1918, when the Eighty-third Division occupied the area as its depot division. At that time the depot as projected contemplated the construction of eight divisional camps, each to accommodate 26,000 men, and two forwarding camps, one with accommodations for 25,000 men and the other for 15,000. In other words, the camp eventually was to accommodate a quarter of a million troops. No military center in the United States compared in size with this project.

At the time of the armistice the development of Le Mans had made good progress. It could then maintain about 120,000 troops. On December 14, when Le Mans was officially designated as the embarkation center, its capacity had been increased to 200,000. Shortly after the armistice began, its transient population jumped to 100,000, and it never fell below this mark until the late spring of 1919, when the greater part of the combat divisions of the A. E. F. had embarked for the United States.

The Le Mans center had the duty of completely preparing for embarkation all troops received in the area. Theoretically every man who passed through Le Mans was prepared to go directly to a transport. This meant bathing and delousing for every man who came to the camp, inspecting his equipment and supplying new clothing and other personal articles if he needed them, and perfecting his service records so that he might encounter no difficulty in securing his final pay and discharge in the United States. To do this important work quickly and well, it was necessary to operate an institution of impressive size.

The dimensions of the whole camp were tremendous. There was nothing like it in the United States. A man could walk briskly for an hour in a single direction at Le Mans and see nothing but tents, barracks, drill fields, and troops lined up for preliminary or final inspections. The task of feeding this city full of guests was so great that the camp administration found it economical to build a narrow-gauge railroad system connecting the kitchens with the warehouses. Food moved up to the camp cookstoves by the trainload, and the same locomotives that brought the supplies hauled away the refuse. A whole adjacent forest was cut down to supply firewood. When the Americans occupied the section there were no adequate switching facilities, nor were there storage accommodations. The Quartermaster Corps, which operated the storage project, cleared a field in the midst of a wood and used the clearing for an open storage space (the surrounding trees giving a degree of shelter), connecting the place with the railroad by constructing a spur track. Thereafter, even after great warehouses had been built in the clearing and it had become the supply depot for the entire camp, requiring the services of 6,000 troops in its operation, the place was known to the camp as "The Spur." As an addition to this storage, smaller covered warehouses were provided at all the divisional sub-depots. At one time the corrals of the camp contained 10,000 horses and mules. In one week in February, 1919, nearly 32,000 troops arrived in camp, a fact indicating the rate at which troops passed through to embarkation. The Quartermaster Corps opened two great central commissaries that were in effect department stores. The camp operated a large laundry, a shoe repair shop, a clothing repair shop, and numerous other industrial plants.

The equipment installed at Le Mans was duplicated in smaller scale at the three embarkation ports. Yet even these port installations could not be called small. Camp Pontanezen at Brest could give accommodations to 80,000 men at once. The largest embarkation camps in the United States were smaller than this. There were thirteen smaller camps and military posts at Brest. The two embarkation camps at Bordeaux could house 22,000 men, but there were billeting accommodations in the district for thousands of others. The construction at St. Nazaire was considerably larger than that at Bordeaux, but not so extensive as that at Brest.

Most of these camps were built after the armistice, and the engineer constructors and the embarking troops elbowed each other as embarkation and construction proceeded simultaneously. Some of the camps had served as rest camps prior to the armistice, but these had to be greatly enlarged and improved in equipment before they could give adequate service as embarkation camps. The weather along the northwestern coast of France is intensely uncomfortable and disagreeable to Americans. In the winter and spring especially, the rains and mists are almost incessant. It was not always possible to choose ideal sites for the embarkation camps in France. The sites had to be near the ports, and in the thickly inhabited countryside the American authorities were forced to accept whatsoever areas they could get, without being too insistent upon such fine points as natural drainage and pleasant surroundings.

This statement is particularly applicable to Pontanezen, which was pitched on high but poorly drained ground. Ordinarily the Army would not have occupied such a location without first making permanent improvements. The continual rains, the lack of strong drainage, and the heavy traffic of men, animals, and trucks combined to make the Pontanezen site in 1919 a morass of quaking mud. Only the strongest of emergencies justified its use. Because of the daily cost of maintaining the A. E. F. and because the expeditionary soldiers themselves wished to return home as soon as possible, regardless of the conditions of their travel, it was decided to make use of these port camps even while they were being constructed, instead of holding up the whole movement until the camp arrangements could be made perfect.

Tales of suffering among our soldiers at Pontanezen came to the United States and were even aired on the floors of Congress, but the suffering alleged was more apparent than real. Those who went through the experience of residence in Pontanezen, even at its worst, were not injured in health. Despite appearances, the camp's sanitary arrangements were of high merit. The medical records of Camp Pontanezen show that its sickness and death rates, leaving the domestic epidemic of influenza altogether out of the comparison, were as low as those of the best camps in the United States.

In the spring of 1919 most of the construction work at the embarkation camps was complete, and they became more comfortable. The camps consisted of miles of one-story, tar-papered, rough-board buildings connected with wooden sidewalks of duck-boards. Pontanezen was a complete American city set down amid the quaint roads of old Brittany. It had newspapers, banks, theatres, stores, public libraries, restaurants, hospitals, churches, telephones, and electric lights, and even a narrow-gauge railway for freighting about its supplies. The entire American military population in the camps at Brest quite outnumbered the French inhabitants of the region. The water system installed by the Engineers to serve all the American establishments at the port was sufficient for the city of 150,000 people. There was a special camp for casual officers. A section of this camp was set aside for the French, English, Belgian, and Italian wives that American soldiers had married abroad. There was a hospital camp, a camp for the white troops on permanent duty at the port, and another for colored troops so assigned. There were numerous small camps for labor battalions, and a special camp for engineer and motor transport organizations. Not far away was a large German prison camp.

In one important respect embarkation in France differed from what it had been in the United States. It was extremely necessary to rid the home-coming troops of body vermin before placing them on the ships. The delousing process at our French ports of embarkation was the most thorough experienced by the doughboy during his foreign service, and this process chiefly distinguished embarkation abroad from that which the soldier had known at Hoboken and Newport News.

Our forebears shared none of the modern aversion to discussion of the louse. One of the great monarchs of France set the stamp of his royal approval upon scratching publicly when one itched, and Robert Burns once addressed a poem to a louse. The louse, however, cannot survive American habits of personal cleanliness; and, justly enough, the insect has become associated with filth and has dropped out of polite conversation. The war revived the fame of this parasite. An inspection at one time revealed the fact that 90 per cent of the American troops at the front were infested. These men naturally wrote home about it, and then the louse, euphemized as "cootie," became a national figure.

There was a serious aspect to the situation, however, that the military authorities could not overlook. Besides being a source of discomfort, the louse is the sole carrier of one of the most dread diseases that afflict mankind—typhus fever. In bygone times typhus was known variously as army fever, camp fever, or jail fever. It was particularly prevalent in this country at the time of the Revolution, and it existed to some extent here during the Civil War—an indication of what must have been the condition of individual American soldiers in those days. Typhus exists to-day practically as an endemic on the central plateau of Mexico, the range of the disease touching the border of the United States. The disease cannot invade this country, however, because of the lack of carriers. But if the A. E. F. had returned to the United States with its 2,000,000 men lice-infested, the demobilized soldiers might have distributed typhus carriers from one end of the country to the other and exposed the nation to a terrible menace.

The sanitary regulations of the A. E. F. kept typhus away from the troops by controlling the lice. The Quartermaster

Corps operated a number of mobile delousing plants just behind the front lines and in the billeting areas to the rear. It is interesting to note that these plants had to be camouflaged because the airmen of the enemy sometimes mistook them for batteries of artillery and directed gunfire upon them. As these plants increased in number and efficiency they reduced the lousiness of the combat troops to a scant 3 per cent.

As long as our troops remained in France largely billeted on the French population, it was unlikely that the field sanitary measures could extinguish the louse altogether; but the command of the expedition determined that at the ports of embarkation the American doughboy should bid good-bye to *P. vestimenti* forever. The importance of completely delousing the troops was emphasized in the same G. H. Q. memorandum that had set up the embarkation system.

In pursuance of this policy every embarkation camp in France was established in two isolated sections. One section was known as the "dirty" camp and the other as the "clean" camp. Upon arrival from the front the troops first took quarters in the "dirty" camp. Between the two sections lay the buildings in which the camp administration conducted all the various processes of preparing soldiers for embarkation for the United States. One of the most important of these activities was bathing and delousing the troops. As far as scientific measures could prevent it, not a louse was permitted to cross from the "dirty" camp to the "clean" camp. The measures were highly effective. Only a few men were found to be infested upon arrival in America. For these there were final delousing facilities at all our debarkation camps. When the overseas veterans took trains for home at the Atlantic ports they were completely verminless. The medical officers at the demobilization centers in this country failed to discover a single exception.

The embarkation plant at Bordeaux was known to returning soldiers as "The Mill." Its processes were typical of those at all the embarkation camps in France. The Bordeaux mill ground swiftly, yet ground exceeding fine. To it came the raw material—dirty, ragged, weary humanity. It reached out for this material, whirled it into its machinery, and a little while later delivered from the other end its finished product—clean, well-clothed, deloused, and comfortable American soldiers, their service records compiled up to the minute, American money in their pockets, and a mighty self-respect swelling their chests.

To France America sent the best clothed and best equipped army that had ever stepped on European soil. The two million men arrived in France outfitted almost completely in new clothing and equipment which they had received in the American embarkation camps just before they boarded the transports. In 1919 we brought home the first American army that had ever fought in a great war and returned in anything but rags. By special act Congress gave permission to each discharged soldier to keep his uniform and certain other equipment when he returned to civilian life. Even though, for most of the men coming up into the embarkation ports in France, their final discharge was only a few weeks away, nevertheless the military organization there saw to it that every man was decently clad before he began the return voyage, and this often meant the issue of entirely new articles. The Quartermaster Corps abroad wanted to win from the folks at home the verdict, when they had looked over their restored boys—"Guess they took pretty good care of you over there, after all."

The "mill" at Bordeaux was housed in a long, low hut with separate departments for the chief operations necessary to the preparation of troops for embarkation, the steps being arranged progressively. At the entrance end were the executive offices. Here the soldier, as he passed through, received his service records, withdrawn from his company's files, and also a Red Cross bag in which to carry his personal trinkets and his record cards and papers on the journey through the "mill." Next he came to the records inspection section, where officers perfected the entries in his record. Here he also received a copy of the orders under which his unit was traveling, his pay card, and a card known as the individual equipment record. On the equipment card appeared the printed names of all articles which a completely outfitted American soldier should wear or carry wherever he went. Next the soldier stood before an inspector who examined the worn equipment, noted wherein it was incomplete, labeled any damaged or worn-out articles for discard and salvage, and checked on the equipment card such new articles as should be issued to the soldier later on. The standard equipment of each returning soldier was as follows:

1 Barrack Bag	1 Comb
2 Undershirts	1 Piece of Shaving Soap
2 Pairs of Drawers	1 Towel
2 Pairs of Socks	1 Cake of Soap
1 Pair of O. D. Gloves	2 Identification Tags
2 O. D. Shirts	1 Belt
1 Pair of Shoes	1 Razor
1 Pair of Laces	1 Ammunition Belt
1 Pair of Breeches	1 Pack Carrier
1 O. D. Coat	1 Haversack
1 Overseas Cap	1 Canteen
1 Pair of Leggins	1 Canteen Cover
1 Chevron (for noncommissioned officers)	1 Condiment Can
	1 Meat Can
1 Shelter Half	1 Cup
3 Blankets	1 Knife
1 Overcoat	1 Fork
1 Slicker	1 Spoon
1 Shaving Brush	1 First Aid Pouch
1 Toothbrush	1 First Aid Packet
1 Tube Tooth Paste	

The soldier next went to the disrobing room, where he divested himself of all clothing except his shoes, which he was to carry through with him. The cootie would not cling to leather. Then he passed on to a medical examination for infectious disease. If he passed this safely, he proceeded to the bathing department, where, under the watchful eyes of a sergeant, he soaped and scrubbed himself thoroughly, first in a hot shower bath and then in a cold one. Experience had taught that the greatest enemy of the louse was plain soap and water and plenty of it. Meanwhile certain of his discarded garments, if they were in good condition or if they could be repaired for future wear, had been sent from the disrobing room to the steam sterilizer in another part of the building. The sterilization process took thirty minutes, which was just about the time it took the soldier to go through the "mill."

Scrubbed and clean, the soldier went from the bath into another room where doctors examined him for diseases of the throat, lungs, and skin. After that, the barber shop and a hair cut. The barber shop at the "mill" was equipped with fifty chairs.

At last the object of these official attentions reached his goal, the equipment room. What he had feared in the process were the two medical inspections, either of which might stop his progress instanter and send him scurrying to a camp hospital for observation or treatment. In either circumstance, his embarkation would be deferred indefinitely. But if he were allowed to reach the equipment room, he knew he was safe. Here he found great bins containing large quantities of the articles named on the equipment card. As he passed the bins every soldier received clean socks and underclothing, new tape for his identification tags and a clean shelter half in which to carry his equipment. He also received such new articles as were checked on his equipment card.

In the dressing room beyond, he found waiting for him a uniform and the serviceable portions of the outfit he had brought with him to the "mill," all the textile articles having been thoroughly deloused and sterilized. He found his old uniform, if that had been in good condition; otherwise, a new one or a respectable one from the repair factory. Sometimes his old uniform came back shrunken and faded by the hot steam of the delousing plant. In that event a serviceable uniform was substituted for it.

The final station in the "mill" was the pay office. It some-

Photo by Signal Corps

1. ENTERING "MILL" AT BORDEAUX

Photo by Signal Corps

2. RECEIVING CLEAN CLOTHING IN "MILL"

Photo by Signal Corps

3. THE "MILL" BARBERSHOP

Photo by Signal Corps

4. THROUGH "MILL" AND READY FOR HOME

times happened that troops came up for embarkation with their pay months in arrears. Now, with his records perfected, the soldier received all his back pay. Thanks to the exchange system set up by the A. E. F. in the embarkation camps, he received his pay in American money, perhaps the first he had seen in many months. The "feel" of the familiar bills and the jingle of the silver were like a taste of home. Clean, neatly clothed, restored once more to man's estate, the soldier emerged from the "mill" and made his way to quarters in the "clean" camp, his heart light because he knew now that he was going home "toot sweet." The sense of well-being moved one soldier-poet to praise of the "mill" as follows:

> "Ye go in one end dirty, broke,
> So dog tired ye can't see a joke.
> Ye come out paid, an' plum' remade,
> A self-respectin' soldier."

The embarkation plant at Bordeaux, if pressed, could cleanse, delouse, equip, and otherwise prepare for the home voyage 180,000 men in a month. During the busy times in 1919 a continuous column of men filed through the departments. They went through in blocks of twelve. In each of the various departments were ten booths, each accommodating twelve men.

The processes at the other embarkation camps were essentially the same. In each of the Le Mans divisional camps was installed a bathing and delousing plant with a capacity of 1,200 men an hour. For the sterilization of clothing in the area there were three large central "disinfesting" plants, five smaller stationary steam sterilizers, and more than a dozen mobile sterilizers.

The two port camps at Bordeaux were known as Camp Neuve and Camp Genicart. After the armistice these two camps were reorganized and enlarged. Camp Neuve became the "dirty" or entrance camp. It accommodated 5,400 men. Camp Genicart was designated as the "clean" or evacuation camp, and its barracks could house nearly 17,000 men. The busiest day for Bordeaux was Sunday, May 11, 1919, when 6,399 men passed through the "mill" and made ready to embark. St. Nazaire handled 15,306 embarkations on June 17, 1919, its record day.

Salvage was an important operation at all the embarkation points in France. Thousands of articles of apparel discarded by the returning troops were not so worn but that they could be made serviceable again. The salvage plant at Le Mans could repair 1,700 pairs of shoes, dry-clean, sterilize, and repair 4,000 pieces of clothing, wash 10,000 garments in the laundry, and disinfect 10,000 blankets every day. The plant occupied eight buildings, and the average value of clothing repaired monthly was over $150,000. There were salvage plants also at Brest, St. Nazaire, and Bordeaux, the one at Brest being of great size.

The task of feeding men at the embarkation camps gave the Quartermaster Corps one of its chief problems. Each divisional sub-depot at Le Mans carried at all times sufficient food to supply the appetites of 25,000 men for fifteen days, and in addition the central warehouses contained 500,000 emergency rations to substitute for the garrison rations if anything went wrong with the food supply. In December, 1918, the subsistence services in the area had been built up to the capacity of 500,000 rations cooked and served each day.

At Brest also the feeding arrangements were laid out on an immense scale. The men ate food prepared in standard kitchens, each capable of providing subsistence for thousands. The cold-storage and other storage spaces of one of the standard kitchens were large enough to hold such items as 10,000 pounds of beef and 6,000 pounds of bread. The kitchen facilities included a meat cutting room, a tool room, a scullery, a garbage incinerator, a great mess hall, and finally the galleys, each of which contained four large hotel ranges with work-tables, serving tables, and all necessary cooking utensils. Ten men did the cooking in each galley. Each mess hall was 280 feet long. End to end, its metal topped tables measured 495 feet in length. Galleys, storage rooms, and mess halls had cement floors. The whole plant was illuminated by electricity.

Each mess hall at Brest was operated on the cafeteria plan. Each was equipped to feed 20,000 soldiers. The men entered the hall marching in column of squads. They passed through the galleys, filling their kits with hot food, then secured places at the tables, ate, and left the hall at the opposite end, where there were refuse cans in which to scrape off their dishes and also tanks of boiling, soapy water and hot rinsing water. Here they cleaned their equipment. The facilities were such that each kitchen could serve a brigade of troops entering the building at the ordinary marching pace. Frequent inspections kept the food up to standard. The camps at Brest also maintained night soup stands at which any soldier could get bread and hot soup between the hours of 8:30 p.m. and 2:30 a.m. The force that operated the messing facilities at Brest numbered 1,600 officers and men.

At Bordeaux the troops temporarily occupying the embarkation camps cooked their own meals at the mess halls, drawing their supplies from the camp organization. At St. Nazaire the messes were similar to those at Brest. The old army transport *McClellan*, which had crossed to France in the first American convoy in 1917, was stationed at St. Nazaire, where it served the subsistence organization as a floating refrigerator with capacity for 3,000,000 pounds of food. The *McClellan* was too old to stand the buffeting of the North Atlantic, and the Embarkation Service, unwilling to risk bringing her home, turned the ship over to the A. E. F. After the expedition had returned to the United States the Government sold the *McClellan* to France.

To the individual soldier, quite the most important branch of the embarkation organization was that one which paid the money due him from the Government. It paid him his money in francs, either in the currency itself or by check, and then saw to it that he exchanged his French money for its equivalent in American currency. Both of these enterprises in finance—disbursement and exchange—were in the hands of the A. E. F.

Quartermaster Corps. The disbursement offered little difficulty, although the monthly pay roll at Brest sometimes contained as many as 100,000 names, while those at St. Nazaire and Bordeaux were proportionately large. The question of foreign exchange presented more of a problem.

Soon after the van of the A. E. F. reached France the Treasury Department at Washington requested the War Department to pay all its troops on foreign soil in the money of the country in which they chanced to be stationed. This meant that most of the men of the expedition received their pay in francs. Before the armistice, questions of currency exchange were of slight concern to the overseas soldier. After the Government had deducted his allotment to his dependents, his monthly premium payment for war risk insurance, and his partial payment for any Liberty Bonds he might have purchased through the Army, there was not much left for him, anyhow. When francs were cheaper he received more of them from the pay officer than he had expected, but as long as he stayed in France and spent his money there the rate of exchange made little difference to him.

French exchange continually strengthened during the sojourn of the expedition in France—until after the armistice began. The normal value of francs is 5.18 to the dollar. In July, 1917, the rate was 5.70. This rate gradually improved until at its strongest point it stood at 5.45. The few wounded men and casuals returning to the United States during this period were thus able to benefit financially by exchanging their French savings for American currency.

After the armistice, however, and during the very time the expeditionary troops were returning to the United States in greatest numbers, the exchange value of the franc slumped badly. Shortly after November 11, 1918, the rate was 5.80 to 1. It continued to fall steadily until in the autumn of 1919 it took 9.70 francs to purchase one dollar. It follows that the provident soldier who had saved the francs paid to him on a basis of less than six to the dollar lost heavily when he was forced to convert his savings back into dollars again on a basis of nearly ten francs to the dollar. The loss was particularly heavy upon officers who maintained drawing and savings accounts in French banks or who had not cashed their pay checks. Sometimes, too, officers lost their checks. Later they obtained duplicates, which the declining exchange had made less valuable. The War Department considered itself bound to protect soldiers from losses on this account. Congress is now considering a war department bill which, if enacted into law, will provide for the reimbursement of losses incurred by soldiers because of variations in foreign exchange.

It was good financial policy for the A. E. F. to leave all its French currency behind as it embarked for the United States, and to bring home only American money. Yet it would have resulted in confusion in the A. E. F. finances to have changed the pay system at the ports of embarkation. Therefore the Quartermaster Corps did the next best thing: it paid off the embarking troops in francs as usual and then immediately converted their francs into American currency. Since both payment and exchange were at the same rate of exchange, there was no loss to the troops in this transaction.

In order to provide the American money for this exchange it was necessary for the Treasury to ship to France great quantities of currency. It took the A. E. F. some time to convince the Treasury Department of the necessity for such shipments. The day after the armistice began, the command of the A. E. F. cabled to the Treasury requesting the immediate shipment of $500,000 in currency, an order afterwards increased to $2,000,000. This money did not actually reach the A. E. F. until the last day of January, 1919. By that date the expedition was beginning to embark rapidly. There was not enough American currency in Europe to buy all the French money of the expeditionary troops, and only by the most strenuous efforts could the Quartermaster Corps provide money for exchange until the first shipment of currency arrived from the United States. Finance officers were stationed in Paris, London, and at the principal seaports with orders to buy all the American money they could secure. By combing the banks and the countingrooms of brokers and by maintaining in Paris a fund from which shipments were rushed by motor convoys to the ports as these exhausted their supplies of currency, the Corps managed to keep the exchange system running. After the January shipment of $2,000,000 the Treasury Department arranged for an automatic supply of $10,000,000 every month.

Meanwhile, at the ports the Corps had built up the exchange plan. Booths were set up on all docks, and a force of disbursing quartermasters was organized to go on board all transports and exchange the money of soldiers who had failed to make the exchange on shore. The A. E. F. passed an order making it compulsory for all soldiers to exchange their cash before sailing. Notices to this effect were posted conspicuously in all the embarkation camps. In the larger units the officers attended to the matter, collecting the French money from their men, receiving American money for it from the exchange officers, and then distributing the familiar currency among the troops. Individuals and men traveling in small units attended to their own exchange. The quartermasters at Brest distributed as much as $400,000 in American currency in a single day. Up to July 1 Brest had paid out $60,000,000 in American money to troops boarding ship there.

By the late spring of 1919 most of the combat divisions, except those on active duty with the Army of Occupation, had crossed the ocean or had started for home. By that time the facilities at the base ports had been developed to a capacity that enabled them to handle all further embarkations, and the command of the expedition closed and abandoned the embarkation center at Le Mans. All of the physical equipment there went to the French Government under the terms of the general sale consummated in August of that year. On June 30 Bordeaux was closed as a port of embarkation. It had embarked 258,000 troops. St. Nazaire officially ceased to exist as a port of embarkation on July 26, although thereafter it embarked a few casuals. Approximately 500,000 American soldiers said farewell to France at St. Nazaire.

A million and a quarter American expeditionary soldiers departed from Brest for the United States. Brest was the last of the ports to close. The embarkation of the millionth American at Brest seemed almost as momentous as the arrival of the millionth American in France a year earlier. In August General Pershing and the historic First Division sailed from Brest, and the last of the combat troops had gone. On October 1 American troops were stationed in France only at Brest and in Paris, but Brest continued in operation as the port of embarkation until the last American had departed. On October 1 there were a few thousand men still to sail, but the A. E. F. no longer existed in France. Its headquarters had moved to Washington. The great task was done.

CHAPTER III

THE TRANSATLANTIC FERRY

ON the first day of the armistice, before Washington knew its exact terms or could form an estimate of how great a force we should have to maintain in France pending the conclusion of permanent peace, General Frank T. Hines, the Chief of the Embarkation Service, which had administered the great work of transporting the 2,000,000 men of the A. E. F. to France and had carried nearly half of them across the ocean in its own ships, placed before the Secretary of War a plan for the return of the troops.

It can be said that the outlook for the speedy repatriation of the overseas soldiers was not bright. It had taken nearly seventeen months to transport the expedition to Europe, and more than half of the men had crossed in the ships of other nations. England had been the chief contributor of tonnage to our overseas movement prior to November 11. To build up on the western front the numerical superiority that was the chief factor in the victory, the British Empire combed the seas for suitable passenger ships, cut her own civilian requirements to the minimum, and devoted to our transport service every ton of troop-carrying capacity she could procure. France and Italy had each supplied a few vessels.

With the immense fleet thus assembled the War Department transported men across the Atlantic with an intense concentration of effort never before known. First in the determination that the Germans should not conquer, later in the assurance that we ourselves should win, the Department shipped the troops over with scarcely a thought of how they were going to get back again. Future events were to be allowed to take care of themselves.

Photo by Signal Corps

KITCHENS AT LE MANS

Photo by Signal Corps

STREET IN LE MANS AREA NO. 5

Photo by Signal Corps

CASUALS ON TRANSPORT LEAVING BREST

Photo by Signal Corps

BOARDING TRANSPORT FROM LIGHTERS, BREST

Now such events had come to pass. England, faced with the sudden necessity of returning her own colonial soldiers to their native lands, and looking ahead, too, to the restoration of her all-important foreign commerce, immediately withdrew her tonnage from our service. France and Italy did likewise. The magnificent "bridge of ships" on which the American Expedition had crossed the Atlantic melted away, and 2,000,000 Americans found themselves partially marooned in a strange land.

Yet not completely marooned. The fleet of American-flag troopships assembled during the war had on the day of the armistice a one-trip capacity of 112,000 military passengers. Operated in armed and guarded convoys, this shipping could not quite average one round-trip transatlantic voyage a month; its transporting capacity under war conditions was somewhere in the neighborhood of 100,000 troops a month. The armistice did away with the need of steaming in convoy and allowed the transports to be operated by the much more efficient system of individual sailings. Under such conditions the monthly capacity of the American-flag fleet was about 150,000 men. This capacity was to be discounted somewhat by the fact that practically all of the vessels had reached a point of having to be retired for a season of reconditioning and repair. It was evident that, unless this fleet were aided, it would take it, under the most favorable conditions, over a year to bring home the A. E. F.; and it was likelier that, actually, the spring of 1920 would be at hand before the last of the overseas soldiers set foot once more on their native soil. General Hines's plan provided for such aid. It discounted in advance the subsequent fact that the Allies withdrew their passenger ships, and turned to our own resources for increased transport capacity.

It appeared that we should have considerable tonnage available for such use—tonnage released by the armistice from other service. For one source, there was the Navy. Its battleships and cruisers variously had been protecting the coast, convoying transports, and holding themselves ready in the combined Grand Fleet to meet the expected German naval attack in force. These duties had come to an end. The Hines plan contemplated the temporary conversion of a number of war vessels into troop carriers by the installation of berths and messing accommodations. Although all foreign tonnage was to be withdrawn at once, the Transportation Service hoped to secure some additional capacity by chartering passenger vessels from foreign owners under new arrangements.

The most promising source of new capacity, however, lay in the fleet of army cargo transports which, on the day of the armistice, represented about 2,500,000 deadweight tonnage* in the aggregate. The armistice immediately rendered a great part of this tonnage no longer necessary to the Government in the maintenance of a vast overseas supply service. The A. E. F. was thereafter to exist on a garrison basis, requiring only the ordinary garrison supplies of food and clothing. The great cargoes of ordnance and aircraft, of raw steel and semi-finished materials for the French and English munitions plants, of horses and mules, of railway and engineering supplies—the tonnage which had laden the cargo fleet in the past and had heaped up at the Atlantic terminals—were to cross the ocean no more. It was proposed to take the best of the cargo transports and convert them immediately into troopships.

The War Department adopted the entire plan, and the first act of the Transportation Service was to begin a survey of the cargo fleet to determine what vessels were most suitable for conversion. Only the larger and faster boats would serve, and of course they had to be ships with holds adapted to the installation of troop quarters. Specialized vessels, such as tankers and ore carriers, would not do.

For the Transportation Service the armistice was but an episode. It merely changed the character of its work and added to the volume of it. The peak of the operations curve, so far as troop transportation was concerned, was not reached until eight months after the armistice had been in effect. The thousands of troops in the Transportation Service yearned for dis-

* Deadweight tonnage represents the weight of cargo it takes to sink a vessel in the water from her light-load line to her deep-load line.

charge and home as ardently as did the rest of the Army; yet these men realized that it would be months before their work could end. Meanwhile they would have to see hundreds of thousands proceeding to demobilization camps as rapidly as steamships and trains could carry them, with never a thought of the transportation men who had made their early discharge possible.

The resulting drop in morale was one difficulty which the Transportation Service faced at the outset of its labors in demobilization, but one which it met and solved successfully. Another more concrete one had to do with the operation of troopships. Early in the war the Army had turned over to the Navy the task of operating most of the troopships at sea, principally because the military authorities found themselves unable to compete with the high wages of the munitions industries in securing civilian crews for vessels. The Navy, with the uniform it offered and its appeal to patriotism, had no such trouble; and consequently it assumed the operation of the troop transports and manned them with bluejackets. These young Americans enlisted for danger and adventure and had no stomach for the work of operating a collection of prosaic ferry-boats across the now safe Atlantic. The Navy Department, seeing that it could not hold them in service, notified the War Department to take back its ships. This the Transportation Service did, hiring civilian crews and placing them aboard the troop transports at a rate that relieved the Navy of the work entirely by the summer of 1919, except that the Navy continued to operate three or four troopships with crews made up of men serving under term enlistments.

While the Transportation Service was contemplating the conversion of many of its cargo carriers into troopships and the consequent use of the vessels for a number of months to come, it was subjected to pressure from the owners of some of these same ships, who demanded that the Government give them up. Practically all of its cargo tonnage the Army held under charter from private ownership, the charters running during the emergency. After the armistice the vessel owners naturally desired to get back into the race for foreign commerce. It was to the interest of the United States that the military tonnage be so employed at the earliest possible time, but the early return of the overseas expedition was even more important, and it received the priority.

Another obstacle in the way of carrying out the Service's demobilization plan swiftly and efficiently was the congested condition of the American shipyards, practically all of which were engaged to the limits of their capacities in new construction for the Emergency Fleet Corporation. This congestion not only hampered the project to convert the cargo vessels into troop carriers, but it also strung out the necessary work of overhauling the regular troop transports already in commission. For over a year these vessels had been driven mercilessly through fair weather and foul, with never a let-up for the general repairing and reconditioning which every ship needs at intervals. Large forces had been carried on all of them as part of the crews to keep the vessels going somehow by making emergency repairs whenever needed. Only conditions as they existed before the armistice warranted such abuse. The armistice occurred opportunely for most of these vessels, and particularly for the ex-German liners. War or no war, they had about reached the point where they had to be drydocked, regardless of the effect upon the overseas movement. After the armistice it would have been folly to set this tonnage at another great task without first putting it in good condition. To do the work the Transportation Service had at its disposal only its own repair yards at New York and the drydock and ship repair yard of the Newport News Shipbuilding Company. Because of this limitation the shipping was tied up longer than would normally have been necessary.

The survey conducted by the Transportation Service immediately after the armistice designated fifty-eight cargo transports for conversion. They were the largest vessels of the cargo fleet, and conversion equipped them to carry, on the average, 2,500 troops on each. Thus the project added 125,000 accommodations to the trip capacity of the troop-carrying fleet as it existed on the day of the armistice—more than doubling it in size. By December 13 the survey was complete and the marine architects were drawing the conversion specifications for the individual vessels; and on that day the Service awarded the first of the contracts, that for converting the *Buford* (which later carried the exported radicals to Russia and gained fame as the "Soviet Ark"). The cost of remodeling the *Buford* was $70,000, and the contractor completed the work in twenty-eight days. By the end of the year twenty conversion contracts had been placed. Others followed at intervals until April 29, 1919, when the last of them was signed. Before June 1 all fifty-eight ships were in service as troopships.

In spite of adverse conditions in industry the ship contractors made extraordinarily good time in remodeling these vessels. Such conversion was practically a rebuilding job. It meant tearing out practically the entire interiors of the hulls and rebuilding to provide troop quarters, galleys, mess rooms, and sanitary facilities. The average time for completing this work was forty-one days and the average cost was more than $161,000. The total cost was about $9,000,000.

It will be seen that the project, because of its expense if on no other account, was a bold step for the Transportation Service to take. The cost of conversion per passenger accommodated was about $72—more than the cost of a single steerage passage across the Atlantic on a commercial liner. Looked at in a broader way, however, the expenditure of the $9,000,000 was really an economy, for it enabled the Government to bring home and discharge several hundred thousand soldiers weeks and even months sooner than would otherwise have been possible.

This single act of converting the cargo transports into troop carriers did more than any other one thing to expedite the return of the A. E. F.; yet the aggressiveness of the Transportation Service did not end there. Under the terms of the peace treaty Germany agreed to turn over to the Allies under charter most of the remnant of her formerly great passenger-carrying merchant fleet. For nearly five years these vessels had swung at their moorings in German harbors and rivers. At her pier in the river Elbe was the *Imperator*, the largest ship in the world, exceeding in size her sister ship *Vaterland*, which had become the U. S. Transport *Leviathan*. The Allied Maritime Transport Council, which had allocated world tonnage in the struggle against the submarine, decided to divide this fresh German tonnage equally between Great Britain and the United States, giving us all the larger vessels because we possessed harbors that could accommodate them. The smaller ships England was to use in repatriating her Australian troops.

General Hines, the chief of our Transportation Service, took part in the proceedings in London, securing from the Council ten large German vessels. At once a U. S. navy board, headed by Admiral Benson, chief of the Bureau of Operations during the great struggle, went to Germany to put the allotted ships in condition for service. Repairs were quickly made, and presently all ten ships, propelled by machinery unfamiliar to American sailors, sailed out of the German harbors and into the harbor at Brest, manned from bridges to firing rooms by Yankee bluejackets and their officers.

From the London conference General Hines went to see various shipping concerns in European Allied and neutral countries and secured by charter thirty-three passenger ships in all—thirteen from Italian owners, twelve from Spanish and Dutch ownership, and eight from French interests.

Long before this event the Navy had taken fourteen of its battleships and ten armored cruisers and by the installation of berths and other accommodations had turned them into passenger boats capable of carrying 28,600 troops at once. These vessels added to the homeward movement more than a division of troops a month.

Thus was the Atlantic rebridged after the armistice and with a structure even broader and more capacious than the one on which the expedition had crossed to France. On June 23, 1919, the troopship fleet reached its greatest expansion. On that day it consisted of 174 vessels with trip accommodations for 419,000 troops. It could have transported the entire

Photo by Signal Corps

TROOPS ON BATTLESHIP READY FOR MESS

Photo by Signal Corps

WARSHIPS WITH TROOPS DOCKING AT HOBOKEN

Photo by Signal Corps

EMBARKING FOR UNITED STATES

Photo by Signal Corps

MESS ROOM ON CONVERTED CARGO TRANSPORT *OHIOAN*

A. E. F. in five trips, with room to spare. It was greater in capacity than the combined facilities at our disposal before the armistice, yet practically all of it sailed under the Stars and Stripes. In number of ships it was four times as large as the troop fleet which the Army held in charter and ownership on November 11. It outnumbered by forty vessels the combined fleet both of American and of Allied troopships at our disposal before the armistice. Yet on the day of the armistice we seemed to have exhausted the possibilities of ocean shipping!

Always courageous and swift in action, the Transportation Service was one of the first of the war department bureaus to anticipate the armistice and the consequent demobilization. On November 1, ten days ahead of the armistice, upon the confidential intelligence that the German Government had ordered its fleet out to give battle to the Grand Fleet of the Allies, and further assured that the defeat of Germany on land was in sight, the Transportation Service stopped the overseas movement of all combat troops. Primarily this action was taken to avoid a disaster to our troop transports, a disaster almost bound to occur if in the expected forthcoming naval engagement any of the German warships were by chance able to slip through the Allied cordon and reach the Atlantic. After the armistice the anticipatory act of the Transportation Service proved to be of material benefit in demobilization, for it had kept away from France at least four divisions of troops, diminishing by so much the work of bringing back the expedition.

On the fifth day of the armistice General Pershing named thirty divisions that were to conduct the advance of the Army of Occupation to the Rhine and hold open the communications, designated the supply troops to support the divisions, and released the rest of the Expeditionary Forces for return to the United States as soon as transportation facilities could be provided. This order freed nearly half the expedition for demobilization. A million men were thus ready to return home at once.

While the authorities in France were preparing for the embarkation to come, there was at hand a job in overseas transportation to which the Transportation Service could turn with such troopships as were available for immediate use. In England on the day of the armistice there were stationed more than 70,000 American soldiers, most of them members of the air service squadrons undergoing training in the British aviation camps. Their embarkation through the large British seaports offered no particular difficulty. On our own regular transports and in such space as the Army could secure on British commercial liners, this whole force was set down in the United States within six weeks after the armistice began.

The embarkation of the A. E. F. in France may be said to have started about the middle of December, simultaneously with the appearance of the order establishing the three embarkation ports and the embarkation area at Le Mans. From then on week by week the embarkations of home-coming troops steadily increased in number. In January the first of the converted cargo transports joined the troopship fleet. A little later some of the chartered foreign tonnage appeared in the service. About that time, too, the Navy began adding its increment of war vessels fitted out as troop carriers. In the late spring we secured the German tonnage. In June, 1919, the American troop sailings reached a maximum never before attained in any military or civilian movement. In that month 368,300 American soldiers embarked on transports in France, and 343,600 landed on American soil. The movement exceeded by 60,000 men that of the greatest month in the transport of the A. E. F. to France. In taking the forces to France we had been assisted by the merchant marines of the principal Allies to the limit of their combined capacities, but we brought back the expedition single-handed.

This great record was made possible not only by the utilization of all tonnage that could be adapted to such service, but also by the operation of the shipping at its highest efficiency. The drop in morale among the *personnel* of the Transportation Service in the first disheartening weeks of the armistice was soon offset by the spirit of the transportation men in early

1919 when they realized the great value of the service they were rendering to their comrades of the expedition and to the country at large. When it bore into their consciousness that they were exceeding all expectations in delivering troops from France to the United States, they fell to with a spirit unexcelled even in the days when every soldier set down in France was so much added insurance of a speedy end to the war. Ship vied with ship to cut down steaming time, and the ports competed with each other in dispatching vessels to sea.

Under such circumstances all records for shipping efficiency fell. In 1918, with every energy bent upon the attainment of maximum efficiency, the average turn-around, or round voyage across the ocean and back, of the American troop transports was something over 36 days. In 1919 during the return movement it dropped to 32.6 days.

The oil-burning transport *Great Northern*, which was bought outright by the War Department in the spring of 1918, proved to be the fleetest thing that ever plied the Atlantic. Leaving Hoboken on June 24, 1919, with a few passengers, a fews days later she landed them at Brest, took on 2,999 troops by moonlight, and recrossed to Hoboken—all within twelve days, five hours, and thirty minutes. No other vessel, military or commercial, ever equaled this speed. The *Great Northern* also established the record of eighteen transatlantic cycles at the average rate of twenty-three days for each; and in the whole war enterprise she transported more troops per ton of capacity than did any other troopship. She was closely crowded for honors, however, by her sister ship *Northern Pacific*.

The vessels alone could not write such records except through the coöperation of the port organizations on both sides of the Atlantic. Before the armistice the capacities of the ports, especially of those in France, were a sharper limitation upon the expansion of American power at the front than was the shortage in ocean shipping. After the armistice the improvement in shipping efficiency was attained largely by speeding up the loading and unloading of transports in port. On May 17 the transport *Maui* at Brest took aboard 3,612 troops and sailed for America in three hours and thirty-five minutes after arriving. These soldiers had to be carried out to her in lighters, and they boarded her at the rate of sixty-five a minute. On the same day the transport *Cape May*, one of the converted cargo vessels, arrived at Bordeaux and sailed on the same tide with a load of 1,928 troops, having been dispatched in one hour and nineteen minutes. These were extreme instances, but they were indicative of the efficiency of the port machinery.

At first the Transportation Service would fix no schedule for the return of the expedition, except the general one that it hoped to bring back the last man before January 1, 1920. By the beginning of spring, 1919, the situation looked so much better that the Service brought out a schedule showing the probable troop-carrying capacity available in the French ports by months, and estimating this capacity for several months ahead. The schedule promised a gradual increase until the shipping reached a goal of 250,000 embarkations a month. On the basis of this schedule the command of the A. E. F. fixed priorities for embarkation and published both the schedule and priority dates, to the excitement of the men of the expedition, most of whom were then still in France. To be sure, the authorities promised nothing definitely and informed the soldiers that the schedule would be met "if practicable"; yet the men of the A. E. F. banked on the Transportation Service to fulfill its predictions.

The goal of 250,000 embarkations a month was the extreme maximum which the Service thought it might attain if everything went right. Yet three months later, when embarkations approached 400,000, the goal had been passed by 50 per cent. The actual performance brought 300,000 overseas soldiers home two months ahead of schedule, and 300,000 others beat the schedule by one month. Here was the equivalent of 900,000 men returned and discharged from service one month earlier than the nation had any reason to expect. The cost of maintaining such a force in arms for one month is approximately $66,000,000, a saving which must be set down to the credit of the administration that made it possible.

The days spent at sea by the returning troops were not time wasted. Although the embarkation officers in France did their best to send out with each soldier a complete record of his service, in the press of the work it was not always possible to attain this ideal. It was unjust to hold back a soldier from embarkation because his records were incomplete; yet before he could secure his discharge his papers had to be in perfect shape. The Transportation Service, through its debarkation camps in the United States, took it upon itself to perfect the individual records of the soldiers, and it did most of this work on the ships at sea. In special schools at Hoboken and Newport News the Service trained a force of traveling *personnel* adjutants for assignment to the transports. As soon as a troopship started out from France the *personnel* adjutant aboard opened an office, and from that moment until the ship docked he was busy from morning to night smoothing up the service records. He also compiled the papers which the debarkation camps would need and instructed the troops in the procedure to be followed after landing.

Unexpectedly, the Transportation Service found itself obliged to bring home in first-class accommodations many more persons than it had carried to Europe in that style. Thousands of officers had crossed before the armistice in commercial liners, and so had crowds of red cross and other welfare workers. Numerous soldiers had acquired wives in Europe. Military regulation gave these women and their husbands accompanying them the right to occupy first-class quarters on transports. After the armistice several congressional committees and hundreds of experts employed by the Government in the peace negotiations traveled first-class on the transports in both directions. The result was that on July 1, 1919, at the ports in France awaiting first-class transportation to America there were 32,000 persons over and above the capacity of such accommodations in sight for several months to come. To have brought them all back in the state to which they were entitled would have made necessary the full operation of the entire transport fleet for three months beyond the time when the return movement actually ceased. To settle the matter the Service adopted the expedient of bringing home several thousand junior officers quartered in the troop spaces of certain of the larger and faster vessels. Although some outcry arose over this treatment, the majority of the officers were too glad to get home at all to be critical of the mode of their transportation.

Not a man of the 2,000,000 passengers lost his life as the result of marine disaster after the armistice. The worst accident occurred shortly after midnight on January 1, 1919, when, during a blinding rainstorm, the great transport *Northern Pacific*, with a load of 2,500 troops, two-thirds of whom were sick and wounded men, went aground on the Long Island shore near the entrance to New York harbor. The sea was rough, the wind making, and as the ship turned port side to the beach and worked up on the sand, pounding heavily, rescue for the time was impossible. The weather was cold, the ship's machinery was out of commission, and she was lightless and unheated. It took three days to rescue the passengers; yet, despite the severity of the experience, no person on board suffered seriously from it. The pounding had so damaged the ship's hull that many of the plates had to be renewed. A more serious injury was a broken stern-post. In former marine practice such an injury meant the casting of a new post in steel. The Navy, as in the instance of the broken machinery in the interned German ships, resorted to the electric welding torch for repairing the broken stern-post, saving several months in time and perhaps $50,000 in money.

The A. E. F. sold most of its property in Europe. The cargo transports brought home about 850,000 tons of military freight—a small fraction of the property held by the expedition at the time of the armistice. The goods were sold abroad at a loss, the average recovery being considerably under that received from the sale of similar goods in the United States. Yet it was good policy to do what was done. Europe needed the supplies and we needed the ship-space for other purposes. If

Photo by Signal Corps

SAILING DAY AT ST. NAZAIRE

Photo by Signal Corps

TRANSPORT *MAUI* LOADING AT ST. NAZAIRE

Photo by Signal Corps

SOUVENIRS OF HIS SERVICE

Photo by Signal Corps

EMBARKING AT ST. NAZAIRE

the materials had been returned to the United States for sale, out of the proceeds would have had to be deducted the transportation cost; and the Government was little, if anything, out of pocket by the transaction.

Among the materials freighted home were 100,000 tons of road-making machinery. This the War Department turned over to the Department of Agriculture to be used in the construction of highways in the United States. The cargo transports also brought back large ordnance stores, principally artillery, much of it of British and French manufacture. The shipments included a large number of captured German cannon, brought back for distribution among American communities as war trophies.

While the returning troop movement was at its height the Transportation Service was winding up its war business and returning to a permanent peace footing. This program consisted principally of disposing of its vessels and its shore establishments. On November 11, 1918, the Service was operating 580 vessels with a total deadweight of nearly 4,000,000 tons. At the end of 1919 the army fleet consisted of only the few transports actually owned by the Government through purchase, construction, or seizure from Germany or Austria.

Most of its vessels the Army held under charter from private owners. The best interests of the United States required the return of these ships to their ownership just as soon as the Army could do without them. The cargo boats were first to go. In February, 1919, the Transportation Service began turning them back—redelivering them, it was called—at the rate of three ships a day. In July, when the peak of the overseas troop movement had passed, the Service began disposing of its chartered troopships (including the converted cargo transports), redelivering the last of them in December.

The Government faced tremendous costs in these transactions. The charters provided that the Army must restore the shipping to its owners in its original condition, ordinary wear and tear excepted. Nearly every ship had been remodeled to a greater or less extent to make it more serviceable to the Army.

All the domestic shipyards and repair yards were glutted with work, and it was evident that it would be a long time before the Transportation Service could recondition the vessels. Meanwhile the Service would have to maintain all of this idle shipping at a heavy continuing expense.

Instead of reconditioning the ships, therefore, the Transportation Service adopted the policy of returning vessels as they were, at the same time compensating the owners with lump-sum settlements for damage done by war service. In most instances the owners were glad enough to accept such an arrangement. To protect the Government in the settlements, joint boards of vessel survey, each consisting of an army, a navy, and a United States shipping board official, were set up at all the ports where ships were to be redelivered. Expert marine surveyors under their direction made detailed examinations of all the ships. With these surveys in hand, and with the complete history of each ship and of the service it had undergone while in the War Department's possession, the survey boards were able to arrive at a close estimate of the amount of the Government's financial liability in each case. The owners also employed their expert surveyors, and out of the two examinations grew negotiations which arrived at compromise settlements.

In December, 1918, the Service redelivered ships of approximately 189,000 deadweight tons. In January the redelivered ships aggregated 461,000 deadweight tons; in February, 470,000; and in March occurred the heaviest redelivery, amounting to approximately 532,000 deadweight tons. Redeliveries crossed the two-million-deadweight-ton mark shortly after the middle of April. By June most of the cargo transports had been restored to their owners, except those which had been converted into troop carriers. On June 15 the Army began dispensing with the use of battleships and cruisers, the last of the twenty-four being withdrawn on August 1. The break-up of the troop fleet began in earnest on August 1, and by the first anniversary of the armistice most of the chartered troopships had gone back to commercial work.

Many questions of admiralty law arose in connection with the restoration of the transports to the merchant marine. The legal branch of the Transportation Service on the day of the armistice consisted of but two lawyers. By that time a large number of maritime claims awaiting adjudication had accumulated, and it was recognized that such claims would multiply during the progress of negotiations leading to the redelivery of the vessels. With much difficulty the Service built up a force of twenty admiralty lawyers. In fact, the War Department, after the armistice, was so badly in need of lawyers for use in the liquidation of war business, that for several months it was forced to maintain the rule that no man of legal training should be discharged from the military service.

In breaking up the fleet of troop transports the Transportation Service found opportunity to create for the War Department a large permanent reserve of troopships without expense to the Government for their maintenance. The German and Austrian ships seized by the Government at the outset of the war became in large part the property of the Army. Most of these vessels were admirably adapted to war service, but they were too large and too costly in operation to justify their continuance in the transport service of the peace-time establishment. Consequently the Transportation Service turned thirteen of them over to the Shipping Board under an agreement providing for their charter to private operators, subject to their recall by the Army in the event of another war. These ships can accommodate approximately 50,000 troops at once. All of the special military fittings have been classified and stored away ready for use again, if it ever becomes necessary.

When the war traffic ended, the Transportation Service found itself in possession of enormous port facilities. Prior to the armistice the Government had seized or leased over seventy steamship piers at various Atlantic and Gulf ports; but even such facilities being entirely inadequate to the vast amount of shipping contemplated, the Government began the construction of seven great port bases located at Boston, Brooklyn, Port Newark, Philadelphia, Norfolk, Charleston, and New

Orleans. Not one of these projects was complete on November 11. One of the early demobilization questions to be settled was what to do with these installations. Should the Government abandon them and set down as loss the millions spent, or go ahead with their erection and perhaps make the whole enterprise profitable by leasing the facilities to American commerce? The latter course was chosen. The contractors completed the construction at a total cost of $143,000,000. As the new piers became ready for use the Transportation Service turned back its leased piers to their owners. Then, as the military traffic dwindled, the space in the base terminals was leased to private ship operators. These terminals, among the largest and finest in the United States, are now rendering an important service to our foreign trade, but on terms ensuring their instant availability to the Government in the event of a future emergency.*

* In the spring of 1919 the Transportation Service brought back to America from Archangel the American troops, about 4,500 in number, sent to northern Russia in September, 1918, to combat the Bolsheviki. It also, in late 1919 and early 1920, transported from Vladivostok to American Pacific ports about 10,000 American troops who had been sent to Siberia at different times to aid Czecho-Slovak, Japanese, and other Allied forces in operations against German and Austrian troops aiding the hostile native Russians in Siberia. In 1920 the Transportation Service, acting as an independent contractor, undertook to repatriate 30,000 of the Czecho-Slovak Siberian troops cut off from escape to the Balkans by the successes of the Bolsheviki in southern Russia. To the government of Czecho-Slovakia the Service named the price of $12,000,000 for this work, a price criticized in this country as too low. The last of the 30,000 Czecho-Slovaks were landed at Trieste about January 1, 1921, and the whole job had been carried through at a cost of approximately $8,000,000. The Service employed twelve U. S. transports for one or more trips in the movement of the Czech expedition, and two of them—the *America* and the *President Grant*, both ex-German liners—circumnavigated the globe in the process of the work, proceeding from New York to Vladivostok *via* Panama and thence to Trieste *via* the Indian Ocean and the Suez Canal, and from Trieste to New York *via* Gibraltar. The Czechs traveled under American military discipline with what that implies in cleanliness and sanitation, and therefore moved without the epidemics of disease that have usually accompanied the progress of Balkan forces.

CHAPTER IV

EBB TIDE

BEFORE the American Expeditionary Forces could be disbanded in this country it was necessary for the training camps, most of which were to become demobilization centers after the armistice, to be evacuated by the home forces occupying them. The fluvial system leading into that sea of humanity which we knew as the A. E. F.—main river crossing the ocean, chief tributaries leading up to the ports in this country, beyond them their branch creeks and brooks, and the rills at the sources—was running bank-full on the day of the armistice. Demobilization, which inverted many of the processes of war and changed familiar names into their antonyms, abruptly reversed the direction of troop-flow, as if some tremendous power had uplifted the reservoir and the mouth of the main stream in France above the ultimate sources in this country. Before the expeditionary sea could drain out, the home channels of troop supply had to discharge their contents into the nimbus of civilian life.

The process of dissolution began within the hour in which the news of peace came to Washington. It happened that November 11 was the first of five days during which the Army planned to absorb 250,000 soldiers inducted into service under the terms of the Selective Service Act. Although it was evident that an armistice was at hand, the Railroad Administration went ahead with preparations for the transportation of these men to the training camps, and even dispatched the draft trains on the morning of November 11 to pick up the selectives, although the morning newspapers had announced that the armistice was indisputably to begin at eleven o'clock in

France. The only preparation looking toward demobilization had been to set up telephone and telegraph circuits over which the officials in Washington could stop and turn back the troop trains in a minimum of time. Immediately after receiving General Pershing's message announcing the start of the armistice, the Secretary of War notified the Troop-Movement Section of the Railroad Administration to stop the draft trains. This was done within an hour, although the trains were then in operation in every section of the United States. Some thousands of young men who had taken the oath of allegiance that morning, and who at the approach of noon were on troop trains proceeding to military camps, found themselves back at home, civilians once more, before the embers of the celebrating bonfires had died out that night.

Hard on their heels came the hundreds of thousands of soldiers who made up the combat divisions in training in the United States. These were the men last to don the uniform—men who were only partially trained, and who could be of no service to the War Department in the activities of demobilization. Their disbandment was not a difficult undertaking. They had been in the service so short a time that there were no complications of back pay and incomplete records to hinder their discharge. Moreover, they were geographically homogeneous—*i.e.*, their homes were generally in the regions surrounding the training camps—and therefore their demobilization brought about no problem in transportation. As a rule they were paid off and discharged at their training camps and allowed to make their way to their homes.

Quite apart from the divisional troops, there was another great body of soldiers in the United States on the day of the armistice. These were men undergoing training in special camps, such as those of the Air Service and the Quartermaster Corps, and also the troops engaged in maintaining the great war establishment in the United States. The demobilization of these men was more difficult. It was for them in the first place that the War Department set up the demobilization system which was to be seen in the perfection of operation later on when the A. E. F. began reaching the United States *en masse.*

Soon after the armistice the War Department established by order a system of thirty-three demobilization camps, or centers, as they were called. In large part these centers were former training camps. Practically all the National Army cantonments and some of the National Guard camps were so used. Other military posts and stations were added so as to distribute the demobilization centers evenly throughout the country according to the distribution of population. The War Department's policy was to discharge soldiers in as close proximity as possible to their former places of residence.

The special troops on duty in this country lacked homogeneity in the regional origin of the members of the various units. Many of the organizations were composed entirely of men chosen because of special aptitude for special service. Single units were therefore made up of men from widely separated parts of the United States. When the time came to disperse these troops it was found impossible to send the units intact to demobilization centers and there to disband them, except at a great waste of transportation. Throughout the whole activity the War Department husbanded transportation. Before the armistice it had been the general policy to move men always to the eastward, since east was forward. The armistice inverted the policy; and in order to avoid expensive duplication of travel, the Army in assembling its demobilization units moved its men always essentially westward until at length they reached the camps where they were to be discharged.

Throughout the winter of 1918-1919 the disintegration of the home forces proceeded rapidly, as the great subordinate services of the Army tapered off their war activities and released their men. One or two of the services, such as the Medical Department and the Motor Transport Corps, held on to their troops for a few months in order to carry out necessary duties connected with the disbanding of the Army and the restoration of the military establishment to a peace footing;

but the others, such as the Air Service, the Signal Corps, the Corps of Engineers, and the Quartermaster Corps, reduced strength as rapidly as the country could absorb the men. These men lost their unit identity as they proceeded toward the demobilization centers and finally found themselves once more grouped with their neighbors, regardless of what service any of them had performed.

By the end of February, 1919, more than 1,600,000 officers and enlisted men had been discharged from the Army. At that time only about 300,000 of the expeditionary troops had reached the United States. The great body of the A. E. F. was still to come, but the demobilization centers in the United States were empty and ready for it.

The policy of discharging troops at centers adjacent to their homes rested upon a sound foundation. As the country faced the demobilization of 4,000,000 troops, young men most of whom had been held for many months under the rigid restraints of army discipline, there was a widespread apprehension that the discharged soldiers might congregate in the larger cities and create profound economic disturbances. Upon the War Department there was no compulsion of law to transport the troops to their own neighborhoods before discharging them. Obviously the easy and convenient thing was to discharge them wherever they happened to be—at the thousand and one camps in the United States, or at the Atlantic ports upon their arrival from France—discharge them there, pay them off, and so farewell to them. Such, in fact, had been army procedure before the World War. The Army discharged its men at the posts where they were serving and paid to them the travel allowances granted by law. Whether they used their money to pay for actual transportation home was no concern of the Army's. They were all free, and most of them white and twenty-one. As long as discharges were relatively few this procedure had no effect upon the economic life of the nation. But what would have been the result if the War Department had continued this practice when disbanding the 4,000,000 troops in uniform on the day of the armistice? Most of them would have been turned loose in the vicinity of the large cities of the United States—more than 1,000,000 of them at New York alone. Their pockets would have been crammed with money. Congress by special enactment raised the travel allowance for discharged soldiers to five cents a mile, payable for the distance between the place of discharge and the soldier's home, whether the entire journey could be accomplished by railroad or not. Congress also granted a bonus of $60 to every soldier—payable also at discharge. Thousands of soldiers, when they came up for discharge, were entitled to back pay. Thus every man received a considerable sum of money with his discharge certificate, and for the overseas soldier this sum probably averaged more than $100. The streets of our cities would have been thronged with such men during the first six months of 1919. After their hardships the temptation to have a fling at metropolitan entertainments would have been well-nigh irresistible. They would have been fair game for gamblers and sharp practitioners. The rare individual might have bought his ticket and gone soberly home, but the majority could scarcely have been expected to show such restraint. In a little while, pockets that had jingled with money would have been empty, the streets would have been crowded with stranded soldiers, and the burdened municipalities would have had to face a severe civic problem.

This was what the War Department sought to avoid, and what it did avoid, by its demobilization policy. There was also another consideration—that of financial economy. The War Department could carry troops at a cost of much less than five cents a mile per capita. Therefore, by distributing the Army about the country and discharging every man within his own native section the War Department was able to save millions of dollars which otherwise would have been paid out in mileage allowances.

The good offices of the Government to the demobilized soldier did not end when the War Department had paid him his money and discharged him. As a special inducement to demobilized soldiers not to linger in the communities near the demobilization centers, the United States Railroad Administration made a special travel rate to them of two cents a mile. In order to secure the cut rate, however, the soldier had to buy his ticket within twenty-four hours after receiving his discharge. Thus it was to his direct financial advantage to go home at once. Nor did the Railroad Administration permit him to overlook the opportunity. All the principal demobilization centers had their own railway terminals, from which special trains for discharged soldiers departed at intervals. The Railroad Administration set up railway ticket booths in the offices of the camp finance officers, so that each newly discharged man, as he turned away from the disbursing window with his money in his hand, faced the railway ticket booth. At his elbow were Red Cross, Y. M. C. A., and other camp welfare workers to urge him to buy his railway ticket at once and leave on the first train. The path of least resistance led straight home, and he was indeed a headstrong individual who did not follow it. As a result of the whole system the demobilization of the Army went through without any trouble at all.

The policy had an effect upon the mode of troop travel that was to be observed even beyond the ports of embarkation in France. The original plan had been to bring all the expeditionary divisions back to the camps in which they had been organized and trained, and there to disband them. There seemed to be nothing in the way of so simple a solution of the problem. In organizing the divisions in the first place, it had been the policy, to which there were but few exceptions, to create divisions of men originating in the territory contiguous to each training camp. As the divisions started for France they possessed definite territorial identity; and the divisional names which they commonly adopted for themselves—the New England Division, the Sunset Division, the Buckeye Division, the Keystone Division, and so on—usually indicated the geographical origin of the men of the organizations. It was thought that, by transporting the overseas divisions back to their original training camps in this country, each would be placed in the demobilization center most convenient to the respective homes of its soldiers.

The attempt to put this policy into practice quickly showed the fallacy of it. Immediately it was discovered that the composition of the divisions had radically changed during the service in France. Men had died in battle, fallen sick, been transferred to other organizations, and their places had been taken by replacement troops shipped from the United States. Whole divisions had been rearranged. In the autumn of 1918 the expeditionary divisions were no longer representative of separate districts of the United States; each was in effect a cross section of the whole of America.

One of the first organizations to come back from France was a minor unit, a company, which had received its training at Camp Cody, Texas. The unit was sent to Camp Cody for demobilization and discharge. There it was discovered that, of every ten men who had joined the unit when it was in training, only four remained. The other six were newcomers, and to reach their homes they had to travel to points scattered from Oregon to the Atlantic coast.

Had this system been followed throughout the disbanding of the expeditionary units, it is evident that it would have cost the Government heavily in travel allowances paid to discharged soldiers, without saying anything about the tremendous traffic burden upon the railroads of the country. There was nothing to do but to break up the whole organization of the A. E. F. before sending it to the demobilization centers, and to assemble the men once more in units that possessed geographical identity.

The A. E. F. received instructions to attempt this break-up in France—at least to begin it there. It was found impossible to regroup the services of supply troops to any extent, because the embarkation ports in France, at which the supply troops were prepared for embarkation, were neither organized nor equipped to handle such a difficult work. More could be done with the divisional troops at Le Mans. Thereafter, whenever a division came into the area of Le Mans those soldiers who had joined the division after its training had been complete, and who did not live in the district centering in the original training camp in America, were detached and assembled with neighbors of theirs into territorial demobilization units, which became known as overseas casual companies. When the division itself went on from Le Mans to the ports it consisted only of the remnant of charter members who had been with it from the outset.

The prescribed size of an overseas casual company was two officers and 150 men, but it was seldom convenient to send forth companies uniformly organized. Men were not held waiting in France until casual companies could be built up to the prescribed size. One company might consist of fifty soldiers and the next 250, according to circumstances in the embarkation camp.

The principal ports of embarkation in the United States before the armistice had been New York (Hoboken), Newport News, and Boston. To these, in the system for receiving the overseas troops, was added Charleston, South Carolina. Charleston was opened as a port of debarkation principally for soldiers who were proceeding to the southern demobilization centers. The entire fleet of troop transports was divided proportionately among these ports, the greatest number operating between New York and the ports in France and the next greatest between Newport News and France. In the main each port kept its own fleet, but sometimes it became necessary to divert a vessel at sea from her usual course.

Only in a general way did the embarkation authorities in France pay attention to the destinations of the ships. After each loaded transport left a French port the embarkation officials there cabled to the Transportation Service in the United States a full description of the troops on board. If, for example, a vessel bound for Boston were carrying a preponderant number of soldiers from the South, the Transportation Service used the wireless to divert the transport to Newport News or Charleston.

The passenger lists cabled to the United States often con-

Photo by Signal Corps

CASUALS WAITING TO BOARD SHIP AT ST. NAZAIRE

Photo by Signal Corps

BOARDING *EDWARD LUCKENBACH*, CONVERTED CARGO TRANSPORT

Photo by Signal Corps

EMBARKATION AT BORDEAUX

Photo by Signal Corps

LEFT BEHIND

tained the first information received in this country about the departure of units from France. There was no news more eagerly awaited by the people. Cities and states had often made elaborate preparations for the reception of their overseas soldiers. A number of states and cities sent representatives to the ports to welcome the troops home at the gates of America. The harbor boat of the New York Mayor's Committee of Welcome was busy almost every day taking visiting delegations down the bay to meet the incoming transports. In the times when from 150,000 to 200,000 soldiers were on the ocean at once in transports bound for the United States, keeping track of each unit became difficult. The Transportation Service set up a news and information bureau through which the press and the public kept in touch with the movements of organizations crossing from France.

Upon the debarkation camps at the Atlantic ports fell the chief work of splitting up the returning expedition into demobilization units. There were five major debarkation camps—Merritt, Mills, and Upton at New York, and Stuart and Hill at Newport News—besides numerous smaller centers at both ports. At the height of the return movement these camps were insufficient to accommodate the incoming thousands, and the Transportation Service used former training camps as debarkation camps, in both the Hoboken and Chesapeake districts. As long as Boston and Charleston acted as ports of debarkation they, too, made use of neighboring training camps.

Of all of the debarkation camps, Camp Merritt was the largest. In it were to be observed some of the most interesting processes of troop demobilization. It was the principal camp both for reception of overseas casual companies and for the breaking-up of organized units and the formation of casual detachments for distribution among the thirty-three demobilization centers.

During demobilization Camp Merritt was like a great terminal post office. The mail consisted of bulk consignments of soldier members of the disintegrating American Expeditionary Forces. It was the task of the post office to sort the mail for thirty-three principal destinations. The individual soldiers were thrown into receptacles called Hoboken Casual Companies, each, when filled up, consisting of two officers and 150 men, and each addressed to one or another of the demobilization centers. Each bore an identifying number, and the numbers ran consecutively, reaching well into four figures before the work came to an end.

Special trains frequently left the two railroad stations which served Camp Merritt. Sometimes an entire train would be loaded with casual companies bound for the same center. Other trains were made up of special cars destined for different terminals. In the camp new casual companies in skeletal form were constantly being organized. Those scheduled to travel to the less populous sections of the country might be several days in filling up to standard strength. Others reached full size in a few hours. As soon as a casual company was complete, it was dispatched immediately to its proper demobilization camp. For several months in the spring and summer of 1919 the average interval between the time a skeleton company was formed and the time it was dispatched from camp was less than twenty-four hours.

Before the armistice, troops which had been inspected, equipped for the overseas voyage, and otherwise prepared at Camp Merritt, marched east from the camp over three miles of macadamized highway and then down the old Cornwallis trail descending the Palisades, until they reached the little landing on the Hudson River known as Alpine, several miles north of the metropolitan limits of New York. There they boarded ferry-boats and rode on them directly to the transport piers in the North River. After the armistice, soldiers debarking at the piers boarded ferry-boats at the pier ends, rode up the river to Alpine, climbed the Palisades, and marched to Camp Merritt. Those bound for Camp Mills or Camp Upton took ferry to the Long Island Railroad terminal at Long Island City on the East River. Those ticketed for Camp Dix boarded trains which had been run into the Hoboken yard on the spur track constructed there by the Government after it seized the pier property from Germany.

At the debarkation camps the Army applied its final precautions against the importation of European diseases and insect pests. There was a thorough disinfection of all clothing and equipment, and each principal camp maintained a delousing plant. However clean the soldiers might have been when they embarked in France, it was always possible for a few of them to become infested on the transports. So far as is known, not a cootie got through the barrage of steam, superheated air, soap, and hot water laid down by the Army at both ends of the transatlantic ferry route.

Before the return of the A. E. F. was well under way an important change took place in the organization of the official military travel bureau. Before the armistice, military transportation had been in the hands of two independent war department agencies. The Inland Traffic Service had charge of the movements of men and supplies by rail within the United States and up to the ports of embarkation. There the Embarkation Service received both, loaded them on the ships, and delivered them to the ports in France. Beyond those points the Quartermaster Service of the A. E. F. was in charge of military traffic. Both the Inland Traffic Service and the Embarkation Service were branches of the General Staff Division of Purchase, Storage, and Traffic.

In December, 1918, the Inland Traffic Service and the Embarkation Service joined to form a new branch called the Transportation Service, and for the first time the Army had a single organization in charge of all military travel, both freight and passenger, on this side of the piers in Europe. General Hines of the Embarkation Service became chief of the Transportation Service. The union brought about a coördination which made it possible for a limited equipment of railway coaches to carry troops away from the ports of debarkation as fast as the ships delivered them there.

As a rule, the overseas men did not travel so comfortably from the ports of debarkation to the demobilization centers as they had ridden when, months earlier, they had traveled from those same centers up to the ports to board the ships for France. The conditions of military transportation were different. The equipment of railway cars at the Army's disposal was limited. It had never consisted of more than 1,500 sleeping cars—tourist sleepers they were, made by removing the rugs and hangings from first-class Pullman coaches. These 1,500 cars, in full operation, could carry less than 50,000 men at one time. Nevertheless, although before the armistice the Army supplied railroad transportation to over 8,000,000 men, nearly every one who traveled at night slept in a comfortable berth. During that period practically all the long-haul travel was between the training camps and the ports of embarkation. The forces in America proceeded to embarkation by divisions—camp by camp. Thus it was possible to arrange the shipping schedules to allow for the most convenient operation of the military rolling stock. But no such arrangement was possible during demobilization. The system of splitting up the overseas units at the ports in this country and distributing their men according to residential origin made it necessary to maintain practically continuous train service between the various Atlantic ports and the thirty-three demobilization centers. The sleeping-car equipment was not nearly large enough to serve in such an operation, and a great many soldiers rode in day coaches halfway across the continent. They did not grumble too much at the treatment. It was better than riding in French box cars, at any rate, and after all they were getting home.

One of the finest accomplishments of military transportation after the armistice was the distribution of 150,000 sick and wounded soldiers of the A. E. F. among the many military hospitals of the United States. The Transportation Service operated six hospital ships at New York. These vessels took the patients from the general debarkation hospital on Ellis Island and carried them on their way to various special evacuation hospitals in the New York metropolitan district. From there they were sent to general hospitals throughout the country. The Service kept six hospital trains in continuous operation, as well as about 250 hospital cars. No such movement of invalids was ever before known in the United States.

The records of the Transportation Service show that in disbanding the Army it carried over 7,000,000 military passengers in special cars and trains. The average journey was 500 miles. Train accidents cost the lives of only two soldiers and injured only seventeen. This high degree of safety was largely due to the fact that troop trains were held down to a running schedule of twenty miles an hour.

The whole system of distribution and travel would have worked almost automatically except for one thing—the victory parades. Whenever it could do so without too great disruption of the system, the War Department yielded to the desire of communities to celebrate with parades the return of their overseas sons. Nearly 200,000 troops in all marched in more than 450 parades, which ranged from the brief processions of single companies to such great demonstrations as those of the First Division in New York and Washington in September, 1919.

Six parades of returning overseas troops passed under the triumphal arch over Fifth Avenue at Madison Square, New York. Of these, the parades of the Twenty-seventh and Seventy-seventh Divisions, both originally composed almost exclusively of New York men, were closest to the metropolitan heart. Part of the Twenty-eighth Division paraded in Philadelphia on May 15, 1919. The Thirty-third Division paraded in Chicago in three sections in late May and early June.

These processions were but preliminary to the greatest celebration of all—the one which occurred when the First Division, first to go to France, last to come back, returned, with General John J. Pershing, the Commander-in-Chief of the American Expeditionary Forces, at its head. In arranging for the parades of the First Division, the War Department determined to show the spectators a combat division in full field panoply—and that meant equipping it with its transport animals. All divisions had left their animals in France, and solely for these spectacles the Transportation Service assembled in New York before the day of the first parade several thousand horses and mules secured from army posts as far west as Texas and then transported to New York.

The First Division gathered in the debarkation camps at New York. It included as an attached unit the specially trained drill regiment of the Third Army Corps. So augmented, it consisted of nearly 24,000 men and their wheeled equipment of artillery, service trains, repair shops, bakeries, kitchens, and so on, the motorized equipment alone numbering five hundred trucks and sixty motorcycles. The transportation of this great unit to Washington afforded a special problem that would have been impossible of solution by any organization less expert than the one which had administered military travel for so many months past. There were no facilities at Washington for the accommodation of such a number of troops, and therefore it was necessary to hold them in the New York camps and take them to Washington on the eve of the parade itself. After the New York appearance of the Division its motor fleet was sent over the highways to Washington, the vehicles incidentally carrying 1,770 men with them. The freighting to Washington of the animals and horse-drawn vehicles, including the artillery, began immediately after the New York parade disbanded and continued for several days. The twenty-two trains carrying the foot soldiers all arrived in Washington during the night before the parade, the last ones just in time to allow their passengers to find their places in the procession.

The moving spectacle which followed gave the national capital and, through the newspaper accounts, the country, an approximation of the Grand Review that occurred in Washington at the close of the Civil War. For four hours the Division marched between throngs such as Washington ordinarily knows only when a President is inaugurated, down Pennsylvania Avenue, past the Treasury and the White House and the reviewing stand, in which were some of the chief uniformed and civilian dignitaries of the Government, including General Pershing. A roaring squadron of airplanes skimmed the treetops between the capitol and the war department building; an observation balloon swayed in air above the White House;

Photo by Signal Corps

HOME AGAIN

Photo by Signal Corps

WELCOMING RETURNING TROOPS AT HOBOKEN

Photo by Air Service

FIRST DIVISION PARADING ON PENNSYLVANIA AVENUE

Photo by Air Service

VICTORY ARCH IN WASHINGTON

and as the steady procession passed—mile after mile of trig ranks, bronzed faces, showy war medals and regimental decorations, burnished caparisons, regimental bands, field guns, limbers and caissons, ammunition trucks, quartermaster supply trains, ambulance trains, engineering trains with strange implements mounted upon motor trucks, horse-drawn carts for many purposes, rolling field kitchens, and finally the jarring tanks, their caterpillar treads leaving indelible matrices in the sun-warmed asphalt—with emotion the spectator beheld this living presentment of the power which America had exerted in the great war.

CHAPTER V

THE PROCESS OF DISCHARGING SOLDIERS

FOUR hours after the First Division finished parading in Washington, its troops were in Camp Meade, thirty miles away, where the "emergency" soldiers in the division's ranks were to be discharged. There, like the millions who had preceded them into the demobilization centers, they fell into the hands of two expert crews, each competing with the other in speeding up the processes of discharge from the Army.

The two principal operations in the discharge of a soldier were (1) examining him physically and (2) computing how much the Government owed him and paying over to him the amount determined. These two activities were in the hands of central organizations functioning at the demobilization centers. The preparation of the soldier's certificate of discharge and of the papers for his permanent record, to be retained in the government files, was in the hands of his company officers.

For the first time after a great war the American Army retained a complete record of the exact physical condition of every soldier at the time of his discharge. Had the Army done this in the past, doubtless it would have saved the Government much trouble and expense arising from fraudulent claims for alleged physical disability arising from military service. The purpose of the final physical examinations at the camps was not only to give the Government this record, but also to discover any men who might be suffering from contagious diseases or from infirmities susceptible of cure under further treatment in the army hospitals. The Army would not let men go until the Medical Department had done all it could for them.

The boards of physicians and surgeons which conducted the examinations were made up of specialists in seven branches of medicine, including dentistry. As each soldier entered the examination building, he was first taken in hand by officers who explained to him what the Government would do in the way of compensation for disabilities incurred in the Service and who urged him to make claim for any disability from which he knew he was suffering. For this purpose he received a claim form to fill out. He then passed through the seven sections of the examination; and if this scrutiny disclosed no disability, and if he had claimed none, he was granted a clean bill of health and passed on to the pay officers.

The degree of disability was expressed in percentage. A rated disability of 50 per cent meant that in the opinion of the examiners the soldier's earning power in his former occupation had been decreased by half by reason of injury or infirmity incurred in the military service. Under the law the Bureau of War Risk Insurance automatically granted compensation to disabled veterans of the war up to eighty dollars a month (for total disability), requiring only that the disabled soldier prepare his claim on a form sent to him by the Bureau upon its receipt of the report of the examining board at the demobilization center. Disability of less than 10 per cent was not compensatable under the law, and so the examining boards certified to the Bureau of War Risk Insurance only the records of disability amounting to 10 per cent or more.*

At first it took the medical boards a considerable time to give examinations to large units of troops awaiting discharge; but Washington kept putting more and more pressure upon the demobilization centers to speed up, until finally the flat order went forth that all troops arriving at a camp must be

* The disability discovered in these examinations was surprisingly small, affecting a little more than 5 per cent of the soldiers examined. Since the so-called limited-service men—soldiers suffering from physical disability at the time of their induction and accepted for military duties with the proviso that they should serve in capacities where their physical shortcomings would not impair their value to the Government—since these men also went to the demobilization centers for discharge, it is evident that, to show a true picture of the physical condition of the Army at demobilization, the limited-service troops must be subtracted from the totals. With such subtraction made, it is estimated that less than 5 per cent of the men called to arms and accepted for service incurred physical disability of any sort by reason of their experience.

put through to discharge within forty-eight hours thereafter. Since sometimes the greater part of a division of troops, or even a whole division, reached a demobilization camp practically at once, the order meant day and night work for the examiners, until they had cleared away the accumulations of men. At such times the boards raced with the finance crews, the doctors exulting if they passed men faster than the disbursing officers could make out the pay rolls, and the latter crowing when they could twiddle their thumbs and wait for men to come from the examination rooms.

The cash settlement between Uncle Sam the employer and his four million soldier employees was a transaction much more complicated than would appear at first glance. There were many elements to be considered in computing the final pay of a soldier, and to determine these elements for each man of the four million the pay officers had to make a complete search of the records each time.

The records were often voluminous. The private soldier's base pay was $30 a month. His records showed when he was last paid, and the Government owed him for the interval between his last pay day and the date of his discharge, at the rate of $30 a month. But perhaps he had been deducting a certain amount of his pay each month as an allotment to his dependents. He could deduct up to $15 a month, and the Government would match him dollar for dollar when it paid the allotment to his dependents. At any rate, any allotment was deducted from his final pay, too. Was he insured with the War Risk Insurance Bureau? If so, the pay officer deducted a premium from each month's pay due him, and the premium varied with each man's age. Perhaps he had purchased a Liberty Bond through the War Department. In that event the monthly partial payment was deducted. Deductions had to be made for sickness incurred not in line of duty, or to fulfill penalties imposed by courts-martial. After March 1, 1919, every soldier was entitled to draw a bonus of $60, and this was included in his final pay. Finally the law granted him a mileage allowance at the rate of five cents a mile for the distance between his place of discharge and his home. And this did not mean the distance to the railroad station nearest his home, but the distance clear home, to his front door, even though he lived off in the back country forty miles from the railroad. The pay officer had to have at his elbow, not only the tables of railroad distances, but also complete road maps of the district served by the demobilization center.

It should be remembered that pay officers were personally responsible for errors in their work, and if the Government chanced to lose money as the result of error, the unfortunate disbursing officer or his bondsmen had to make it good. In spite of the many elements entering into the pay computations, the finance crews at the centers grew astonishingly expert in making out the pay rolls. It became so that a team of two pay officers could enroll names on the pay sheet at the rate of two names a minute.

To accomplish such a result the Director of Finance, in whose hands eventually centered all the finance activities of the War Department, swept aside hampering regulations and precedents and adopted the direct methods of business. This impatience of red tape was not better shown than in the treatment of wounded men in the American hospitals. The regulations were hard and fast in adherence to the rule that a soldier could be paid only upon the representations of facts as written into his service records. Wounded men, however, picked up unconscious on the battle field, often too sick for months thereafter to look out for their personal affairs, in thousands of instances had lost their service records altogether. The matter came to a focus in early 1919 when the finance officer at Walter Reed Hospital at Washington reported that there were nearly a thousand patients in that institution who possessed no records at all to show what the Government owed them. The Director of Finance thereupon issued instructions that they and all other wounded men in the domestic hospitals should be paid off on the basis of their sworn affidavits setting forth the amounts owed to them by the Government. The finance officer at Walter Reed Hospital collected the affidavits, but, feeling his personal responsibility, hesitated to certify the pay roll; whereupon the Director of Finance showed his courage by certifying it himself, thus setting a precedent which the hospital officers were willing to follow.

That was one departure from tradition. A more important one, because it concerned more men, did away with the individual final statements which all soldiers in the past had been required to make when coming up for discharge. The final statement was an elaborate form which each soldier filled out, at the cost of considerable time and effort. Moreover, the pay officers could not work rapidly from these forms. For them was substituted the final-payment roll which served for an entire company of men and which could be made up quickly by the company officers. Working with individual final statements, a certain demobilization center had been able to discharge four hundred men a day. As soon as the final-payment roll was adopted the same crew at the same camp was able to discharge men at the rate of fifteen hundred a day.

The men who paid off the demobilized troops at the camps were trained for the work in a finance service school established immediately after the armistice at Camp Meigs, in the District of Columbia. The school graduated some 250 experts in army camp finance. These men were distributed among the demobilization centers, working in teams of two men each. For a long time the work of discharging the Army kept these teams at work from dawn until late at night, with never even a Sunday as holiday.

From the pay-roll teams the certified sheets went to another set of finance teams for "change-listing." The final payments to soldiers were made in cash. The "change-listers" took the pay rolls and computed precisely how many bills of each denomination, how many half-dollars, how many quarters and dimes and nickels and pennies, it would require to pay off all the men without requiring one of them to make change at the window. The aggregate change lists went to the camp disbursing officer, and he procured the cash from the nearest bank. The banks nearest to some of the camps were miles away

Photo by Signal Corps

OVERSEAS TROOPS ENTRAINING AT HOBOKEN

Felix J. Koch Photo

VETERANS DETRAINING AT CAMP SHERMAN

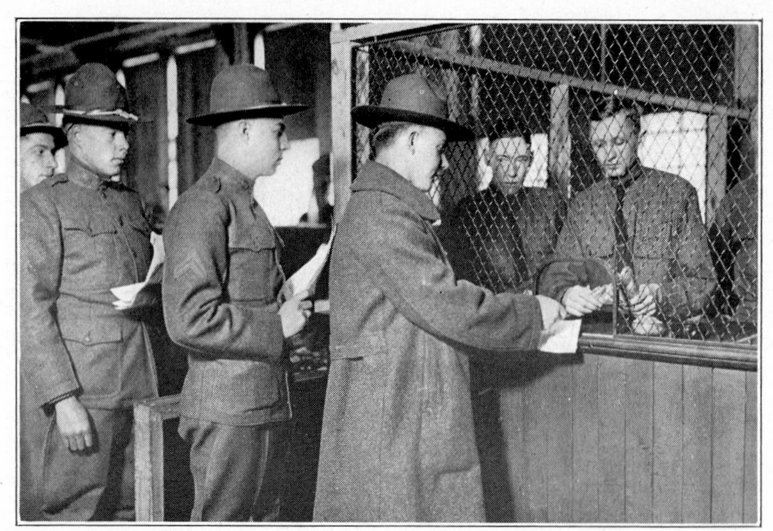

Photo by Signal Corps

DISCHARGED SOLDIERS RECEIVING FINAL PAY

Felix J. Koch Photo

MAKING OUT DISCHARGE CERTIFICATES

through desolate country, and sometimes a disbursing officer had to bring back in his automobile as much as a million dollars in currency. He rode under the escort of a heavy guard and was further protected by armed men in his camp office. Losses incurred through robbery were insignificant.

Every morning the disbursing officer turned over to his assistants the exact quantity of bills and small change needed to cover the payments to be made that day. The men reported to the pay office in companies. Their officers called out their names one by one, and when each man had verified his cash he received his discharge certificate, on the back of which was endorsed the amount of money just paid to him in final settlement. At that moment he was no longer a soldier. He could do as he pleased from that time on, but he usually yielded to the good influences of those urging him to proceed directly to his home.

The Seventy-seventh Division was paid off and discharged at Camp Upton in two days. There were 27,000 men in the division as it reached the demobilization camp. The problem of the finance officers was simplified by the fact that practically all of the men resided in New York City, which made it easy to compute mileage. Each man received an average of $100, including the bonus, an amount which is probably a fair approximation of what was paid to the average overseas soldier upon discharge. The advantage of speed in demobilization was not all to the soldier. It cost about two dollars a day to maintain a private soldier in the Service. Each day's delay, therefore, in demobilizing the Seventy-seventh Division cost the Government $54,000.

A further simplification of methods resulted in promptness in discharging commissioned officers. The disbursing officer at a demobilization camp saw all officers in three classes—those who in service had been accountable for neither government property nor money; those who had been accountable for property only; and those who had been in possession of government funds. The officers of Class 1 could be paid off finally at discharge; but the accounts of accountable officers were subject to audit, and their final pay was withheld until these audits were made. Inasmuch as officers often came up for discharge with two or three months' back pay due them, the withholding of such considerable amounts of money for an extended period imposed a hardship upon them. Under the old system it would have been a long time before all of the discharged officers could have received their final pay. In fact, after the termination of every previous war in which American emergency troops had ever engaged it was a long time before the Government finally settled the pay claims of the accountable officers. The accumulation of officers' accounts in the spring of 1919 became so great as to make it evident that under the existing plan the War Department would be a dozen years at least in auditing all of them; which meant—if the old audit system were to be continued—that it would be 1931 before some of the World War officers received their final pay for their services.

The Director of Finance determined to do better than that. To be sure, the audit of the property accounts was required by law; but instead of continuing the system of auditing them in Washington, the Director of Finance arranged for a force of field auditors to go to the demobilization centers and audit the property accounts as they were presented. The result was that the officers responsible for property were enabled to draw their final pay with their discharge certificates.

Officers responsible for government money occupied a different status, but such officers were relatively few in number. The former plan in use required the audit of their accounts by the Treasury Department, and it was evident that the Treasury Department would be a year or more in making these audits. Meanwhile none of the discharged officers would be able to draw their final pay. This auditing arrangement was a requirement, not of law, but of military regulation, which the Director of Finance was able to sweep aside, paying off such officers finally upon the receipt of statements from them accounting in detail for the money which they had handled. The Government risked nothing by this innovation, because officers accountable for money were required to give bond to indemnify the Government against losses. On the other hand the change made it possible for discharged accountable officers to receive their final pay within a month after discharge.

On February 24, 1919, the President signed a bill granting a cash bonus of sixty dollars to every soldier who had been in uniform before November 11, 1918. The payment of the bonus to soldiers still to be discharged after the bonus law was in effect offered no difficulty at all, since the camp disbursing officers needed only to add the bonus to the final pay of each man coming up for discharge. But on February 24 approximately 1,600,000 troops had already been discharged. The payment of the bonus to these men added measurably to the burden of work upon the Finance Service.

The Director of Finance announced that he would begin paying the bonus on March 1. The Zone Finance Officer at Washington was designated as the official to pay the bonus to officers and enlisted men who had already been discharged. He hastily organized an office with about sixty new and inexperienced clerks. Meanwhile the newspapers, the Red Cross, the American Legion, and all other organizations concerned with the welfare of discharged soldiers spread the tidings of the bonus payment and urged all discharged men to present their claims for it at once. It is doubtful if ever before a national publicity campaign reached its mark with such thoroughness in such a brief period of time. Claims for the bonus snowed upon Washington at the rate of 100,000 a day, and within two weeks practically all of the discharged 1,600,000 had filed their claims. The pay office grew until it numbered more than a thousand clerks. With this force it cleaned up the whole job in two months' time.

Never before had government checks been issued at such a rapid rate. It was necessary to make use of the most modern labor-saving appliances in accomplishing this record of payment. The Bureau of Engraving, which prints the paper money for the Government, engraved a special check with the sixty-dollar amount printed in, so that it was necessary for the clerical force only to date the checks, fill in the names of payees, and then sign the instruments. The Zone Finance Officer himself was the only person in his department authorized to sign checks on the Treasury. However, upon his request the Treasury Department authorized five clerks whom he designated to sign his name for him. The Treasury further authorized the use of the pantograph or multiple signing device, which enabled each designated clerk to sign five checks with one writing of the signature. On the name line of each check was typed in the payee's name, his address, and his army serial number. The Zone Finance Officer adopted a window envelope through which could be seen the recipient's name and address as written on the check inside, and this measure saved the great labor of addressing the envelopes. All checks were typed in triplicate—one original and two carbon copies. Both copies were filed away to be the Government's record of the transaction. The cases in which the duplicates were filed filled a large room.

Soldiers of the surname of Smith received 15,200 of these bonus checks, and these were only the Smiths among the 1,600,000 troops discharged before March 1, 1919. If the same percentage carried through the rest of the Army, it is evident that there were enough Smiths in uniform to make up an entire combat division with a sufficient residue over to provide the necessary accompaniment of supply troops. If pushed to it, the Smith family could fight a respectable war on its own account. But the balance of power is maintained by the Brown army. The Brown family collected 9,000 of the 1,600,000 bonus checks issued from Washington in the spring of 1919.

Although every effort was made to pay off all troops in full at the time of their discharge, there were many men who, through their own fault or the fault of those in command of them, or else because of conditions over which there was no control, failed to receive all of the money rightfully theirs when they left the military service. For such men the remedy was the claim. A financial claim against the Government is notoriously a static thing. At the present day there are Civil

War claims still outstanding and unsettled. The Director of Finance determined that the World War should leave behind it no great body of soldier claimants to haunt Washington and nurse their grievances for years to come. Under the ordinary procedure the claims of soldiers for arrears of pay had to go through the channels of both the War Department and the Treasury Department before final payments could be made. The Director of Finance sought and, on January 30, 1919, received a decision of the Comptroller of the Treasury which permitted the former to settle back-pay claims without reference to the Treasury Department when there was no construction of law involved and the rights of the claimants were evident.

Although the claimants numbered many thousands, the number was relatively small compared to the total number of men in uniform. At the end of the calendar year 1919, less than 5 per cent of the nearly 4,000,000 men who were under arms on the first day of the armistice had filed claims with the War Department. Three-fourths of the claims were for the refund of allotments deducted from pay but for one reason or another never paid by the Government to the allottees; so that only a little more than 1 per cent of the Army left the service with claims resulting from errors in soldiers' pay accounts. Because of the more intricate financial relations between officers and the War Department, the claims of officers were greater in proportion, but the officers' claims submitted up to the end of the year 1919 amounted in number to only 10 per cent of the total number of officers commissioned.

The failure of the Government in many instances to pay over allotments to soldiers' dependents arose from a multiplicity of causes. In the first place, the legal method of paying allotments changed in the midst of the active part of the war. The War Risk Insurance Bureau for many months paid to soldiers' dependents the allotments granted by the soldiers, plus the amount which the Government added to each allotment. In June, 1918, Congress enacted a law requiring that all allotments of this form be paid directly by the War Department, leaving the War Risk Insurance Bureau to pay only those allotments which did not carry government allowances with them. The troops were at once apprised of this change; but because of the failure of individuals to discontinue their deductions to the War Risk Insurance Bureau, or because officers, busy with other things, neglected to do it for men under their command, or because of the loss of papers in the mails, thousands of pay deductions continued to go in to the Bureau of War Risk Insurance long after that bureau had discontinued paying the allotments to dependents. Out of this situation arose thousands of claims from discharged soldiers.

In other instances allotments were made to persons residing in enemy countries or in countries cut off from mail communication, Russia being the principal one of the latter class. Failures to deliver allotments for this reason resulted in claims.

As to soldiers' pay, there were many reasons why payment was not always accurate. Sometimes amounts were withheld by the Government erroneously as court-martial forfeitures or because of alleged losses of government property. Men upon promotion often failed to note on their pay vouchers that they were entitled to the advanced pay, and so failed for a time to receive their increases. Some failed to receive the increase in pay due for foreign service, and some did not get their cash commutations of rations and quarters while on leave at the recreational areas in France. In all there were fourteen major classes of claims for back pay.

There were claims of still another class—claims for personal baggage lost by the Government in transporting the Army.

Although the individual soldier's affidavit was largely used in the settlement of claims, still such a short-cut method of arriving at a judgment was permissible only when the official records were missing. The gradual concentration of records after the armistice, and sometimes the discovery of lost records as the disbanding Army cleared up its quarters, often brought to light papers that had been missing when the troops were discharged. Every claim submitted involved on the part of the Finance Service a search of the records. Since many of the records on which the claim depended were in the possession of the A. E. F. in France, it was impossible for a long time to do much in Washington with such claims. The A. E. F. records returned to the United States in the early autumn of 1919, but it was several months thereafter before they were properly sorted, filed, and made available for research.

During the first fifteen months after the armistice, the claims submitted to the War Department by former enlisted men totaled 184,256. Of these, about 64,000 were paid in that period, 33,000 declined, and 6,400 transferred to some other branch of the Government for settlement—103,000 claims disposed of and 81,000 still in process of adjudication and settlement.

CHAPTER VI

PICKING UP AFTER THE ARMY

EVEN in the United States, with its well-developed trunk-checking and baggage-transfer systems, the management of any considerable amount of personal luggage gives concern to the traveler. In a foreign land, travel with baggage is nothing less than an ordeal; and the man who can convoy a fleet of trunks over a foreign tour and bring them all back without loss to the home port, may safely regard himself as an expert globe-trotter. What, then, of the A. E. F.? It was on foreign soil, in a land where military traffic had almost altogether superseded civilian, and the troops had little benefit of the services which ordinarily look out for civilians. The soldiers, by the nature of things, could not give personal attention to their baggage. You might multiply the troubles of the individual traveler by the two million men of the A. E. F., and still fall short of even half of the baggage problem of that organization.

The baggage problem was one of those unforeseen complications which arose to make the task of maintaining the expedition harder than it had at first seemed to be. It was by no means entirely a transportation problem, although whole organizations, when advancing toward France, often had to leave their baggage behind them to follow by train or ship, and this baggage, entrusted to unfamiliar hands, sometimes went astray. But the greatest losses occurred in France itself, where the troops were quartered. Units were often moved on short notice. Expecting eventually to return to the same billets, the soldiers left their effects where they were and traveled light; but seldom did it happen that they returned to that area again. Other organizations moved into the places thus vacated, themselves later on to move forward and leave baggage behind. In the course of time, literally millions of pieces of American military baggage in France became beautifully and thoroughly lost.

This state of affairs called into being a military unit strange to our army structure—the Lost Baggage Bureau of the A. E. F., established as a branch of the Quartermaster Department. Before the armistice the Lost Baggage Bureau had attempted to do little more than set up certain facilities, notably a central baggage depot at Gievres, the Q. M. headquarters of the A. E. F., in which divisions ordered up to the trenches could store their excess baggage. This arrangement did well enough until the fighting ended, and then for the first time the lost-baggage problem began to make its magnitude manifest. After the armistice tens of thousands of enquiries about lost baggage began to shower down upon the Services of Supply, making it evident that great quantities of American property must be scattered throughout the area occupied by the Yankee troops in France. The little one-horse Lost Baggage Bureau gave way to an extensive organization, known as the Baggage Service of the A. E. F. The function of the new Service thereafter was to manage the transportation of all troop baggage during the exodus from France and to locate, collect, and if possible restore to its ownership, all baggage lost by the soldiers of the expedition.

The Baggage Service went at the problem with a plan drawn true to scale. American troops had been quartered at one time or another in fifty-nine departments of the Republic of France. This great territory the Baggage Service divided for its purposes into twenty-one zones. In each zone it placed a local organization in charge of an officer whose instructions were to go over his district with a fine-tooth comb and collect and forward to the central office at Gievres all lost articles belonging to individual American soldiers or to the Army as a whole. The search which then ensued not only took in hotels, railroad stations, police headquarters, and other obvious places in which lost property might be expected to collect, but it involved also a house-to-house search of all areas in which American troops had been billeted upon the French population. Each day the zone officers sent to headquarters reports which contained the descriptions of the articles found. The central baggage office took this information and indexed it, together with the descriptions of the 90,000 pieces of baggage which had accumulated in the Gievres warehouse up to the time the armistice began. By May 1, 1919, all of the territory occupied by the Americans had been thoroughly searched over and cleaned up, and hundreds of thousands of pieces of baggage, once lost, had been catalogued and stored at the headquarters of the various base sections or in the central warehouse at Gievres.

Although most of this baggage was obviously the property of individual soldiers, the search also turned up a great deal of government property. This included some twenty rolling kitchens in good condition, abandoned for one reason or another, hundreds of rifles and pistols, numerous helmets, many uniforms still wearable, and even bags of mail which had never reached destination. The searching parties came upon a lone army mule resigned to its apparent fate of ending its days as an adjunct to an impressive manure pile in a French peasant's dooryard.

By the time the search was complete and the baggage had been collected, the troops were then moving in such numbers up to the French ports of embarkation for their passage home to the United States that it was found to be impossible to restore their lost property to them *en route*. The Baggage Service in France was able to hand over to their owners only about 50,000 pieces of baggage. In early June, 1919, it was decided to ship all the remaining unclaimed baggage to Hoboken, where the owners could obtain it after their return to the United States. The baggage thus shipped filled sixty-three baggage cars and provided a large part of the lading of an entire cargo transport. With the baggage to Hoboken went the records from Gievres, to be used by the Lost Baggage

Service at Hoboken in restoring property to overseas soldiers returned to the United States.

The A. E. F.'s Baggage Service, besides finding and caring for lost baggage, was charged with the important duty of acting as the baggage agent for the returning expedition. There was no counterpart to such an organization before the armistice. Had there been, the Expeditionary Forces would have had practically no baggage problem at all, so far as the loss of baggage *en route* was concerned; for, on the way home, thanks to the new Service, the troops lost scarcely any baggage. Here, then, was another new military organization called into existence by our experience in the World War; one which proved its usefulness and thereby won a place for itself in any plans for large military operations in the future. The Baggage Service saved its own cost over and over again, for the Government itself is often responsible for the loss of the personal baggage of soldiers and expects to pay in cash the claims presented. Indeed, many claims for lost baggage which had accrued at A. E. F. headquarters were settled by the restoration of the baggage itself to its owners.

In handling baggage for the traveling expedition, the Baggage Service set up branches at all the important A. E. F. troop centers and at all the American embarkation ports in France. The function of the baggage men at the troop centers was to see to it that when units departed their baggage went forward with them, properly marked and routed. The Service took charge, not only of organization baggage, but of the baggage of individual soldiers as well. At the ports its branches acted as checking, storing, and forwarding agents. Brest was the largest of our embarkation ports in France, and at Brest the official baggage office was operated by five officers and one hundred enlisted men. The official "baggage room" at Brest was a whole huge warehouse located on one of the jetties. The military passengers awaiting embarkation at Brest usually numbered well over 100,000, and it took an immense storage space to contain all their baggage.

Officers of the baggage organization met all troop trains

arriving in the Brest area. On these trains were thousands of officers and enlisted men traveling alone or in small groups as casuals. From these the military baggage agents secured their railroad baggage checks, together with cards on which the travelers wrote identifying descriptions of their baggage. Thereafter the individual traveler had no further baggage worries. The Baggage Service secured the pieces from the railroad stations, loaded them on trucks and took them to the central warehouse, and then made out index cards identifying them and showing their location in storage. These cards were made out in the owners' names and filed alphabetically. Whenever a transport was preparing to sail, the embarkation authorities sent to the Baggage Service a copy of the passenger list. The baggage people checked over this list against the record cards, and were thus able easily to assemble the baggage belonging to the passengers to sail on that ship. The baggage was taken out to the transport on lighters, and the canceled identification cards were thereupon stamped with the name of the transport and the date of sailing and then filed away in the dead file. The baggage of organizations was handled in the same way, except that the troop units did not abandon the practice of sending their own baggage details along with their baggage to watch it. These detachments of soldiers remained with the baggage at all times, even when it was stored in the warehouse.

The military organization in the United States had nothing comparable to the A. E. F.'s Baggage Service to take charge of the baggage of traveling troops, but it did have an organization to handle lost baggage. This was not a branch of the Quartermaster Department, as it was in France, but an agency set up by the Transportation Service, an independent bureau of the General Staff's Division of Purchase, Storage, and Traffic. It was called the Lost Baggage Section, and it operated exclusively at Hoboken. Although we had several other ports of debarkation for the returning expedition, Hoboken was designated to receive all the lost baggage from France. When, in late June, Hoboken received the vast accumulation

Photo by Signal Corps

COMMON GRAVE NEAR CIREY

(See page 89.)

Photo by Signal Corps

LOST MILITARY BAGGAGE AT HOBOKEN

Photo by Signal Corps

PREPARING CEMETERY AT BEAUMONT

Photo by Signal Corps

LOADING COFFINS ON COLLECTION TRUCKS

of lost baggage which had been stored at Gievres and at the base headquarters of the A. E. F., the work of the Lost Baggage Section began in earnest. One of the great Hoboken pierheads, with its echoing, barnlike storage room and adjoining offices, was given over exclusively to the Lost Baggage Section, which put to work more than two hundred clerks to handle the voluminous correspondence which sprang up immediately. Individual owners, their relatives, various soldier-relief organizations, and even members of Congress who had interested themselves in soldiers, deluged the Lost Baggage Section with enquiries. When the armistice was a year old the Section had handled 2,000,000 pieces of miscellaneous baggage, and had succeeded in delivering eleven pieces of every dozen received from France.

In the United States, among the troops quartered at the cantonments, camps, posts, and stations of the war-time establishment and traveling over the American railroads, there was no such baggage problem as had fretted the A. E. F., but nevertheless there was one of considerable size. Shortly after the armistice the Transportation Service took cognizance of an accumulation of reports which it had received telling of baggage, ostensibly the property of soldiers, which was remaining unclaimed at railroad stations and at posts formerly occupied by troops. It happened that about that time the general baggage agents of the principal American trunk lines held a convention in Washington. The Transportation Service seized the opportunity of this meeting to request the coöperation of the railroads in returning lost baggage to soldiers. The baggage agents agreed to secure a complete report from the whole United States of all military baggage on hand at parcel rooms, express rooms, and baggage rooms. At the same time the Transportation Service ordered the commanders of all the military camps in the United States to send to Washington inventories of unclaimed baggage at the camps. The next step was to find out what soldiers had lost any baggage. Newspapers and service journals gave publicity to the project of the Transportation Service, and the various welfare societies added their assistance, with the result that the Service was able to restore hundreds of pieces of lost baggage to their rightful owners. Again the United States was saved a considerable sum of money which otherwise it would have had to pay out in settlement of claims.

One task of the military authorities, similar to the restoration of lost baggage, but much more delicate and requiring a high degree of tact and sympathy in its administration, was that of returning to bereaved relatives the baggage of soldiers who had been killed in battle or who had died on foreign soil. This was so obviously a work of its own kind, requiring men peculiarly adapted to the handling of it, that it was placed in charge of a special service, both in France and in the United States. In France the Effects Bureau, as the organization was called, was part of the Quartermaster Department; in the United States a bureau of the same name, and virtually the successor of the overseas organization, was attached to the Transportation Service, and, like the Lost Baggage Section, operated exclusively at Hoboken.

As long as the A. E. F. was in France in force the overseas Effects Bureau handled most of this work. It set up headquarters at the embarkation port at St. Nazaire, and there it checked up all the baggage it could find which was the property of deceased soldiers and forwarded it to the United States. Many of these effects were found in the general search of France for lost baggage, but thousands of pieces were stored at military hospitals and with troop organizations.

The work of restoring the effects to heirs in the United States and elsewhere did not attain any great size until after the armistice, and then it was handled almost entirely by the Effects Bureau at Hoboken. In July and August, 1918, for instance, the shipments of deceased soldiers' effects received in the United States were fewer than one hundred in number: in the month of May, 1919, alone, Hoboken received more than 15,000 packages of such effects. By that date the work of disposing of this property was engaging the attention of one of the largest individual offices connected with the Port of Embarkation of New York. All through the summer of 1919 the Effects Bureau handled a correspondence that averaged 1,000 letters a day.

It was not enough for an officer in the Effects Bureau to be well meaning and kindly intentioned—to fit his place, he had to possess a rare tact, an instinctive knowledge of what to do in circumstances that constantly varied. Early in the episode the Bureau witnessed a striking example of how not to deal with a bereaved family. One of our aviators had been killed in France when his plane crashed to the ground. At the time he had in his pocket six 100-franc notes. These were badly charred in the flames that had nearly incinerated the airman. The misguided effects officer who took charge of the dead aviator's baggage, thinking he was doing a kindness, replaced the mutilated notes with six new ones and forwarded these to the aviator's family, telling in a letter what he had done. The family promptly returned the new notes with the request that the charred currency be sent instead, because they would prize the burned money as a keepsake more highly than they would any amount of new money.

This incident apprised the Effects Bureau, at the outset, of the extraordinary value which the relatives of deceased soldiers were likely to attach to the most apparently trifling possessions. The men of the Bureau had to understand this fact. Moreover, they had to be men of scrupulous honesty. In the effects of men who had died abroad was a great deal of money in cash, and under the circumstances there could be no check upon the people handling this cash. The opportunities of pilfering from the dead were wide open. Consequently the Army picked only men of the highest quality to serve in the Effects Bureau.

The Bureau at Hoboken was compelled to accept responsibility for many unfortunate occurrences in which it was not at fault. The procedure behind a letter telling relatives in this country of the existence of property which they had inherited upon the death of a soldier was approximately as follows: after the man died the officers of his immediate organization made up an inventory of his property; and this inventory, together with the baggage itself, eventually reached the Effects Bureau. It was usually this original inventory which went to the relatives. Often enough, however, the dead man's property was not all in his possession when he died. Perhaps he had been billeted in villages where he had left souvenirs and other cherished but not easily portable trinkets, intending to go back some time and secure his property before he started back for the United States. He was unlikely to have left among his effects any record of these articles; and yet his relatives were quite likely to know of the existence of the property from the soldier's letters home. The baggage search in France raked together a considerable quantity of this property, the ownership of much of which could not be determined by any identifying marks. Consequently, when relatives wrote to the Effects Bureau to reproach that service with not having returned all of the deceased soldier's property the Bureau was often able to find the articles among the lost baggage at Hoboken. Frequently, however, the Bureau had to confess itself unable to locate the lost articles and to bear the brunt of any displeasure that followed such an admission.

After the *Tuscania* disaster the British authorities shipped to Hoboken a miscellaneous collection of unidentified articles of value, such as watches and finger rings taken from the bodies of drowned American soldiers. It seemed to be an impossible task to restore these trinkets to the relatives of the rightful owners, but the Effects Bureau nevertheless made the attempt to do it. The Bureau wrote letters to all the next of kin to the soldiers who went down with the *Tuscania*, asking them to send in descriptions of any articles known to have been in the possession of the soldiers when they boarded the ship. The replies brought back duplicate prints of photographs carried in watch cases, dimensions of finger rings, descriptions, and other identifications, which enabled the Bureau to restore many of the articles to the proper heirs in this country.

After an arrival of identified effects in Hoboken, the Effects Bureau wrote letters to the immediate relatives or other heirs of the deceased soldiers describing the property on hand. With each letter went a legal form, to be filled out and executed before a notary public, establishing the right of the proper heirs to receive the effects. Upon the receipt of executed forms, the Bureau sent forward the effects at the expense of the Government.

The effects piled up in the Hoboken pier contained many a pathetic reminder of the invincible curiosity and enterprise of the American boys in France and of their passion for souvenirs of the war. The dead men had collected from almost every part of Europe thousands of keepsakes of every description. In the baggage of one deceased soldier was found a German machine gun which he had acquired in some manner and had succeeded in identifying as his personal property. Occasionally those going over the effects found the contraband loaded shell and grenades. These were confiscated and destroyed, because of their dangerousness, but all other property was reverently handled and protected. Because of the complete lack of identification for some thousands of parcels, it was impossible to make complete restoration of the effects to the heirs of the American dead. Nevertheless, by the end of 1919 the Effects Bureau had delivered more than 35,000 sets of personal effects of deceased soldiers to their families.

In winding up the affairs of the American Expeditionary Forces in France, there was a final, mournful task for the Quartermaster Service; one of large proportions and unusual difficulty—that of disposing of the soldier dead. During the fighting it had been taken for granted by many that the Americans who fell would be interred in great American cemeteries in France, to be maintained and kept beautiful forever by the American Government; but after the armistice there developed in this country, among those bereft of their sons and brothers, a powerful feeling that the bodies of these boys should be returned to final resting places within the United States. The country, or that part of it immediately interested in the question, divided into two opposite camps and attempted to force the War Department into a definite policy one way or the other.

When the aviator Quentin Roosevelt was killed, his father, the late Theodore Roosevelt, quoted the words of the rugged Old Testament Preacher: "In the place where the tree falleth, there it shall be." This was perhaps the strong attitude, and a considerable number of bereaved relatives of soldiers felt as did Roosevelt; but they were, after all, the minority. Thousands of mothers, sisters, and sweethearts on the farms and in the hamlets, towns, and cities of the United States held rather with the poet, Theodore O'Hara:

> "Your own proud land's heroic soil
> Shall be your fitter grave."

In this contention the War Department took no sides. It did not adopt the wishes of the majority as a government policy, nor yet those of the minority; but it allowed each bereaved family to have its own way. If the family asked for the return of the body, that the War Department agreed to. If the family were willing to have the body remain buried in France, the War Department guaranteed that the grave should always be a hallowed and beautiful spot.

As soon as the A. E. F. began reaching France in force and its command realized that American troops were to bear their full share of the future fighting, the importance of identifying the slain and their graves asserted itself as a major problem. The experiences of the other armies had not been pleasant in this respect, and the command of the expedition did not underestimate the difficulties. The British Army, for instance, had lost the identification of fully 40 per cent of its dead. This was not due to the lack of identification of the dead at the time of burial so much as it was to the obliteration of cemeteries by shell fire as the battle front surged back and forth over many kilometers of ground. After the American Army reached the front in force in the summer of 1918, it never knew a major retreating action; its movement was always forward, and its cemeteries, always in the rear, were never destroyed. The result was that the A. E. F. maintained an extraordinarily high percentage of identification. Less than 2 per cent of its graves, after all the evidence was in, housed unknown dead.

The first step taken by the A. E. F. to accomplish this result was to establish, in the summer of 1917, a Graves Registration Service in the Quartermaster Department. The original plan was for this Service to send out field units to take complete charge of the disposition of remains—burying the dead on the battle fields and elsewhere, acquiring land for cemeteries, keeping the records of burials, and maintaining the cemeteries in the future. Sentiment among the troops themselves brought about a change in this arrangement. As soon as the divisions suffered their first casualties, the comrades of the dead men could not bear to have their friends buried by strangers, even though the strangers were Americans in the American uniform. Consequently G. H. Q. modified the original order, saying that "the dead must necessarily be buried by the units themselves. These units perform this duty as tribute to their dead." Thereafter the Graves Registration Service merely recorded all burials and grave locations and looked after the graves.

Such a system was maintained until the early autumn of 1918. Then the fighting reached its most intense stage, and our advancing forces could spare neither time nor energy for the proper burial of the slain. At this juncture the field units of the Graves Registration Service stepped in voluntarily, without waiting for special orders, and assisted in searching the ground for dead men and in burying them, enlisting such aid in the work as they could find on the spot. This was the time of the heaviest American casualties, and the units of the Graves Registration Service buried in all some 10,000 dead American soldiers.

The work of the Graves Registration Service was rendered particularly difficult by the width and the separation of the areas over which the American troops fought. It was not as if the front had been a continuous line. Some Americans had fallen in Belgium, others with the British at the Franco-

Belgium border, and still others at the southern extremity of the line, where it entered Alsace-Lorraine; but most of the American casualties had occurred in the Argonne when, during the final weeks of the war, the A. E. F. had forced a passage of that rough, forested, and traditionally impenetrable terrain.

In those last weeks in the Argonne the advancing troops had been too exhausted to make any thorough search of the battle areas for the bodies of their slain comrades. Consequently one of the first acts of the command of the A. E. F. after the armistice was to order an immediate, thorough search of all ground where our troops had been in action. Large numbers of divisional soldiers were assigned to help the Graves Registration Service in this work. Through the wreckage and débris of the Argonne went the search parties, sometimes finding unburied bodies and frequently bodies poorly and even only partially buried. To these the Graves Registration Service gave proper interment, marking all these temporary graves so that the identity of their occupants would not be lost. While this was going on, similar searching parties were at work in all the other battle areas in which American troops had been in action, and still other units of the Service followed up behind the Army of Occupation which was advancing through Luxembourg to the Rhine, in order to discover and identify the graves of any Americans who might have died, as prisoners or otherwise, behind the former German front. And the searchers were not content with a single examination of the ground: they went over every square yard of it three times, the final search being a check of the accuracy of the preceding two. Largely to the thoroughness of this work was due the completeness of the identification of the A. E. F. dead.

After the widely scattered graves were located, it was next the task of the Graves Registration Service to concentrate the bodies of the slain into as few cemeteries as possible. The American dead had been buried in approximately two thousand principal places. The concentration of the bodies was able to reduce the number of American cemeteries to about seven hundred. Not only were the bodies in isolated graves

Photo by Signal Corps

1. OVERFLOWED AMERICAN CEMETERY AT FLEVILLE

Photo by Signal Corps

2. TWO MONTHS LATER—BODIES ALL REMOVED

Photo by Signal Corps

1. ROMAGNE CEMETERY, APRIL 10, 1919

Photo by Signal Corps

2. ROMAGNE CEMETERY, MAY 30, 1919

brought in to the concentration cemeteries, but sometimes entire cemeteries were abandoned and all the bodies in them removed. This was particularly true when the emergency cemeteries had been poorly located. The Graves Registration Service would not allow even the elements to be unkind to the bodies of our fallen soldiers. At Fleville the divisional troops had buried a number of their comrades in an emergency cemetery located between a small stream and an embanked road. During the first winter of the armistice the stream overflowed its banks and flooded the little cemetery, leaving only a few crosses sticking up out of the water. The Graves Registration Service sent a force of two hundred men to the place. In three weeks they had built a dam around the entire cemetery and had pumped out the water, after which the bodies of eighty-seven Americans were disinterred and removed to a better burial ground.

The sites of the American concentration cemeteries were carefully selected by the French Government itself, which set up special commissions for that work. Each commission included within its membership various engineers and sanitary experts, as well as officers of the American Graves Registration Service. The first of the American concentration cemeteries was established soon after the action at Château-Thierry. Most of them, however, were created after the armistice. As soon as the site for a permanent cemetery had been secured by the A. E. F. and a few of its sections plotted and marked off, the Graves Registration Service set labor troops to work digging rows of graves, each five feet deep, and at the same time started out collection parties to bring in bodies. The concentration cemeteries gathered bodies in from distances as great as fifty miles. While the bodies were being brought in and reburied, engineers were at work laying out roads in the cemetery, grading, and perfecting the drainage, surveyors marked off new sections, and landscape gardeners planted shrubbery and prepared lawns.

The work of gathering the bodies fell into a dreary routine. Each collection party consisted of an officer and eight or nine men, and its principal piece of equipment was a motor truck. From each cemetery the collection parties ordinarily started out each morning before daybreak,* each party taking half a dozen empty coffins on its truck. The officer in command had with him cards showing the location of the bodies to be disinterred and transferred. Sometimes the party could obtain all six bodies from a single place, but more often it was necessary to visit four, five, or even six places to get the whole gruesome load. It was an experience common enough for a collection party which had started out before daybreak not to get back to the concentration cemetery until after midnight. In this way, 20,000 officers and enlisted men, operating 2,000 trucks, worked for months, until at the end they had visited 40,000 graves, scattered over 90,000 square kilometers of ground, and had removed all the bodies to new graves in concentration cemeteries.

The American concentration cemeteries designed to be permanent resting places for the bodies of such American soldiers as are to remain where they fell, are hundreds in number. The principal ones, their locations, and the number of American soldiers buried in each (December 31, 1919), are as follows:

Name	*Location*	*Number of burials*
Argonne	Romagne	23,061
St. Mihiel	Thiaucourt	4,233
Sedan	Letanne	774
Seringes-et-Nesles	Seringes-et-Nesles (Aisne)	3,792
Belleau	Belleau (Aisne)	2,045
Ploisy	Ploisy (Aisne)	1,954
Fismes	Fismes (Aisne)	1,712
Juvigny	Juvigny (Aisne)	411
Bony	Bony (Aisne)	1,766
Waereghem	Waereghem (Belgium)	689
Villers-Tournelle	Villers-Tournelle (Somme)	549
Bouvillers	Bouvillers (Oise)	297
Vaux-sur-Somme	Vaux (Somme)	234

* This work was practically all done after the date of the armistice and before the advent of spring in 1919—in other words, during the time of the year when the days are short and the nights long.

In addition, 357 Americans were buried in the British military cemetery at St. Souplet, Nord, and 122 others in the British military cemetery at Poperinghe, Belgium.

All of the cemeteries named above were carefully located in the first place and carefully planned thereafter, art aiding nature in making them fit places for the permanent interment of American soldiers. In addition to them there were hundreds of others, laid out on a smaller scale, but no less carefully planned. When the concentration cemeteries were filled, American soldier dead lay sleeping in many American national cemeteries on foreign soil—in rugged Scotland, on the Irish coast, in peaceful English villages, in sunny Italian fields, under the snows of North Russia and of Siberia, in Germany and in Austria, and along the whole battle front in France and Belgium.

In its search for bodies the Graves Registration Service came upon one common grave at Cirey, a village which had been held by the Germans. This grave was marked with a wooden cross bearing the legend in German: "*15 tapfere Amerikaner*" (15 brave Americans). The French inhabitants of Cirey swore under oath that these men had been prisoners massacred in cold blood by machine-gun fire. A complete investigation, however, made it seem likely that the villagers were merely repeating rumors, and led to the conclusion that the Americans had been members of a raiding party which, being surrounded, had preferred death to surrender. After a long investigation the Graves Registration Service succeeded in identifying all the bodies in the common grave. All fifteen were given separate burials.

Upon the Graves Registration Service fell the duty of identifying the unknown dead, and in this work it rendered one of its most valuable services. The work was essentially detective work, the following up of clues and the assembling of circumstantial evidence. The case of L—, an aviator, demonstrates the methods used. The men of the Service found behind the former German lines a grave containing a body which had apparently been stripped of every identifying mark. The cross on the grave designated the occupant thereof merely as "A brave American." The graves registration officers, examining the body minutely, found, pushed up so high on one arm that it had evidently not been seen by the Germans, a wrist watch engraved with the name L—. A subsequent investigation showed that one L—, an American aviator, had fallen to the ground within the German lines at about that spot; and thus the identification was made certain.

A much more remarkable feat was the identification of the body of Private Walter L—, a former member of one of the infantry regiments of the First Division. Near the isolated grave of an unknown American at Ploisy one of the graves registration men found on the ground an old, faded, water-soaked, and nearly illegible letter addressed to the single name "Walter" by one who was evidently a sister living in California. The Graves Registration Service communicated with this woman and learned that her brother was Private L—, of the —— Infantry. The chaplain of that regiment offered evidence that L— had been killed in action near the place of the unknown grave. Thus another grave was identified.

Second Lieutenant T—, an aviator, was killed in action early in November, 1918. The Graves Registration Service found a lonely grave in the commune of Letanne marked "Unknown First Lieutenant, A. S., U. S. A." The body was examined. The uniform bore the mark of a manufacturing tailor at Rochester, New York. A letter to this tailor from the Graves Registration Service induced him to make an independent investigation among the retailers who had sold his uniforms during the war. About three hundred retail clothing establishments answered to his enquiry. Several dealers, judging from the description of the dead man, thought they might have sold him the uniform; but one retailer in Texas said he had sold a uniform to a man answering the description, who was then an aviation cadet in training. His name was T—. This seemed to the Graves Registration Service to be a good clue. Pursuing the line of enquiry in the Air Service, the Service established that T— had been last seen alive flying toward

Letanne, and, since he never returned from that flight, he might have been shot down at Letanne. This circumstantial evidence together with other corroboratory details, justified the Graves Registration Service in identifying the unknown dead man as T—.

Upon the Graves Registration Service fell the duty of communicating with the kinsfolk of fallen American soldiers to learn their wishes as to the final disposition of the remains. The Service sent out nearly 75,000 letters to the relatives of deceased soldiers. In reply 44,000 asked for the return of bodies to the United States; 19,000 expressed willingness to leave the bodies in Europe; and some 300 others requested the removal of bodies to cemeteries in countries other than the United States. The rest did not reply.

On the first anniversary of the signing of the armistice a transport reached New York bringing the bodies of 115 American soldiers who had died on foreign soil. These bodies, the remains of men who had died in northern Russia, were the first to come home. The French law prohibited the disinterment and shipment of bodies until after the expiration of a considerable period of time after burial, and for that reason the return of remains to the United States did not begin immediately. At present (1921) frequent shiploads of bodies are arriving in the United States. They are received at New York and from there they are transported under military guard to the cemeteries chosen for their final resting places.

CHAPTER VII

SOLDIER WELFARE

THE World War brought to America a new and enlightened discernment of the Government's responsibility toward the men whom it had called to the uniform. In former wars the military hierarchies had, in effect, regarded the individual soldier as a piece of cannon bait; and when he was no longer able to serve this purpose, they were done with him. In the World War the attitude of the Government toward its four million soldiers was much less impersonal, much more paternalistic. Its first solicitude was, to be sure, the soldier's expertness as a soldier, but after that came a real and helpful regard for his physical, mental, moral, and economic well-being.

Particularly was this true after the armistice. Before that day the various welfare activities conducted by the Army and its auxiliaries had been mainly directed to the end that the soldier might be made physically and morally fit as a fighter. After the armistice the undertakings in soldier welfare began looking to the time when the troops would resume their places in the workaday world once more.

When the fighting stopped, the American Expeditionary Forces faced a long interval which was bound to elapse before the shipping of the United States could possibly repatriate the two million Americans in France. This might easily have been a period of stagnation for the temporary exiles. Those in command, however, seized the opportunity to establish within the A. E. F. a vast school system. Wherever American soldiers were quartered in any numbers, classes were organized and instruction proceeded, the curriculum including practically the entire range of subjects taught in the public schools of the United States, from the three elementary R's to the Latin and algebra of the high schools. Those who desired it could receive instruction in trade and business subjects. As an auxiliary to this system the Young Men's Christian Association conducted at its huts courses similar to those given by that organization in its buildings in this country. A surprising amount of illiteracy was discovered among the troops raised in 1917 and 1918, foreign-born soldiers being classed as illiterates if they could not read and write the English language, even though they might be proficient in reading and writing their own. It is estimated that, during this period when the expedition was waiting for the ships to take it home, 100,000 men of the A. E. F. were taught to read and write English.

The public school system of the A. E. F., to call it that, was rounded out by a great soldiers' university established after the armistice at Beaune. In the ranks of the expedition were thousands of young men who, in order to join the Army, had interrupted their studies in colleges and other institutions of higher education in America. For these and for others to whom it was practicable to give such training, the General Headquarters of the expedition organized the A. E. F. University, occupying French army barracks, schools, and other public and private buildings at the town of Beaune. A large faculty was recruited almost entirely from the men in uniform, although a few college professors came from the United States to assist in the work. The faculty organized a curriculum which in scope would do credit to any large university in the United States. About 10,000 soldiers registered as students. Distinctions of rank ended at the classroom doors, and it was not uncommon to see private soldiers conducting classes in which sat officers of as high rank as lieutenant colonel. The university's brief career ended with the advent of the summer of 1919. Colonel Ira L. Reeves was president of the university.

Besides these educational advantages, the A. E. F. arranged for scholarships for some of its men at various French and English universities. Practically every university in

France, including the Sorbonne, admitted designated A. E. F. soldiers to its classes during that winter and spring, as did also Oxford and other famous educational institutions in England. Brigadier General Robert I. Rees was in charge of all educational activities of the A. E. F.

Yet it was not all study and work and no play for the men of the A. E. F. during the waiting time after the armistice. Athletics were organized on a tremendous scale. Near Paris the expedition established a great athletic field, called the Pershing Stadium. There, in the spring of 1919, were held the military athletic championship contests, to which the British, French, and other armies of the Allies sent their competing teams. Military drilling after the armistice became competitive in spirit, and out of such competition came the crack drill regiment of the Third Army Corps, known as "Pershing's Own Regiment," which paraded with the First Division in New York and Washington in September, 1919. The drill regiment was organized and trained by Colonel Conrad S. Babcock. Nearly every division in France conducted a horse show after the armistice. The expedition numbered among its members men of high talent in almost all callings, including that of the stage. At Tours the A. E. F. organized an expert theatrical producing company, the performances of which equaled in merit the productions seen on the American stage. This central troupe also conducted a training school for amateur actors of the expedition. The various areas in which the American soldiers were concentrated sent their local Thespians to Tours for training, after which they returned to their stations to organize and produce plays. It was a small community indeed which did not have its theatrical performances at regular intervals. The taste of producers and audiences alike ran strongly to musical comedies.

There was nothing which contributed more to the welfare of the men of the American Expeditionary Forces, or to their spirit and morale, than the *Stars and Stripes*, the service newspaper of the A. E. F. This unique adjunct to a modern army originated in the ranks, was written, edited, and published by

Photo by Signal Corps

COLONEL IRA L. REEVES, PRESIDENT OF BEAUNE UNIVERSITY

Photo by Signal Corps

STUDENTS AT BEAUNE UNIVERSITY

Photo by Signal Corps

ART STUDENTS IN A. E. F. TRAINING CENTER, PARIS

Photo by Signal Corps

A. E. F. STUDENTS IN UNIVERSITY OF LYON

men from the ranks, and to the end of its famous existence was primarily and always the organ of the enlisted man, with the enlisted man's point of view. No other army in Europe possessed an expeditionary newspaper, but it is unlikely that any great American army of the future will ever be without one. The value of the *Stars and Stripes* was beyond dispute.

Three men—Private Hudson Hawley, Field Clerk James A. Britt, and Corporal John T. Winterich—were the founders of the *Stars and Stripes.* All three had had training in the making of newspapers—Winterich had been one of the editors of the Springfield *Republican.* At Neufchâteau one winter night early in 1918 these three foregathered to descant upon the growing American Expeditionary Forces and—like the fraternity of reporters the world over—to talk shop; and these men agreed that the chief need of the expedition was an agency which might put the various American military elements in France in touch with each other, tell every man what the expanding force was like and what it was trying to do, and build homogeneity and singleness of purpose within the expedition such as no other agency could evoke—in short, the A. E. F. needed a newspaper. The idea was communicated to General Pershing, who promptly approved it. Thus was the *Stars and Stripes* officially born.

The first number was published in Paris on February 8, 1918, and regularly every Friday thereafter the paper appeared until June 13, 1919, when it was discontinued, and the editorial staff joined the homeward migration. At its summit of popularity the *Stars and Stripes* attained to a circulation of 526,000, which was close to the permitted limit of one copy for every three soldiers in the expedition, a stricture made necessary by the shortage of paper in Europe. This was all paid circulation, obtained without direct solicitation other than the advertising appearing in the paper itself. The *Stars and Stripes* was printed in the Paris plant of the London *Daily Mail.* The total net profit earned by the newspaper was about $700,000, a sum which went to the credit of the Quartermaster Department. After the armistice the collectors in America awoke to the historical value of this publication and offered large sums for the few complete files which had been saved.

At about the third issue of the *Stars and Stripes* Private Harold W. Ross, who had had an extensive experience as an executive in newspaper offices of the Pacific coast, became the editor-in-chief. The three originators of the newspaper were on its staff until the end. Sergeant Alexander Woollcott, who before and after his army experience was the dramatic critic of the New York *Times*, became the battle correspondent of the paper. His accounts of the engagements in which the American troops appeared were not excelled by those of any correspondent with the Army. After the armistice Sergeant John W. Rixey Smith joined the staff. These names all became well known to the men of the A. E. F. Nor should the two artists, C. LeRoy Baldridge and A. B. Wallgren, both private soldiers, be forgotten. Their work on the *Stars and Stripes* resulted in fame and fortune for both of them. The latter, as "Wally," made himself, with his whimsical nonsense, about the most popular figure in the American Expeditionary Forces. Baldridge was the possessor of a delicate and subtle talent. Practically unknown in his own country before the war, he returned after it to take his place among the foremost American illustrators.

These and other men connected with the publication were formally organized as a unit of the A. E. F., bearing the name 1st Censor and Press Company. The officers in charge were Major Mark Watson and Captain Stephen T. Early, both of them experienced in newspaper work.

The military authorities granted an extraordinary editorial freedom to the *Stars and Stripes*. At one time the paper was making a satirical onslaught against the army practice of fencing off the rank and file from the more desirable cafés and other gathering places with the placard "Officers Only." A high general of the expedition took umbrage at this campaign and sent to the publication office a peremptory order for the attack to cease. The editorial staff at once appealed to General Pershing, who replied with a written order that there was to be no interference with the editorial direction of the *Stars and Stripes*. With such a charter the *Stars and Stripes* threw itself whole-heartedly into various projects for the good of the A. E. F. and its *personnel*. Its chief military contribution was its "Berlin or Bust" campaign, undertaken in the summer and autumn of 1918. In this it directed its energies chiefly to the improvement of the unloading efficiency at the American ports in France. By citing publicly the labor units which made good records in the unloading of vessels, the newspaper created, among the stevedore troops, a spirit of competition which had a marked effect upon the efficiency of the ports. The newspaper induced American troop units in France to "adopt" for one year more than 3,000 orphans of deceased French soldiers, and many of the units continued their guardianship after they returned to America. In this campaign the *Stars and Stripes* raised over 500,000 francs for the care of French war orphans, and most of this money was contributed by men in the trenches. The newspaper also conducted a service department in which it answered more than 500,000 enquiries coming from American soldiers. After the armistice it co-operated in the expedition's educational enterprise.

In this volume, however, we are not so much interested in welfare activities within the Army as we are with those which bore directly upon the difficult business of demobilizing the troops without shock to the economic organization of the country. The activities in soldier welfare directly connected with demobilization were of two classes—those benefiting the sick and wounded and those helpful to the able-bodied.

To the officers and enlisted men of the Medical Corps in this country the armistice meant only an increase of work. Therefore, in common with the other military departments the *personnel* of which after the armistice could see no immediate prospects of discharge, the Medical Department experienced a sharp drop in corps morale. Many of the officers and enlisted men attempted to get out at once, and some of them succeeded, but for the most part they were held in uniform; and later, when the men realized how badly their services were needed and what good they were accomplishing, they became contented and worked with good spirit until the corps could be placed on its permanent peace footing.

While the Army was expanding, the most noticeable work of the Medical Corps in this country had been that of examining the men who sought entrance to the training camps, sorting out the physically fit from the unfit. The care of military patients did not become a predominant medical activity in the United States until the late summer of 1918, when, simultaneously, the A. E. F. began sending home its first shiploads of wounded men and the influenza epidemic invaded the training camps. Meanwhile the care of war's disabled had taken on a new meaning for the American military medical authorities. In former wars, as soon as a sick man or a wounded man had gained strength enough to travel, he was usually furloughed to his home, there to win his own way back to health if he could. In the summer of 1918 the War Department adopted the policy of not discharging disabled men from the Service until they were as nearly rehabilitated physically as medical science could make them; and even then a patient was not turned adrift, but might seek the services of other governmental agencies for specialized treatment and for reëducation that should enable him to take a place in civilian life at least as useful as the one he had left in order to join the military service. This policy had a marked effect upon the layout of the machinery which conducted the demobilization of the Army. It not only resulted in maintaining the Medical Corps, equipment and *personnel*, at war strength for many months after the armistice, but it also set up within the Government great new agencies for carrying out the Government's beneficent purposes toward the ex-service men.

On the day of the armistice there were 200,000 patients in the A. E. F. hospitals in France. It was at once realized that the best interests of these men demanded their prompt return to the United States; for nowhere else could they secure the treatment most certain to restore them to complete health. The Medical Corps at home was ready for them. For months it had been constructing throughout the United States a great chain of specialized hospitals in anticipation of a heavy American casualty list in France.

Many of the 200,000 hospitalized members of the A. E. F. recovered in time to recross the ocean as members of regular military units, but more than half of them returned as patients needing more or less extended treatment in the military hospitals in this country. The policy in France was to move these men either in ambulances or in hospital trains from the interior hospitals up to hospitals near the ports of embarkation. There they were placed aboard the special hospital ships or given accommodations on the regular transports. Practically all of them debarked either at New York or at Newport News. New York could accommodate 24,000 patients at once in its regular and special debarkation hospitals. The two regular debarkation hospitals in New York—one located in the Greenhut Building and the other in the Grand Central Palace—each had beds for over 3,000 patients, and in addition the Army could call upon thirteen additional hospitals in New York in an emergency. At Newport News there was a regular and emergency equipment of 10,000 hospital beds for incoming overseas patients.

Harbor hospital boats and ambulances distributed the patients from the ships to the debarkation hospitals. There they were classified according to the sort of treatment they required. There were eighty interior hospitals which received overseas patients. The policy of the Army was to send patients whenever practicable to the hospitals nearest their homes. In the distribution of patients from the ports to the interior hospitals, the Medical Corps operated four hospital trains—three out of Hoboken and one out of Newport News—and twenty unit cars, one of which, attached to a train of regular Pullman or tourist sleepers, enabled such a train to serve as a moving hospital. Each of the regular hospital trains was made up of seven hospital cars, and carried comfortably 141 patients and 31 doctors, nurses, and orderlies. The unit cars were equipped with diet kitchens, in which could be cooked food enough for

250 patients. With this equipment 139,000 overseas patients were handled up to the end of the year 1919, and of these, 103,000 entered the country through the port of New York. On the first anniversary of the armistice thirty-six of the eighty general hospitals had been closed, an indication of the rate of convalescence among the military patients.

In its treatment of patients in the military hospitals, the Medical Department of the Army went beyond the realm of pure surgery and medication in order to reconstruct physically and mentally, when necessary, the men left disabled by the war. To this end it enlarged its Sanitary Corps to include persons skilled in physical and occupational reconstruction. The plan permitted the employment by the Corps of civilian women, who, after putting on the distinctive blue uniform adopted for them, were known as reconstruction aides. These women were skilled in two branches of therapy—occupational therapy (the teaching of new occupations to invalids as a curative measure) and physiotherapy (including baths of various sorts, massage, heat and electric treatments, and gymnastics). Most of the general hospitals were fitted with workshops, gymnasiums, physiotherapy departments, and educational buildings. An elementary school system was inaugurated at the general hospitals, and several thousand illiterate patients were taught to read and write during their convalescence. Organized recreational activities were conducted at each general hospital engaging in reconstruction. Outdoor games, setting-up exercises and other gymnastic exercises, military drills, and organized play of many sorts vied with concerts, plays, boxing matches, and other amusements for the interest of the convalescents. One important work of the physiotherapists was to teach men with amputated limbs how to dress, feed, and otherwise care for themselves, and how to use the artificial legs or arms which the Government supplied to them. Nineteen former training camps were converted into convalescent centers operated by the Medical Department. To these places the general hospitals sent 50,000 convalescent soldiers to be

Photo from Engineer Department

AIR VIEW OF PERSHING STADIUM, PARIS

Photo by Signal Corps

AMERICAN SOLDIERS AT UNIVERSITY OF GRENOBLE

Photo by Signal Corps

A. E. F. SOLDIERS AS COMEDIANS

Photo by Signal Corps

JUDGING COMEDY HORSE AT 4TH ARMY HORSE SHOW

finally hardened by curative work and play for their reëntrance into civilian life.

After patients were finally discharged from the Army and from the army hospitals, the Government by no means washed its hands of them. Congress had set up three great new federal agencies looking to the welfare of the discharged soldier. One of these was the Bureau of War Risk Insurance, which, in addition to offering low-priced life insurance policies of the standard sorts to all ex-service men, determined, granted, and paid the monthly allowances given by the Government to all Americans disabled by service in the uniform during the World War. Then, too, Congress had greatly enlarged the function of the old Public Health Service by making it responsible for the medical care of all ex-service men discharged from the Army or Navy and from the military hospitals but still needing attention on account of disabilities incurred during the war. Finally, Congress established by law the Federal Board for Vocational Education, an act which outdid in gratitude and generosity anything which the American Government had ever before offered to disabled war veterans.

After the Public Health Service began expanding its facilities for the care of disabled veterans, the Medical Department adopted the policy of discharging its patients rapidly and turning them over to the Public Health Service. Not only were those two classes of war victims requiring extended medical treatment—the mental and nervous cases and those suffering with tuberculosis—so treated, but men still suffering from wounds and sometimes requiring major operations and long periods for convalescence thereafter were released from the Army and committed to the ministrations of the Public Health Service. The immediate result of such a transfer was to entitle the disabled soldier to receive from the Government his disability allowance, which could be paid only after a man's discharge from the military service, and it often allowed him to secure medical care in the vicinity of his own home. Another important result was that, during 1920, although thousands of the victims of the war still required constant medical attention, the Medical Service of the Army rapidly contracted toward its prewar proportions, with a consequent expansion of the branch of the Public Health Service which dealt with disabled veterans.

There was not nearly so much tuberculosis in the Army as the medical authorities had anticipated. In the expectation of a wide prevalence of the disease resulting from the severity of field conditions in France, the Medical Corps established nine tuberculosis hospitals in the United States. Afterwards, although 100,000 of the 4,000,000 men were sent to hospitals as tuberculosis suspects, the positive diagnosis of pulmonary tuberculosis was confirmed in less than 15,000 cases. The result was that at no time did the Army use more than seven of its tuberculosis hospitals, and after it adopted the policy of discharging tubercular patients on certificates of disability it maintained only two of these hospitals. Discontent and homesickness are deterrents to the cure of tuberculosis, and the Medical Corps generally allowed sufferers from the disease to continue their own cures at home under instructions or to enter the hospitals and sanitariums of the Public Health Service near their own homes.

The other class of disabled ex-service men in need of extended medical treatment were the nervous and mental cases. Such victims were turned over to the Public Health Service, and they constituted the largest class of cases treated by that agency after the armistice.

After a disabled man was discharged from the Service, he automatically became eligible for vocational rehabilitation under the direction of the Federal Board for Vocational Education. The only four conditions were that the man must have been honorably discharged after April 7, 1917, that he must have a disability incurred in, aggravated by, or traceable to, the military service, that the disability must be, in the opinion of the Federal Board, an actual vocational handicap to him, and, lastly, that vocational training was a feasible thing for him. In other words—to clarify the final condition—the Vocational Board would not give training to a lunatic or give training of any sort beyond a man's mental capabilities. Within these necessary restrictions, however, there was practically no limit to which the Federal Board could not go. Most of its beneficiaries, to be sure, received training in the purely mechanical vocations in shops and factories; but the Board could and did send men to colleges and even to the postgraduate schools of universities. The objective of the Board was not only to overcome by training the man's physical handicap, but also to carry him forward in training as long as his progress and his mentality warranted it. More than one war veteran found that his disability brought to him educational opportunities which might otherwise never have come his way. The Board possessed funds to pay not only for tuition, textbooks, and incidental expenses, but also for the maintenance of the student and his family, if he had one, while he was in training. According to the number of persons dependent upon the student, the Board was authorized to pay for maintenance as much as $150 a month. At first the disabled men were slow to make application for vocational training; but, once they understood the advantages which were theirs for the asking, there was a great rush to avail themselves of the opportunities thus freely offered by the Government.

The three rehabilitation services, though interdependent in their operation, were independent of each other in their management and control. The Public Health Service conducted the physical examinations on which the War Risk Bureau rated men for their disability allowances. The War Risk Bureau certified men to the Public Health Service for medical treatment, and for vocational training to the Federal Board for Vocational Education. A man could not legally receive his disability allowance from the War Risk Bureau while receiving a training maintenance allowance from the Federal Board. While in effect, therefore, conducting three branches in the single main enterprise of caring for the men left disabled by the war, the three federal agencies were independent in their executive managements. This anomalous arrangement resulted in such distressing delays and stirred up so much discontent among the ex-service men that in the spring of 1921, upon the insistence largely of the American Legion, the veterans' own organization, the three services were brought together under a single direction.

The agitation which led to the amalgamation of the three welfare services undoubtedly created a wide impression that the Government had neglected the ex-service men. Nothing could have been farther from the truth. The complaint was not against the generosity of the Government, but against the method of administering that generosity. It was often difficult for the ex-service man to obtain the benefits which Congress had provided for him. The lavishness of the hand of Congress is shown by the fact that up to the present (June, 1921) its appropriations of money for ex-service men have amounted in sum to about $800,000,000. This is more money than the Government provided for veterans of the Civil War during the first thirty years after the conclusion of that conflict. The appropriations to date include the money for the physical and vocational rehabilitation of disabled World War veterans, for death claims paid by the Bureau of War Risk Insurance, and for allowances paid by the War Risk Bureau to disabled ex-soldiers, but they do not include the sixty-dollar bonus paid to all ex-service men in 1919. This bonus accounted for about $200,000,000 of the Government's money. Altogether, therefore, the Government has either paid out or obligated itself to pay out about one billion dollars for the benefit of men who served in the American forces during the World War.

So much for the post-armistice care of the wounded and otherwise disabled. The other principal phase of welfare work for the Army after the armistice had to do with the able-bodied soldiers; and, concretely, it meant getting jobs for them. The War Department did not regard a soldier as completely demobilized until he was once more placed in an occupation in civilian life. The Department could exercise no authority over the veteran once he had received his discharge, but it could and did exercise a friendly solicitude as to his economic future. Therefore the War Department led a nation-wide movement under the slogan, "Jobs for Soldiers"—and that meant jobs for approximately 4,000,000 men thrown suddenly into the labor market just at the time when industry was going through the critical transition from war to peace.

In demobilizing the men of the Army, the War Department adopted a policy the diametric opposite of the British policy of discharging soldiers by trades as they were needed in industry. With our enormous and varied industry, we had everything in our favor to make a success of the industrial plan of troop demobilization; but, nevertheless, the War Department settled upon the questionable policy of discharging the troops by military units, regardless of the effect such a policy might have upon general industrial conditions. As it was, the United States faced an economic crisis in the transition of its war industry, and to inundate the country with unemployed ex-soldiers was only to add to the difficulties of those who were trying to bring industry safely through the readjustment. Later on, the War Department modified its policy by providing that any soldier who faced unemployment after discharge might, upon his own request, be held in the service for a reasonable time while he tried to locate a job for himself in civilian life, and that, on the other hand, if work were waiting for any man not yet in line for immediate discharge, such a man might, upon submitting proper proof that there was a civilian demand for his services, receive his discharge forthwith. The Department permitted officers to take thirty-day leaves of absence with pay while they sought work.

There was, of course, danger that the wholesale outpouring of ex-soldiers upon an industrial field already complaining of a labor surplus would precipitate a business crisis; yet it seemed certain that a wise guidance of the internal affairs of the nation could avert such a calamity. The world was short of almost everything which man consumes, and it seemed evident that it would take several years of brisk production in every field to build up the reserves wasted by war and overtake industrially the demands of the consuming public. It was evident, in short, that there was plenty of work for all, if business did not become hysterical in the face of a difficult transition. The part for the Government to play was to conduct a skillful graduation of war industry into the pursuits of peace and at the same time to take the lead with its own agencies in infiltrating the demobilized troops into the ranks of trade and industry.

Fortunately, for this latter purpose, the Government possessed an agency at hand—the United States Employment Service, a branch of the Department of Labor. The war had built up this organization to great size and usefulness. Its branches covered the United States. Before the armistice it had been instrumental in staffing some of the more important war industrial establishments, particularly the new shipyards and the government powder plants. This agency would have been competent alone to secure employment for all discharged soldiers, but for the circumstance that, in the spring of 1919, there came into office a Congress of a political complexion the opposite to that of the administration. This Congress at once adopted a program of economy, but it was a spurious economy to the extent (which was considerable) that it arbitrarily cut down appropriations needed for important projects. The United States Employment Service received a scant $5,000,000 with which to finance the work of securing civilian employment for 4,000,000 men, when twice that sum would not have been overabundant. The result was that in this final scene of the war the Government was forced to call upon outside and volunteer aid in the conduct of an essential war activity.

At this point the semi-governmental Council of National Defense stepped into the breach. Shorn of most of its purely industrial functions, the Council of National Defense had become largely an organ consolidating and directing all volunteer civilian effort in aid of the Government in its war and demobilization problems. It had built up a field service covering the entire United States, consisting principally of the state and local councils of national defense. Meanwhile, with the expansion of the United States Employment Service restricted by lack of money, the Secretary of War made plans to use some of the emergency war funds in the soldier-employment project and called to Washington Colonel Arthur Woods, the former police commissioner of New York City, making him an assistant to the Secretary of War in charge of all war department activities in reëstablishing service men in civil life. The Director of the Council of National Defense created, in March, 1919, its emergency committee on employment of soldiers and sailors, with Colonel Woods as chairman. The membership of the committee linked up the United States Employment Service and other interested governmental bodies in an emergency organization for Colonel Woods to command. The committee also tied in all state and municipal employment agencies, welfare societies everywhere that were taking part in the solution of the employment problem, and also the thousands of community councils of national defense. Thus was evolved in brief time a fairly efficient employment service of national scope.

The success of the project was beyond question. The so-called bureaus for discharged soldiers, sailors, and marines were set up in practically every community in the United States. Since the work was so largely voluntary work, no strict system of reports was ever put in force, but the figures from 500 principal American cities and towns showed that when the year 1919 ended, 1,326,000 discharged service men had applied to the employment agencies, and more than 927,000 had been placed in jobs by the organization. A general survey in the autumn of 1919 disclosed only about 20,000 ex-service men out of work.

The men of the A. E. F. came in contact with the Government's employment organization before they left foreign soil. The United States Employment Service sent several representatives to France soon after the armistice. These advance agents carried cards, which were distributed to the troops of the expedition as they came to the embarkation ports in France. With the cards went the Government's assurance that it would use every effort to restore every soldier to a useful place in civil life. Any soldier who desired to avail himself of these good offices was instructed to fill in a card during his voyage home, telling his qualifications, what sort of job he desired, and where he wished to be employed. Hundreds of thousands of these cards were collected by the federal employment agents at the ports of debarkation in this country. The cards were sorted and sent to the proper local employment bureaus throughout the United States. Thousands of men were engaged for work before they received their discharges. The fact that jobs were waiting for them undoubtedly helped to avert the congregating of idle service men in cities after they had been turned off at the demobilization centers.

The overseas soldier had been serving his country for a dollar a day while others had stayed at home in bomb-proof jobs and drawn the highest wages ever paid in America. The returning veteran often felt, and felt justly, that it was his turn now to reap some of the financial rewards. Travel had broadened these boys; the harsh experiences of war had sobered them and often quickened their ambition. Such men were not content to go back to the jobs they had left in 1917 and 1918. They demanded something better, and often they got it, because employers were prone to accept their point of view. Events justified this attitude, too, as was testified to in hundreds of letters received by the employment bureaus from satisfied employers, who wrote that the demobilized soldiers were better and more ambitious workmen for their war experiences.

The success of the reëmployment campaign was largely an achievement for publicity. The publicity was directed both to the soldier and to the employer. For reaching the soldier one of the most valuable devices proved to be a booklet entitled *Where Do We Go from Here?*, written by Major William Brown Meloney. This pamphlet was filled with good advice for the demobilized soldier. It took into account his stirred ambition, but showed how impossible it was for every man to get the place in civil life he desired, and therefore urged each man to take what job he could get and make the most of it.

Photo from Federal Board for Vocational Education

DISABLED VETERANS TAKING FEDERAL TRAINING

Photo by Signal Corps

EDITORIAL CONFERENCE OF *STARS AND STRIPES*

Photo by Signal Corps

POSTER USED IN REËMPLOYMENT CAMPAIGN

Felix J. Koch Photo

EMPLOYMENT OFFICE AT CAMP SHERMAN

The War Camp Community Service printed and distributed 3,000,000 copies of this booklet.

The American Red Cross sponsored a poster by Dan Smith, the artist, bearing to employers the slogan: "Put Fighting Blood in your Business!" A file of helmeted Yanks obliquely below a shield on which were inscribed the names of the principal engagements in which the A. E. F. participated; below that, the lines: "Here's his record. Does he get a job?"—such was the display.

Publications of every sort, motion picture theatres, ministers in their pulpits, and school-teachers in their classrooms joined in the effort to make the whole United States think of its obligations to the returning troops. The War Department conferred a so-called citation upon employers who agreed to take back all of their former employees who had joined the Army or Navy. The leading business organizations of the country worked with their members to secure a complete re-employment of former service men. The thoroughness of the effort accounts for the large degree of its success.

At the same time the War Department constituted itself an employment agency for placing soldiers with technical training in the best positions that could be obtained for them. Such soldiers were usually commissioned officers. The Department asked these men to send to Washington statements of their qualifications and their wishes as to employment. The Department then circularized some 25,000 business firms of the United States as to their needs for men with technical training. By this method about 8,000 men were placed in responsible positions at good salaries.

The employment organization encountered and overcame an abuse of the army uniform that was particularly flagrant for the first few months after the armistice. On the streets of most large cities were men in uniform, wearing the red chevron indicating their honorable discharge from the service, selling cheap or worthless articles or begging outright. There may have been a shadow of excuse for this during the early weeks of the winter of 1918-1919; but as industry recovered and revived it became possible for every ex-service man who desired a respectable job to secure one. Street solicitation, however, was highly profitable, and many professional beggars and sharpers, who had never been in the Service at all, secured uniforms and posed as discharged soldiers. The American Legion instituted a campaign against these men, urging the public not to give money to them. The reëmployment forces persuaded local authorities to refuse peddling licenses to men in uniform. Thus the evil was largely stamped out after a few months.

Not even the assurance of an immediate job and the other official inducements which made the road home the path of least resistance could always induce the discharged soldier to go home directly, particularly if he left the demobilization camp with his pockets full of money. Around some of the demobilization centers ranged bands of thieves and outlaws who, having evaded military service, now during the demobilization wore the army uniform and posed as discharged soldiers in order to prey upon the ex-service men. If a soldier leaving the camp listened to their fraternal "Hello, Buddy!" and fell in with them, he usually later found himself fleeced to his last penny. To offset this evil the American Red Cross established a chain of soldiers' banks at the principal demobilization centers. In these banks the discharged men could deposit their money, drawing it out by check after they reached their homes. The deposits in the camp banks passed $4,000,000 in amount.

In one respect only was the reëmployment campaign unsuccessful. The War Department had hoped to use the demobilization of troops as an offset to some extent to the steady drift of population from American farms to the cities. In pursuance of this ambition the Government distributed among the troops at the demobilization centers nearly 1,000,000 copies of a booklet entitled *Forward to the Farm! Why Not?* Yet, although most country boys in the Army were willing to return to the farms, the Government could not induce the city dwellers to take up country life. However, it is noteworthy that in June, 1919, when the Kansas wheat crop was in danger for want of labor to harvest it, the reëmployment organization was able to send nearly 50,000 ex-service men into the Kansas wheat country during the harvest at wages of $5 to $7 a day, lodging and board thrown in.

CHAPTER VIII

WAR CONTRACTS

OF all the business activities of the American Government in the World War, none aroused in the business men of America more interest or more concern than the Government's employment of its function of making contracts with industry for the production and delivery of war supplies. There is little danger of putting too much emphasis upon the importance of the war contract. After the declaration of war, the Government rapidly assumed unprecedented powers over business, until in the heavy productive months of 1918 it occupied a supreme position. The War Industries Board had virtually commandeered all important raw materials and was distributing them at fixed prices. The Government had become the sole dealer in wool; it was closely regulating the prices of, and determining priorities in the use of, such commodities as copper and steel; through the United States Fuel Administration it was in full control of the production, distribution, and use of fuels; and its position was equally monopolistic toward all other important basic materials. Of the labor, the machinery, and the processes which normally manufactured these materials into the commodities of American commerce, the Government had become almost the only employer; only now it had woven these facilities, the industrial facilities of the largest of industrial nations, into the intricate texture of an arsenal. Mechanical industry for private enterprise had almost disappeared. On the day of the armistice the factories of the United States were working practically as a unit in the production of munitions. While the Navy, the United States Shipping Board, and the military missions of the principal Allies were also prosecuting extensive war industrial projects in America, the War Department alone had entered into some 30,000 contracts directly with builders and producers, these contracts upon their consummation obligating the Government to pay out a sum in excess of $7,500,000,000. Of this production, less than half (reckoning it in money value) had been completed on the day of the armistice.

It follows that the instrument which commanded and set in motion all this effort—the war contract—must have been a thing exceedingly important to America. The 30,000 war department contracts, as a body, constituted in themselves the charter under which the preponderant part of American industry existed for nearly two years. As wisdom or unwisdom appeared written into the provisions of the war contracts, so fared well or badly not only the half of the population directly associated with industry, but the other half as well, and the Government, too. As an example, it was charged with some degree of justice that one great class of war department contracts, the so-called cost-plus contracts, was the chief factor in the rapidly mounting cost of living during the war. In other ways also these writings, which defined the terms of existence for American industry, profoundly affected every person in the United States. We may leave to lawyers and economists the discussion of the academic legal questions involved in the war contracts and still find in them plenty of interest common to all.

When an individual person goes out to buy anything, he normally procures it by paying the price fixed by the seller. Business houses, too, commonly follow this custom in procuring their usual supplies. If, however, the individual person or business house is going into some relatively large operation in which he will require goods and services in extensive quantity, then it is customary to ask for bids from those in a position to supply the needs, and to contract thereafter with the concern which offers to supply the goods and services at the best price. The law requires the Government to follow this procedure in procuring practically all its supplies. Each federal department must advertise its needs publicly, giving complete specifications, must call publicly for bids to supply the materials specified, and must allot the business to the one tendering the best bid; provided only that the bidder is responsible and is known to have the ability to produce goods of the quality desired. The courts have held that a contract written under any other conditions is void.

The law, however, permits certain exceptions. The War Department, for instance, is permitted by law to increase the size of a contract already properly made. It can deal directly, without advertising, with a manufacturer who is a sole source of supply, provided that previous advertising has elicited no bids. These exceptions are the reflection of experience in governing, exceptions granted by Congress to the end that the Government's necessary business may not be impeded by the operation of the legal checks and balances.

Now there was to the federal contracting rule one other exception which was, for our purposes here, the most important of all. The law authorized the Secretary of War to enter into contracts without the formality of advertising and soliciting bids, *in the event of a national emergency*. We had not yet been a week at war with Germany when the Secretary of War issued proclamation declaring such an emergency to exist. His signature to this document swept away the most serious legal restrictions which circumscribed the War Department's contracting powers. The hand of the Department had been further strengthened by the National Defense Act (passed in 1916), which empowered the Secretary of War, "in time of war, or when war is imminent," to command a manufacturer to produce supplies for the United States at prices fixed by the War Department itself; and if the producer refused this arrangement, then the Act empowered the Secretary to commandeer and take over the producer's business, paying the producer, however, a fair and just compensation.

Competition for the Government's contracts under the normal procedure would have been fatal to both speed and secrecy in the procurement of war supplies, and therefore the law wisely permitted the War Department to abandon competition in the emergency of war. But, with the safeguard of the competitive bid abandoned, it is reasonable to suppose that the officers of the War Department, if they were faithful servants of the public, would seek to protect the Government against the extortioner by the substitution of other devices not open to the objection either of delaying the war manufacturing program or of betraying its nature and extent. And so they did. And although the methods of applying the protection were numerous, the essence of it was that the contractor was required by the terms of his contract to produce war supplies at cost, plus a profit for himself, the profit being reckoned in various ways. A contract of this sort was known as a cost-plus contract. Contracts of the normal, older sort, in which the Government dealt with the lowest bidder or with a producer with whom the law empowered the federal purchasers to deal directly without competition, were known as fixed-price or lump-sum contracts.

The cost-plus contract was not entirely unknown to American business before the war, but it had been employed only sparingly. The war brought the form into great prominence, since much of the most important war business was conducted on the cost-plus plan. It is noteworthy that the form has persisted to some extent in American private business, and particularly in the building industry, since the armistice.

Although under the circumstances the cost-plus contract was a necessity and its advantages were many, nevertheless the form was endowed with an inherent weakness (from the Government's standpoint) most difficult to overcome. In a lump-sum contract the profit of the contractor increased according as he was able to keep down his costs. If his costs ran too high, he faced actual loss. In the cost-plus contract of the simplest form—cost of production, plus a percentage of the cost as profit—it was just the other way. The higher a producer's costs, the greater his profit; and though a producer might not deliberately seek to augment his costs, yet if he were relieved of the necessity of maintaining a normal business wariness, bargaining for his raw materials, and resisting wage advances, the best interests of the Government might not be served.

There is no question that the elementary form of cost-plus war contract in the early months of the war added considerable impetus to the procession of higher costs of living, higher wages, and higher costs again in the vicious circle. It was to retard this tendency, to add an inducement to the producer to control and keep down his costs, that the Government evolved the many modifications and refinements of the cost-plus contract.

At several points in these narratives we have called attention to the train of evils which followed the attempt of the War Department in 1917 to conduct its enterprise in the production of munitions with an organization feudal in character and, one might almost say, in antiquity. Five virtually independent bureaus—the Ordnance Department, the Quartermaster Department, the Corps of Engineers, the Signal Corps, and the Medical Department—and, later, after the creation of the Construction Division, the Air Service, and the Chemical Warfare Service, eight, set forth to procure their own war supplies as competitors, each determined to attain its own ends at the expense, if necessary, of the others. This plan of operation soon drew up near the edge of disaster, as factories and the more accessible industrial districts were overloaded with war contracts by the undirected distribution of the Government's business, and transportation both on rail and ocean was nearly throttled by the congestions of freight at various seaboard and inland terminals.

Here again, in considering the war contracts, we stumble once more across the trail of this faulty organization. The war contracts were practically as diverse in their provisions and types as the Government's contracting agencies were numerous; and here it should be noted that some of the main procurement bureaus were in turn subdivided into smaller purchasing agencies, each of which drew its war contracts according to its own lights. About all the early war contracts had in common were the legal provisions protecting the Government against fraud and graft. There was no such thing as a standard contract, and no uniformity anywhere. The Government was being obligated in contracts to the tune of billions by contracting officers almost out of touch with the responsible heads of the administration.

The Government was soon forced to take cognizance of this state of affairs. In the spring of 1917 the Secretary of Commerce convened the so-called Interdepartmental Conference to consider the war contracts—the first attempt to bring harmony into the confused business situation. To the conference came the representatives of the various departments, boards, and administrations interested in contracts, and to the sessions of the conference also the opponents of the cost-plus contract brought their objections to it. There were those who held it almost solely responsible for the great increase in costs of all sorts during 1917.

It was soon evident to the conferees, however, that the cost-plus contract had come to stay in the war business, regardless of its obvious dangers and disadvantages. If an evil, it was a necessary one. True, the Government could still go into fixed-price contracts for the procurement of many important war supplies. These were such supplies as food, clothing, and tools—commodities essentially like those produced and consumed in time of peace. The producers of these commodities were not perplexed by costs; their facilities and processes were ready to begin production; and therefore the War Department could, and did until the end of hostilities (except when shortages made it necessary to deal with single responsible manufacturers in order to gain early deliveries), procure such supplies on fixed-price contracts let after competitive bidding. But such supplies, although they bulked large in the cash balance, contributed little to the solution of the main munitions problem. It was in the production of artillery, of airplanes and airplane engines, of ammunition, of explosives, even of buildings in which to house the war department enterprises, that the cost-plus contract had become a necessity.

There was no way of telling in advance what would be the costs of producing these more important supplies. Many of them were of types and designs entirely new to American manufacturing experience. It was hard enough for the government agents to induce manufacturers to undertake these contracts even on a cost-plus basis. Had the War Department attempted to advertise the specifications of such a mechanism as the French hydropneumatic recuperator, it would never have received a bid. The only possible terms on which any sane manufacturer would take such a contract would be the payment of his costs, plus a profit.

Many of the contracts for the more difficult sorts of supplies were bound to continue over an extended period before all the deliveries could be made. It was often impossible for such contractors to make commitments in advance for all their raw materials. Therefore they faced a rising market and prices which they could not predetermine. They also faced almost certain increases in the wages paid to their employees; yet here again they could not anticipate what these increases would be. The costs of a maker of optical instruments for the Army depended partially upon what he should have to pay for optical glass, but the glass was to come from a new war industry which had not yet begun production and therefore could not estimate what it would charge for glass. With its designs for war implements the War Department did the best it could, founding its specifications upon the latest and best information at its command. Yet so rapid was the evolution of war materials resulting from their intensive use that sometimes the Department found a design obsolete before its production was fairly begun. Its designers therefore made changes in the specifications at the factory, and these changes involved heavy manufacturing costs. Every contractor knew that his work was to be subject to such changes in the specifications; yet no one could foretell whether changes would be made or what they would cost.

These purely manufacturing considerations were enough in themselves to explain the prevalence of the cost-plus contracts. Another element was the time required to prepare specifications and advertise for bids—time not to be spared in war. But there was still another reason to account for the cost-plus contract, a reason in war finance, even more cogent. The successful prosecution of the war meant that practically the entire industrial equipment of the United States would have to be devoted to the production of war supplies. Before the war only large concerns with great financial resources were able to put through great government projects in which the delivery dates were far removed from the dates of starting the work. A war contract often involved a tremendous preliminary expenditure of money in factory expansion and in commitments for raw materials. The Government's practice was to pay for supplies only upon their delivery. Under such conditions the small manufacturer could not work for the Government. In normal times, perhaps, the possession of a government contract might have enabled him to finance his operation through the banks in the usual way, but with every manufacturer needing special financing, the effect upon the banks was to make them less liberal in their commercial loans. The banks had their own solvency to look out for first.

The cost-plus contract proved to be one of the solutions of this problem. Most of the cost-plus contracts provided that the War Department could pay the manufacturing costs as they accrued, in installments. Thus, by securing partial advance payments from the Government, the small producers, and the large, too, were able to finance their projects and even to take advantage of the cash discounts in their purchases of raw materials. Naturally, the War Department was careful to make such arrangements only with contractors of recognized probity, men who were deserving of confidence, but who often lacked working capital to enable them to become successful producers of war supplies.*

The Interdepartmental Conference, far from disapproving or attempting to abolish the cost-plus contract, recognized its

* The financing of war factories, and particularly of those which had to make large and expensive plant additions before manufacturing could proceed, was effectively aided by the War Credits Board of the War Department. In the autumn of 1917 Congress authorized the War Department to advance to contractors amounts up to 30 per cent of the total contract obligations. The War Credits Board administered this work. In all, it lent to war department

necessity, but registered a preference for forms of it which best protected the interests of the people and of the Government. The elemental cost-plus contract obligated the Government to pay manufacturing costs, plus an agreed-upon percentage of the costs as profit. Costs included not only the charges for labor and materials, but also certain overhead and depreciation charges. This contract form was vicious in principle, and the Conference did not approve it. Meanwhile various contracting officers of the Government had been improving the cost-plus contract with provisions which either removed the tendency for the contractor to increase his costs or added inducements to him to keep his costs down. One of these improvements was a cost-plus form providing for a fixed profit to the contractor, regardless of what his costs might be. This form removed the incentive to increase costs. A still further refinement made it of material advantage to a contractor to keep down his costs and penalized the man who was careless about costs. In this form the Government agreed to pay all costs and a fixed profit, but the contract also fixed in advance an estimated unit price for the product, this price being known as "bogey," a term borrowed from the ancient and honorable game of golf. If the contractor succeeded in holding his costs, plus his fixed profit, under the unit bogey price, he was paid a share of the saving. If, however, his costs and profits ran above bogey, then he was penalized a percentage of the excess, the penalty being subtracted from his fixed profit when the War Department came to pay for the supplies. This form not only put a premium upon plant efficiency, but it stimulated the speed of production; for the briefer the factory processes, the smaller the costs, as a rule, and the sooner the contractor would get his money. The Interdepartmental Conference approved both these forms.

This was not yet the desideratum of standardization in contracts, but it was a step in that direction and perhaps as much

contractors about $250,000,000. On June 1, 1921, it had recouped all but $14,500,000 of these loans. Its total losses were not expected to run over $150,000, while the profits (interest, of which $8,000,000 had been collected) were estimated at $12,000,000.

as could be done in an organization as ill-articulated as that of the War Department then was. The Interdepartmental Conference possessed only advisory powers, but it was able to establish a policy for the Government in its contracting function. By pointing to the more desirable forms of contracts, its report was at least a moral force in securing greater uniformity in war contracts. It must be remembered, too, that most of the contracting officers were men of considerable business experience and ability. Many of the leading business men of the country were serving the United States either in uniform or as officers of such agencies as the Council of National Defense and the War Industries Board, and the procurement bureaus had the benefit of their study and advice in the making of contracts.

Under such conditions a great volume of war department business was placed in the latter part of 1917 and during the early months of 1918. Then the conditions of war industry finally forced a reorganization of the War Department, bringing all of its supply activities (with one or two important exceptions) under the single direction of the Division of Purchase, Storage, and Traffic, of the General Staff. The Division of P., S., and T., as it was called, was created early in 1918. One of the first acts of its director was to appoint a committee to study the various forms of war department contracts in use and to recommend standard forms which should keep errors at a minimum and make the War Department certain at all times as to its rights under its contracts.

Simultaneously the new Division was assuming a centralized control of war department contracts. Early in June the Secretary of War appointed a Surveyor of Contracts, who in turn appointed a board of contract review within each procurement bureau. A bureau board was to pass upon all proposed contracts drawn by contracting officers, except the few contracts which involved the Government for trivial amounts of money. This system, with the Surveyor of Contracts dictating policies and passing them on down through the bureau boards, was effective control of the contracting function under a single direction; but in late July the Secretary of War still further strengthened the scheme by appointing the Superior Board of Contract Review. The Director of Purchases and Supplies and the Surveyor of Contracts were the general members of this Board, and each procurement bureau sent to it a member, who was either the chief procurement officer of the bureau or a member of the bureau's board of contract review. This Superior Board of Contract Review became the great policy-forming agency of the War Department in respect of its contracting activities.

Note, however, that not yet had there been any standardization of contracts. In early August the committee appointed by the Director of Purchase, Storage, and Traffic to study war contracts and recommend standards, made its report. The Superior Board of Contract Review received this report, and early in September promulgated, on the basis of the report, a series of twenty-four standard contract provisions, nineteen of them to be included in all war department fixed-price and cost-plus contracts, and five particular provisions pertaining either to cost-plus or fixed-price contracts, but not to both. Most of the standard provisions, except perhaps in their phraseology, were not new, but had been used in substance variously by the contracting officers. The importance of standardization was that it required the use of all of them in the war contracts and also dictated the phraseology. One or two of the standard clauses, particularly those which anticipated the end of the war and the termination of the war industry, were new and most important.

The first six provisions dealt with the Government's obligations to furnish raw materials and component parts to the manufacturer, with the packing and marking of supplies, with the changing of specifications and the Government's assumption of increased costs or savings wrought thereby, with inspection, with the storage of finished products at plants, and with extensions of the time of the contract under certain conditions.

The seventh provision anticipated the end of the war by

Photo by Signal Corps

SENDING OUT THE *STARS AND STRIPES*

Photo by Signal Corps

GRADUATE A. E. F. STUDENTS AT EDINBURGH UNIVERSITY

Photo by Howard E. Coffin

REVIEW OF "PERSHING'S OWN REGIMENT" AT COBLENZ

Photo by Signal Corps

GAMES IN LE MANS EMBARKATION AREA

providing for the cancellation of contracts under certain circumstances, one of which was if the public interest required it. This was a new thing in war contracts. The provision set forth the reimbursements which the contractor should receive in the event of cancellation.

The eighth forbade contractors receiving advance payments from the Government to mortgage or otherwise pledge articles partially completed. Thus, if the contract were canceled, the Government could take over the unfinished work without involving itself in a mesh of legal complications. The next provision dealt with protection of war plants. The next was the statutory one forbidding the transfer of contracts.

The eleventh provision dealt with subcontractors, normally not of any interest to the Government, but in war of vital interest, since the failure of a subcontractor might greatly delay an entire project, and since also a cost-plus contract offered an opportunity to a prime contractor to conspire with a subcontractor to increase costs. The provision gave the Government full control over the subcontracting and extended to the subcontractors the Government's rights of cancellation.

The twelfth was the statutory one forbidding any member of Congress from sharing in the benefits of a contract, except that a congressman was permitted to own stock in a corporation accepting war contracts.

The next provision wiped out the horde of fly-by-night commission brokers who had flocked to Washington to grow rich on commissions paid by gullible producers who accepted the theory that it took pull and influence to secure a war contract. Since these commissions went into the manufacturer's costs and therefore were paid eventually by the Government, the Attorney General had issued a ruling forbidding the government departments to pay manufacturing costs that included brokers' commissions. Established selling agencies, however, were exempted from this rule. The thirteenth standard contract provision wrote this prohibition into the contracts themselves.

The next provision dealt with indemnifications for the invasion of patent rights. The fifteenth provided for the settlement of disputes and claims arising out of questions of performance or nonperformance under contracts. Later the Board of Contract Adjustment was organized to fulfill this function. The next three provisions dealt with hours of labor, the settlement of wage disputes, and the conditions of labor at war plants. Then came a provision requiring the producer to make periodic reports of the progress of his work, one defining what costs would be allowed in a cost-plus contract, one allowing the contractor to appeal to the Board of Contract Adjustment in the event that a contracting officer of the Department disallowed costs in excess of $5,000, one providing for uniformity in contractors' cost accounting, one forbidding the payment of wages above current local rates, and a final provision vesting in the United States the title to all materials in course of manufacture under a cost-plus contract.

Such were the standard contract provisions, protective and fair to the Government and the producers alike. They were not adopted until the end of the summer of 1918, and therefore no important amount of government business was placed on their identical terms. As stated, however, most of their requirements in substance had been written into the war department contracts previously drawn.

The cost-plus contract under which the immense building construction program of the War Department was carried through was of a peculiar form, not used elsewhere. It was known as the cost-plus-with-sliding-scale-and-fixed-maximum-fee contract. The distinguishing feature of it was that each contractor was paid a percentage of the cost as profit up to the extent of a fixed maximum profit, and he could not be paid more than this profit whatever the cost of the job. The profit percentage diminished on a sliding scale as the cost mounted. In its latest form this contract paid a profit of 7 per cent to contractors on jobs costing less than $100,000, and the profit declined gradually in percentage until it reached the low mark of 2½ per cent paid as profit for work costing more than $9,650,000. No building contractor, however, could be paid more than $250,000 profit on a job, whatever its cost; and out of his "profit" he still had to pay his overhead operating expenses.

In its building program the War Department became one of the largest employers of labor in the country, and its building contract was roundly attacked as a chief element in the swift rise in wages. To meet this attack the Department convened a board of construction engineers and other experts to study the contract. Instead of condemning the form of contract, the report of this board endorsed it in unqualified terms and declared that, if anything, the contract tended to check extravagances in the work.

While the tendency was all toward the cost-plus-fixed-profit form of contract, when it came to the production of materials entirely new and strange to our industry the War Department could not escape the cost-plus-percentage form. The Government's powder-bag-loading plants were operating on the basis of the payment of operating costs, plus 14 per cent. Several of the shell-loading plants worked under contracts providing for the payment of costs, plus 10 per cent. Silk cartridge cloth was manufactured at cost, plus 10 per cent as profit. This profit, as the skill of the cloth weavers increased, was gradually stepped down to 3 per cent. The Modified Enfield rifles were made at cost, plus 10 per cent. When the War Department commandeered plants, it engaged operating companies to run them on a basis of costs paid, plus a fixed monthly remuneration. Certain patriotic contractors built large munitions plants for the Government at cost, plus the statutory $1 as profit.

Then there was the combination contract, adopted for work new to our industrial experience—a cost-plus form graduating into a fixed-profit form as the actual work developed what the costs would be. The Browning machine guns were produced under contracts of this sort.

Contracts for the production of aircraft were not brought under the centralized administration of war department contracts. The aircraft contracts provided for the payment of costs by the Government, plus fixed profits, with bonuses for the producers if they kept under the estimated costs.

CHAPTER IX

THE SETTLEMENT OF THE WAR CONTRACTS

IN the preceding chapter we have been discussing chiefly the written, formal contract, the tangible, visible document, duly signed and witnessed, which could be submitted to any court as prima-facie evidence of the obligations of both the producer and the Government. If, however, the impression has been given that all the war business was conducted under the authority of such instruments, let it now be dispelled; because thousands of manufacturers did war work for the Government, and the Government itself became involved for hundreds of millions of dollars, under another set of arrangements, which became known, after the armistice, as the informal, or "Bevo," contracts. These agreements, while embodying the same terms as those of the formal contracts, were drawn with no such attention to the niceties of federal procedure, without which the law says that a government contract is not enforcible. The informal contracts were a product of the hurry and rush to get things done. There were several sorts of them, some being formal in type but defective in detail, others existing in written records, such as correspondence, but not in formal contracts, and still others being merely oral agreements between the producers and the agents of the Government as to what work had to be done.

The law, in theory, assumes that the Secretary of War himself makes and signs contracts for the production of army supplies. He is permitted by law, however, to delegate his contracting function to accredited deputies, who are called contracting officers. In normal times these contracting officers are able to make all the necessary contracts; but during the war, with all industry aligning itself in the munitions organization, it became physically impossible for the regular contracting officers to handle all the business, and they in turn appointed deputies or proxies, and conferred on them (quite illegally, as it afterwards appeared) the right to sign contracts. Then, in the urgency of the occasion, the procurement officers, who were frequently business men commissioned in the military service, adopted the common business expedient of allowing correspondence to stand as evidence of contractual engagements, expecting to follow up this correspondence with formal contracts when the ponderous executive machinery of the Department could get around to it. Sometimes the producer did not even have the protection of correspondence, but, after coming to an oral understanding with the contracting officer as to what was to be done and on what terms, hurried back to his factory to spend, it might be, hundreds of thousands of dollars in preparation for some large manufacturing effort, without a scrap of writing to secure him in these investments. Finally, there was an extensive class of contracts which lacked correct form. New officers, unfamiliar with the restrictions which hedge about the governmental administrative acts, restrictions which the public calls red tape, took the short cut of making out direct purchase orders, which stipulated quality, quantity, price, method of payment, time of delivery, and so on; and the producers accepted such orders in good faith as binding agreements.

All went well with this informal procedure until the armistice brought the necessity of terminating the war business. The question was, How might the oral and other informal contracts be settled? And then the Comptroller of the Treasury rendered the absolutely stunning decision that all these informal arrangements, including the formal contracts which had been signed by proxies of the constituted contracting officers, were illegal and without standing before the Treasury, and that not a penny of government money could be paid out in settlement of the obligations of the Government under the terms of these agreements, except that the Government could pay for goods actually delivered. At that time the outstanding contracts and agreements of all sorts involved the Government in the sum of approximately $7,500,000,000. The informal contracts, thus declared void, accounted for $1,500,000,000 of this sum. The Government, if it chose, could refuse to reimburse a dollar of hundreds of millions expended freely by patriotic manufacturers, careless of their own interests in their eagerness to give their utmost service to the prosecution of the war.

Of course, repudiation of these agreements was unthinkable, if only for the reason that such action would have brought on an unprecedented business panic and sent many concerns crashing down into bankruptcy. Yet the only remedy was legislation to permit the Government to settle up its obligations under these contracts just as if they had been properly drawn in the first place. Such legislation, known as the Dent Act, was eventually passed by Congress, the law being approved by the President on March 2, 1919. In the interim between the armistice and that date, the holders of informal and irregular contracts were subjected to an unavoidable injustice, the nature of which will be plain when we have somewhat examined the War Department's method of terminating its war industry.

The modern contract is the foundation stone of industry and commerce. If the integrity of that foundation be impaired, we come into a condition of anarchy of which Anglo-Saxon civilization knows nothing. The man who breaches a contract can be held in court to indemnify the other party to it, and the Government itself cannot escape such liability. On the first day of the armistice there were 30,000 outstanding war department contracts. Three thousand of these, involving a government expenditure of over $1,500,000,000, either were so near completion or called for the production of materials so necessary to the maintenance of the demobilizing Army or for the future preparedness of the United States that they were allowed to go through undisturbed. The other 27,000 contracts bore a face value of $6,000,000,000. Under many of them there had been extensive deliveries of finished supplies to the Government, these deliveries (including the deliveries made while the industries were tapering off their production and adjusting themselves to peace conditions) amounting to approximately $2,000,000,000 in value. Thus there was left to the War Department a contractual obligation amounting to $4,000,000,000, which huge sum would go to pay for a great mass of materials for which the Government could have no possible use. It was highly desirable to terminate the unfulfilled portions of these contracts; yet few of the contracts contained termination clauses. It will be remembered that the standard termination clause did not appear as a common feature of the war contracts until the final six weeks of hostilities. Thus the majority of the 27,000 contractors possessed the plain legal right to go through with the performance of their contracts, even though the war had ended, and thereafter to hold the Government to the full payment of the face value of the contracts. The sum of such determination, had it been unanimous, would have cost the United States $4,000,000,000 with nothing to show for it except a great collection of useless munitions which could be sold to the junk dealers.

Upon the administration of the War Department rested the responsibility to save for the people as much of this sum as could be saved. Not all of it could be saved. Millions had been spent by the contractors for machinery and other equipment, for materials, and to pay manufacturing costs during the early stages of production. These millions the Government was bound to reimburse in any event, together with a reasonable profit upon work already done. The closer the administration could come to paying these legitimate costs and nothing else, the more successful would be its conduct of the industrial demobilization. The question was, what procedure to adopt.

To be sure, the departmental heads might have adopted the policy of canceling the contracts outright; but such a course would have meant ruin for many manufacturers, it would have thrown into the courts a mass of litigation that would have congested them for the next two generations, and it would have shattered the faith of business in the Government and rendered difficult all governmental contracting in the future.

Instead of that, the war department heads adopted the shrewd measure of requesting the producers to suspend work on their contracts. They made termination a voluntary act on the part of the contractor. It is obvious that it was fully as much to the interest of the producers as to that of the Government to liquidate the war business amicably and, it may be said, inexpensively, since these very men would be the ones called upon to contribute most heavily in taxes to the payment of the war debt. Nevertheless, it was greatly to the credit of American business men that their response to the general request to terminate war contracts was nearly unanimous. There was scarcely one who stood on his full legal rights. The business of industrial demobilization was largely that of negotiating with the individual producers as to the terms under which they would consent to terminate their contracts. When the terms were adopted, they were written into the original contracts as supplemental agreements and thus given legal force. The decision which resulted in this procedure was one of the great administrative acts of the War Government. It saved billions of dollars to the Government and it sent the war producers away fairly well content with the treatment they had received.

The preliminary steps in industrial demobilization were taken before the armistice. For one thing, in those final days when it was apparent that the end was close at hand, the War Department adopted the policy of terminating the war contracts by agreement. For that purpose, the war department administration added to the standard contract provisions already adopted standard forms of supplemental agreements, to the end that the liquidation of war industry might be carried out uniformly. On November 9 all production bureaus of the Department were notified to be ready to enforce the termination clauses of contracts when the fighting ended. This order, of course, applied only to those contracts containing termination clauses; but at the same time provision was made for the suspension of war work when the public interest required it. This suspension was to be preliminary to the adoption of arrangements whereby war industry could be gradually stopped down and readjusted by easy stages. On this date, too, the Department adopted a policy from which it never afterwards deviated: not to pay to a producer any profits on prospective production under his contract, but to allow a profit as high as 10 per cent of the cost on work that had actually been done but from which no actual production might have resulted. Thus from the very first the Government showed a spirit of conciliation that promised well for the producers of war supplies.

On the morning of November 11, after the receipt of the official news of the armistice, the Secretary of War, the Secretary of the Navy, and the Director of the United States Shipping Board announced after a conference that all Sunday work and overtime work on government contracts would cease at once, and that war industry would be tapered off by the various procurement agencies in consultation with the Department of Labor and the War Industries Board. These two organizations, the one in contact with employers and the other with labor, were in a position to guard the interests both of labor and of industry. Meanwhile the procurement bureaus of the War Department, following the recent instructions, had sent out generally requests to suspend the manufacture of munitions. These orders were soon modified to allow production to continue at most of the war plants, but the brief interim of idleness gave the procurement officers time to survey the situation and also served as a notice to the manufacturers that the war was over and that they were to incur no further obligations in pursuance of their contracts.

Simultaneously with issuing the suspension requests, the procurement bureaus in Washington began making out what were known as termination schedules. These were detailed statements of proposed reductions in war work compiled by individual contracts, by manufacturing projects, by entire commodities that were being consumed by the Army, and by entire production programs. These schedules were first sent for approval to the Director of Purchase, Storage, and Traffic, who also secured the approval of the War Industries Board and the Department of Labor. The approved schedules were then sent back to the bureaus for action, except that the bureaus were instructed to terminate the production gradually so as not to disturb industry in any particular localities. The terminations, of course, were made by agreement with the producers, the agreements embodying the terms under which the manufacturing ceased.

So expeditiously was this work started that the first termination schedules reached the Director of Purchase, Storage, and Traffic on November 12, and the schedules poured in upon him every day thereafter. Within a few days the prepared schedules involved the termination of a billion dollars' worth of work. Each schedule was the product of a comprehensive study of the industries affected, made by the production bureaus, which were in intimate touch with those industries. On December 5 the terminations and reductions reached a total of $2,500,000,000. A large part of the war industry had been reduced or terminated without serious detriment to the condition of business and employment. Consequently, it was decided that no such precautions as were being taken were longer necessary, and a change in the liquidation system went into effect. Thereafter the stoppage of war industry was placed entirely in the hands of the district production officers of the War Department. These men were to consult with the local officers of the Department of Labor as to the effect of terminations upon employment, and were also to make frequent regular reports to the Director of Purchase, Storage, and Traffic. For the rest, they were free to act according to their own best judgment.

The various supply bureaus were well organized to conduct the demobilization in this way. Before 1917 the bureaus had administered the production of supplies directly from their headquarters in Washington. After the war came, the volume of business grew beyond the capacity of such a system to handle it efficiently; and the principal production bureaus thereupon divided the country into manufacturing districts and placed district organizations, subsidiary to the bureau headquarters in Washington, in charge of them. The bureaus in Washington continued to execute contracts, but the work of superintending manufacture, inspecting products, and paying for supplies was placed in the hands of the district organizations. The Ordnance Department, for instance, established twelve manufacturing districts in the United States and one in Canada. The Director of Purchase, in charge of the production of quartermaster supplies, established fourteen such districts, which were called zones. The Air Service had eight districts and the Chemical Warfare Service four. All production for the Signal Corps, Engineers, Construction Division, and Medical Department was administered directly from Washington.

This decentralization of the field administration of war industry had a marked effect upon its efficiency. The administrative officers in charge of a manufacturing district were men of high standing in the business and industry of their respective regions. They knew the manufacturers in those regions. They were always right at the spot when difficulties arose in securing raw materials and fuel and shipping priorities. Even more important, each district organization had within it a representative of the Finance Service of the Army. The War Department was empowered to make advance payments on contracts up to a considerable percentage of the value of work done or supplies actually delivered. These advances, as we have said before, enabled the munitions producers to finance their projects. The district organizations, maintaining finance officers in the field as they did, enabled the producers to obtain these advances in a minimum of time.

Frequently the chief executive officers of the manufacturing districts were civilians. Each district board maintained a strong legal department and also numerous technical assistants, not the least among which were the cost accountants. Since a great portion of the war supplies were produced on the cost-plus plan, the war brought the cost accountant into great prominence, during both the period of production and the period of liquidation afterwards.

These district organizations, in immediate contact as they were with the producers, comprised an organization ready built for the delicate work of terminating war industry. Washington might fix policies and specify the classes of supplies the production of which was to be stopped and the sorts which were to be produced after the armistice in full or curtailed quantities. It was for the district administrations to say how the terminations and reductions should be carried out. Consequently, after the armistice the organizations in charge of the manufacturing districts were changed over into what were variously known as district claims boards and district boards of review. Whatever they were called by the bureaus creating them, their duties were essentially the same—to terminate contracts by mutual consent, to agree with the producers upon the terms of settlement, to take over in the name of the War Department such finished products, raw and semi-finished materials, machinery, buildings, and other equipment as became government property under the terms of the settlements, and to dispose of the materials thus taken over, some being selected for permanent retention among the nation's war assets, some being turned over to other branches of the Government which could make use of them, and others being disposed of by sale. To assist it in this work, each district board maintained a subsidiary organization known as the district salvage board, which collected the government property and disposed of it.

To supervise this field activity, each procurement bureau of the War Department established at headquarters in Washington a superior board known as the bureau claims board. Each of these supervisory boards, in turn, created as an adjunct to itself a bureau salvage board, which maintained executive control over the district salvage boards. For several weeks there was no specific executive agency to direct the work of this organization, except that all the bureau and district boards were under the general authority of the Director of Purchase, Storage, and Traffic. He unified and controlled their work through what were known as supply circulars, a medium of administration which had come into great importance after the creation of the Division of Purchase, Storage, and Traffic. Through the supply circulars the administration of war industry issued its general and class directions to the production bureaus. The standard contract provisions, for instance, had been brought to the attention of the contracting officers by publication in the supply circulars. The series of supply circulars thus came to be the code of unified army supply.

The Director of Purchase, Storage, and Traffic, however, had many duties other than those of directing the demobilization, though none more important. It was realized that the system needed a controlling head, the sole function of which would be to administer the entire liquidation of war industry. Therefore, late in January, 1919, the Secretary of War created the War Department Claims Board, into which were to focus, through the bureau boards, all the field activities in industrial demobilization. The Assistant Secretary of War became the president of this board. Mr. G. H. Dorr, who was also the assistant Director of Munitions, and Brigadier General (later Major General) George W. Burr, who had succeeded General G. W. Goethals as Director of Purchase, Storage, and Traffic, were the first regular members of the War Department Claims Board. There were also three special members and a recorder, and as time went on the Board was expanded by the creation of subcommittees of experts in various legal and industrial subjects.

The process of liquidation, therefore, originated with the district boards. In settling with a contractor, the district board appraised all the articles completed under the contract. It examined the expenditures which the contractor had made and the obligations he had incurred looking toward the finished production. Under the demobilization policy adopted, the Government was responsible for both of these costs. It paid for completed supplies (the price including the contractor's profit), for raw materials purchased for the contract but not used, for semi-finished materials, for the contractor's obligations to his subcontractors (including the costs of canceling the subcontracts), and, finally, for all general operating costs, including the contractor's "overhead" expenses, factory and machine depreciation costs, and the amortization of new facilities built at the Government's behest. To the most important production costs (but not including depreciation or amortization costs or interest on money invested in materials) the claims boards were authorized to add 10 per cent of the sum as the contractor's profit. The Government paid no prospective profits, but only a fair remuneration for work actually done.

This was the proposition extended to the manufacturer when the Government proposed to him the voluntary termination of his contract. Most of the contractors received the terms favorably: they did not wish to collect money for work not done, even though theirs was the technically legal right to do so. If any producer balked at the policy, he always had the remedy of seeking his full pound of flesh in the Court of Claims. However, the slowness of procedure in the Court of Claims made this a weak remedy; and even if the Court of Claims finally granted him his exactions, then he must wait for his money until Congress passed an act appropriating it from the Treasury. Only recently Congress passed a bill to reimburse the estate of a long-deceased individual who was wrongfully deprived of a horse during the Civil War. Such was the prospect which faced the contractor unwilling to accept the War Department's terms of settlement. With this coercive potentiality in the Government's position, the Government itself fixed the terms of settlement, at least in broad outline; but the terms were, in the main, fair to all concerned.

The district boards proved to be able to liquidate most of the contracts without dispute. From these boards the settlement agreements went up for approval first to the bureau claims boards and finally to the War Department Claims Board, with certain exceptions to be noted later. If agreements could not be reached by the district boards, appeals could be taken to the bureau boards and, after them, to the War Department Claims Board. The last-named body designated one of its members to sit with each bureau board and to exercise the authority of the War Department Claims Board in approving all settlements after action by the bureau board. The approval of the special member, acting in the name of the Secretary of War, constituted the final step in the settlement, which then passed to the finance officers for payment. Thus only a few of the 27,000 suspended contracts reached the War Department Claims Board for detailed consideration. Nearly all of them came up to the highest authority as agreed-upon settlements, needing only the approval of the proper special member of the War Department Claims Board before being embodied within the original contracts as supplementary agreements. Occasionally questions of fact arose as to the fidelity of a contractor's performance under the terms of his contract. Such questions were carried by appeal, not to the War Department Claims Board, but to the Department's Board of Contract Adjustment, which, it will be remembered, was, by inference, set up as arbiter of such questions by one of the standard contract provisions. The Board of Contract Adjustment had other and more important duties in connection with the industrial liquidation, as will be shown later.

Now this settlement system was able to render an important service to American industry during the demobilization. Many of the contractors had gone to the limit of their resources in procuring buildings, machinery, materials, and work in the prosecution of their contracts. As long as production was continuing, the Government could finance the expansion by making advance payments to the cost-plus contractors and by advancing money to others through the War Credits Board. But when the contracts were terminated, the Government could no longer follow this financing system, and the contractors faced a period of months or even years before they could conclude their settlements with the Government. During all that time their invested money would be tied up. Some of the more deeply involved—and large concerns they were, too—were perilously near actual bankruptcy as a result.

For the relief of such producers the War Department continued in demobilization its plan of advance payments, with, of course, a difference. Before the armistice the Government, in making advance payments, paid a percentage of the cost of work actually done. After the armistice no work to speak of was being done; yet in practically all the settlements there were numerous items of cost admittedly legitimate and about which there was no dispute. These were such items as materials in sight, appraised, and invoiced to the War Department, and such items as the contractor's obligations to his subcontractors. The War Department adopted the policy of making payments in advance of final settlement up to 75 per cent of its admitted obligations. These payments, amounting in all to more than $143,000,000, enabled the producers to tide over the period between the termination of work and the final settlement with the Government. The practice of maintaining officers of the Finance Service as members of the district claims boards facilitated the prompt payment of these advances. In the final settlements, of course, the Government subtracted from the amounts due from it to the producers all advances made to them.

From this outline it will be seen that the War Department, in striking a balance with war industry, set up within itself what was essentially a system of courts, with a regular procedure and process of appeal and—for such the decisions of the War Department Claims Board came to be—a body of laws and precedents. The court system, however, had the advantage of flexibility, simplicity, and rapidity of action, being hampered by none of the rules and customs that circumscribe the regular courts. The war department courts, if we may call the claims boards that, were courts of conciliation. The claimants partook of their benefits voluntarily. They might, under certain conditions, at any time appeal to the regular federal courts; but there they faced years of litigation before they could reach final settlement. This gave the war department system a great advantage, which the Department utilized to obtain advantageous terms for itself; yet it must be said that the entire liquidation was conducted in a spirit of desire to make the contractors whole for all their expenditures.

We are now in a position to understand the unavoidable

injury done to the holders of the informal contracts during the first months after the armistice. When the Comptroller of the Treasury ruled that the informal contracts were invalid, he foreclosed the War Department from making any advance settlement payments to these victims of patriotism and haste. Many of them were as heavily obligated financially as the holders of the valid contracts, and their solvency was equally precarious. Yet not a dollar of government money could they receive until the wheels of legislation had ground out authority for the settlement of their claims. Some of their circumstances were particularly distressing.

Early in October, 1918, one of the war department bureaus ordered a certain manufacturer to produce 5,000 frames for army trucks on the security that "formal contract will follow." He was awaiting the arrival of this document to justify him in making commitments for materials when he received an urgent message from Washington beseeching him to make early delivery of the frames. He yielded, and without waiting for the formal contract spent over $500,000 for machinery and materials. The armistice was signed before his formal contract was executed, and then, with his production stopped, he was unable to collect a penny of the money due him. Another man spent $400,000 in the prosecution of a contract, only to find after the armistice that his apparently valid contract had been improperly signed and therefore was classed among the invalid contracts.

The Dent Law gave all such claims a legal footing, but that act was not in force until March 2, 1919. Meanwhile, however, the War Department's liquidation machinery had taken up the settlement of the informal contracts along with the others. The district boards had determined for many of them what part of the work had been completed, what amounts the Government should pay for materials delivered, what reimbursements the producers should receive for expenditures made in preparation for production, and in many instances had reached complete agreements as to final lump-sum settlements. When the Dent Law went on the statute books, these agreements needed only final approval to become operative; and therefore the settlement of the informal claims proceeded with great rapidity after the passage of the enabling act.

The Dent Law conferred upon the Secretary of War power to adjust the informal contracts on equitable terms, with the proviso (already adopted as policy in the settlement of the valid contracts) that no prospective profits should be paid. This power the Secretary delegated to the War Department Claims Board, with two exceptions. Invalid contracts made with Canadian producers were to be adjusted by the Imperial Munitions Board, a branch of the British Ministry of Munitions, which had acted as the agent of the War Department in procuring army supplies in Canada. All contracts with other foreign producers—they were principally French and British producers—were to be settled by various foreign agencies and representatives of the War Department.

The informal contracts with American producers were of two sorts—those of which there was written evidence and those of which there was no written evidence. The former were known as Class A contracts and the latter as Class B. The Class A contracts were contracts apparently formal but improperly executed, or procurement orders, or correspondence setting forth the contract terms. The Class B contracts were agreements wholly or in part oral. The Class A contracts presented no difficulty to the War Department Claims Board, and they were put through to settlement by the regular procedure. It required the taking of testimony to establish the terms of Class B contracts, and the War Department Claims Board, with its subsidiary boards, had its hands too full with the regular routine of liquidation to add to its business this new, voluminous work; and therefore it in turn delegated the duty of establishing the terms of the Class B contracts to the Board of Contract Adjustment, the creation of which was noted above.

The Board of Contract Adjustment heard witnesses and then rendered a decision as to the terms of a Class B contract. After that it did one of two things: it referred the now established contract to the proper district board for settlement, or else it determined itself the financial obligation of the Government and issued an award to the producer. In addition to this work the War Department Board of Contract Adjustment, as a convenient agency, also settled contracts of all sorts made by such presidential agencies as the War Industries Board and the United States Food Administration.

After the Dent Act was in operation, the War Department extended to the informal contractors also the privilege of receiving partial payments in advance of final settlement.

Such, in outline, was the system which liquidated the war industry and struck the balance between the War Department and the munitions producers. A few details of organization should be noted. The War Department Claims Board greatly expanded its own organization during the episode by creating various subsidiary bodies. One of these was its Standing Committee (composed of members of the Board), which did most of the actual work for the Board and presented its acts for the consideration of the entire Board in the form of resolutions. These resolutions in time became a body of precedents to standardize the whole procedure. To handle engineering and other technical questions, the War Department Claims Board created its Technical Section, which, in turn, established within itself its Plant Valuation Group, made up of men specially qualified to appraise the contemporary value of plants erected for the War Department by producers with the understanding that the Department would pay for these plants, or an agreed-upon portion of their cost. The Special Auditing Committee of the Board also conducted a work of great importance. During the war numerous manufacturers held contracts with two or more production bureaus of the War Department. After the armistice they filed separate claims for the settlement of such contracts. There was always danger that in these claims there would be duplicate items of such costs as overhead expense and plant deterioration. The Auditing Committee consolidated the claims of individual producers and thus enabled the War Department Claims Board to strike out duplicate items of cost. Numerous contractors followed the old peace-time procedure of filing claims with the auditor of the War Department. So many claims originated from this source that the War Department Claims Board established in the office of the Director of Finance a Classification Board to separate all claims coming to the auditor and to refer them to the proper bureau boards.

This system had nothing to do with the settlement of claims arising out of the War Department's operations in real estate during the war. There were thousands of claims for damage done to property incidental to the training of the Army. To settle such claims the Secretary of War utilized the existing War Department Board of Appraisers, which had been created to establish the values of commandeered property. The commanders of military posts investigated the validity of real estate claims and recommended awards. These, after approval by the Board of Appraisers and the Secretary of War, were paid by the auditor of the War Department. Numerous real estate claims arose under informal and invalid agreements, and the condition of such claimants was usually particularly helpless. When the War Department started to build its great trinitrotoluol plant at Racine, Wisconsin, a large number of persons, home owners and renters, moved off the site without the formality of written contracts. Many of these individuals sold their farm animals and household goods. The armistice cut short the construction of the plant, and then the property owners discovered that they were without legal standing before the Government. The Dent Law enabled the Department to settle these and other real estate claims arising under informal contracts, and the Board of Appraisers made the settlements.

The Canadian contracts, both formal and informal, were adjusted by the Imperial Munitions Board, acting in conjunction with two American officers called assessors, one of whom was a special member of the War Department Claims Board. Mr. D. C. Jackling, the director of United States Government Explosives Plants, adjusted all the outstanding contracts and orders in connection with the construction of the Nitro (West Virginia) Powder Plant. More than 3,200 firms and individuals had received orders for materials for the plant, and a fire at the plant immediately after the armistice destroyed the records of all open orders. The terms of these orders were reëstablished by correspondence with the contractors. A special settlement board within the Ordnance Department adjusted the terminated contracts for the construction of nitrogen fixation plants authorized as a war measure. The Spruce Production Corporation of the Air Service terminated and settled its own contracts with the spruce lumber interests in the Northwest.

On July 1, 1920, the War Department Claims Board, which had conducted the liquidation of the Department's war business (with the small exceptions noted above) ended its work and disbanded, turning over to the regular military organization of the War Department the residue and remnant of work still left. Of the 27,000 war contracts, 26,000 had been terminated and settled by the Department. There were still 995 claims pending, or less than 4 per cent of the original number; but more than half the auditing and other preliminary work on these 995 claims was done. The liquidation was therefore more than 98 per cent complete, and this in little more than a year and a half after the Government halted the mightiest industrial undertaking upon which any people ever embarked. The promptness and wisdom shown in that settlement had allowed war industry to taper off and stop without shock to the economic structure of the country, had stabilized business, relieved the banks of the country of a vast load of debt which they were carrying for the war producers, and thus had brought the nation safely and easily through what might otherwise have been the sharpest business crisis it had ever known. Concretely, in dollars and cents, this work was of great material benefit to the Government and people of the United States. The rate of liquidation of the unfinished portions of the war contracts averaged fourteen cents to the dollar—that is, the payment of fourteen cents by the Government satisfied and wiped out a contractual obligation of one dollar. At this ratio, the settlements effected by the War Department Claims Board saved the people of this country from having to pay out well over $3,300,000,000.

Photo by Harris & Ewing

THE WAR DEPARTMENT CLAIMS BOARD

Photo by Signal Corps

CONVALESCENT READING
STARS AND STRIPES

Photo by Signal Corps

HOSPITAL TRAIN IN UNITED STATES

CHAPTER X

ORDNANCE DEMOBILIZATION

WHEN the average man speaks of munitions, he means ordnance and, even more specifically, guns and ammunition. In this he is nearly half right. Technically, the word "munitions" includes army supplies of all sorts, even to candy and cigarettes, and in this sense the word is used in these volumes; but of the total war business transacted for the Army, the procurement of ordnance supplies constituted 42 per cent. Ordnance was by far the largest class of munitions. Four thousand American manufacturing plants worked on ordnance contracts during the war. Nearly 3,000,000 men labored in these mills.

The mere size of the war ordnance industry would have made the problem of its demobilization a great one, but it was also complicated with peculiar difficulties. The production of most ordnance materials differed radically from that of any articles known in normal American industry. The Quartermaster Department procured for the Army food, clothing, shoes, hand tools, and many other supplies which, though they were frequently of special design, nevertheless were not much unlike the sorts of commodities with which the contractors were already familiar. The Engineer Corps used many materials commonly employed in the peaceful pursuits. Outside of ordnance, the manufacture of aircraft alone took our industries into virgin fields of endeavor.

Therefore, those factories which were making for the Army products essentially similar to products consumed by the civilian population, were ready after the armistice to resume their places in normal commerce with slight internal adjustment. But the ordnance factories—they were a different story. In ordnance production the war had witnessed some factory conversions of the most violent sort. Manufacturers of printing presses built gun carriages of new and difficult design; makers of sewing machines and automobiles undertook the difficult task of producing hydropneumatic recuperators for absorbing the recoil of field guns; producers of typewriters and water meters manufactured time fuses for shell; women's cloak factories sewed silk powder bags; a phonograph maker produced aërial bomb sights; and one producer turned from the modern business of making corsets and took up the ancient occupation of tentmaker. For nearly all these factories the ordnance contracts virtually implied the physical reëquipment of their plants for quite different manufacturing processes. For them, too, demobilization meant a not less severe dislocation of equipment and processes in changing back again to their former work.

It was the problem of the Ordnance Department after the armistice to manage the liquidation of its great war business—to halt the work, to dispose of raw materials and materials left half completed when the wheels stopped, to do something with the special factories and even the complete towns built by the Government or for the Government in the prosecution of the war enterprise, to recoup the millions advanced to finance the ordnance producers, and finally to settle with cash the obligations of the Government to the producers incurred when the contracts were terminated.

Although in size and intricacy this problem was appalling, there was no hesitation in setting about solving it, no period when the enterprise hung in neutral, going neither forward nor backward. Ordnance work was reaching new peaks of production when the Ordnance Department in Washington took the first steps toward its dismemberment. In late October, 1918, when the Argonne-Meuse offensive was striking home and it was becoming evident that the curtain might at any time fall in the theatre of war, the chief ordnance officers held a secret meeting one Sunday afternoon in Washington and for the first time considered the possible demobilization. At this meeting the Chief of Ordnance appointed a commission to make a rapid study of the organization of the Ordnance Department to determine whether that organization was fitted to turn without change to the stoppage of work and the restoration of the industry to its former basis. This same commission later became the Ordnance Claims Board, the agency which supervised the entire demobilization of ordnance industry. It was, of course, like all the other bureau claims boards, subsidiary to the War Department Claims Board. The Ordnance Claims Board was formally created by order on November 2, and thus had been in existence for nine days when the armistice was signed. Its chief was Brigadier General W. S. Peirce. Its members were Colonel R. P. Lamont, who was president of the American Steel Foundries Corporation before and after his military service in the World War; Colonel G. H. Stewart, an ordnance officer of the Regular Army; Lieutenant Colonel M. F. Briggs, counselor at law, New York; Lieutenant Colonel F. R. Ayer, recorder of the Eastern Manufacturing Company, of Bangor, Maine; and Mr. Waldo H. Marshall, president of the American Locomotive Company, New York.

This board found an existing organization—the field administrations of the thirteen ordnance manufacturing districts—admirably adapted to the work of closing up the war business. The district organizations had been created to give the Ordnance Department a mechanism by which it could keep in immediate contact with the process of manufacture without congesting the headquarters in Washington to the point where competent management became impossible. They had been likened roughly to the fire exits of a theatre, distributed to prevent crowding at the front doors. In the district organizations were employed 33,000 civilians, uniformed officers, and enlisted men, and through this great force the office in Washington kept in as intimate touch with the work, the trials, and the accomplishments of its producers as if it had been employing the services of but a single factory. The ordnance field men knew the war factories as they knew their own offices. They were acquainted with the contractors, with the subcontractors, with the shop superintendents and foremen, and often with the workmen themselves. Obviously they were qualified to judge at what rate production could be stopped without injury to the industry or its workmen and to determine the settlement adjustments that would be fair to both sides.

It is worth while pausing a moment to examine the thirteen ordnance districts and to note their headquarters cities, their extent, the characteristic sorts of ordnance supplies produced in each, and the chief production officer of each.

Toronto. Embraced the whole of Canada. Produced principally shell machined and ready for loading, particularly 75-millimeter shell. As noted in the preceding chapter, all industrial demobilization in Canada was carried out by the Imperial Munitions Board, two of the members of which were special representatives of the War Department Claims Board, sent to Canada after the armistice for this purpose.

Bridgeport. Included Connecticut and four Massachusetts counties. Primarily the small-arms district, producing all the pistols and revolvers, all the bayonets, all the automatic rifles, more than a million of the service rifles, most of the heavy machine guns, and almost all the small-arms ammunition delivered under war contracts. Mr. Waldo C. Bryant of Bridgeport was chief of the district.

Boston. Included the rest of New England. The chief producer of soldiers' belts, haversacks, mess kits, and other personal ordnance equipment; produced small-arms ammunition heavily, and produced also boosters and adapters (for shell) and carriages for 155-millimeter howitzers. Mr. Levi H. Greenwood, chief of district.

New York. Included New York City, Long Island, and nine other New York and twelve New Jersey counties. The prime producer of trench-warfare ordnance. Produced much toluol and was a finisher of shell, fuses, and cartridge cases. Loaded more than one-third of all artillery ammunition shipped abroad. Chief, Mr. George J. Roberts, vice-president of the Public Service Corporation of New Jersey.

Philadelphia. Included eastern Pennsylvania, part of New Jersey, and all of Delaware. The chief service-rifle producer and a chief producer of high explosives. Immense shell-loading activities. Chief, Mr. John C. Jones, president of the Harrison Safety Boiler Works.

Baltimore. Included all of Maryland but two western counties, and all of the District of Columbia and the states of Virginia and North and South Carolina. The leading shrapnel-loading district and a great shell-loading area. Contained the largest of the ammonium nitrate plants. Produced all the 37-millimeter guns. Chief, Lieutenant Colonel A. V. Barnes, formerly president of the American Book Company.

Rochester. Embraced all the state of New York not in the New York City district. Chief production was in Lewis machine guns, Enfield rifles, 75-millimeter field guns, shrapnel, picric acid, and optical glass. Chief, Mr. Frank S. Noble, executive officer of the Eastman Kodak Company.

Cleveland. Northern Ohio and three northwestern counties of Pennsylvania. Produced completed big guns, shell fuses, 75-millimeter gun carriages, mounts for railway artillery, and 6-ton tanks. Chief, Mr. Samuel Scovil, former president of the Cleveland Electric Illuminating Company.

Detroit. Included the state of Michigan. Produced gun recoil recuperators, artillery vehicles, large-caliber shell, and trench-mortar shell. Chief, Mr. Fred J. Robinson, president of the Lowery-Robinson Lumber Company.

Chicago. Included northern Illinois and the band of states to the northwest as far as Montana. Produced caterpillar traction for the tanks and artillery, guns, carriages, recuperators, projectiles, and grenades; the district was also saturated with contracts for machinery for the eastern munitions plants. Chief, Mr. E. A. Russell, vice-president of the Otis Elevator Company.

Pittsburg. Included western Pennsylvania except three counties, two counties of western Maryland, two counties of

Ohio, and all of West Virginia. The prime subcontract district for the production of raw steel and steel forgings. Herein was located the Neville Island ordnance plant project. Produced optical glass in quantity. Chief, Mr. Ralph M. Dravo, of Dravo Brothers, contractors, Pittsburg.

Cincinnati. Southern Ohio, Indiana, and the South. Was the chief nitrogen-fixation district and the chief producer of smokeless powder. Included Dayton, with 200 factories exclusively engaged in munitions production. Produced tanks, shell, fuses, optical instruments, and machine tools for war factories. District chief, Mr. C. L. Harrison, a Cincinnati capitalist.

St. Louis. Included southern Indiana and sixteen western states. Produced black walnut, toluol, and picric acid. Chief, Mr. Marvin E. Singleton, former president of the East St. Louis Cotton Oil Company.

After the armistice the manufacturing committees in charge of the twelve American ordnance districts became, without essential change in their organization, the ordnance district claims boards. Each board consisted of seven members—business men and at least one lawyer—with such technical assistants as they needed. The first executive act in demobilization for these boards to make was to determine what war contracts were to be terminated immediately, what ones were to be tapered off with a minimum expense to the Government and a minimum disturbance to industry and labor, and what ones were to be carried through to completion.

It was often advantageous to allow the contractors to proceed undisturbed. Some of these ordnance supplies, which would be valuable and essential items of our military equipment for years to come, were only just reaching the stage of production in the factories, after many months of costly experiment and preparation. It was obviously unwise to interrupt these projects with nothing to show for them except heavy bills of expenses. Then, too, it was sometimes of financial advantage to the Government to allow a contract to go through to completion. A contractor in the Chicago district, for example, had nearly completed the manufacture of several large machines for installation in an eastern munitions plant. To cancel the contract would have cost the Government $90,000 in a settlement and left on its hands a quantity of semi-finished materials having only junk value. The Government no longer had use for the finished machines; yet it would cost only $14,000 more to go on and complete them. This was done, and the Ordnance Department was later able to sell the machines to a private buyer for more than $100,000, thus recovering practically all the money it paid to the contractor.

To provide a basis of fact for all such acts of administration in the demobilization, the district boards first took a rapid but thorough inventory of the ordnance industrial situation. This they did by means of questionnaires sent to all the contractors. Each questionnaire, when returned to the district board, showed the status of the contract at the time and how the contractor's business and his employees would be affected by a termination. The general ordnance policy was to permit contractors (after the first emergency suspension which, it will be remembered, had been requested immediately after the armistice was signed) to continue their work on a diminishing scale for a few weeks, while they made their arrangements to engage once more in commercial work. Some of the contracts, including all the late, standardized ones, provided for the termination of work upon thirty days' notice. If, however, the enforcement of this provision would create any considerable amount of unemployment, the district boards allowed such contractors to complete an average thirty days' production, but to spread out the work over a longer period of time.

There were variations of the general policy when it was applied to special classes of ordnance industry. For instance, the many contractors who were machine-finishing the artillery shell were permitted to keep their plants in full operation until January 31, 1919, when the work had to cease abruptly. All source industries—industries, that is, producing rough forgings and other raw and semi-finished materials for ordnance manufacture—were taken from war work forthwith. Then, too, as noted, in various classes of large ordnance, or ordnance of exceedingly difficult manufacture, the orders were greatly reduced and the contractors permitted to go ahead and complete the residue, no matter how long it might take. Such ordnance included gun carriages, recuperators, tanks, optical instruments, and other supplies of the sort. This reduced production continued for more than a year after the general stoppage of war industry. Some of the Mark VIII tanks (the Anglo-American design) were delivered to the Army as late as June 1, 1920.

So expeditiously was the work of termination carried on in the other classes of manufacture (and these made up the greater part of the ordnance industry) that by January 1, 1919, nearly all war ordnance production had either been terminated altogether or was dwindling to the vanishing point under specific agreements. After February 1 the only war ordnance factories in operation were the exceptional plants noted in the preceding paragraph.

Even as the ordnance industry was being stopped, the Government was coming to an understanding with the ordnance contractors as to the settlement of their claims. To this end, in most of the manufacturing districts the board members traveled from city to city, addressing large meetings of the contractors and explaining to them the general liquidation policy adopted by the War Department. In its broad outlines, this policy was as follows: The Government would take off the contractor's hands at cost all materials which he had specifically purchased for his contract, but which he had not used. The Government would reimburse him for all work done on his contract, for all materials used, for all money paid out in wages, and for all legitimate overhead expense, the Government in return taking over all materials in the various stages of their completion. Further, the Government would regard as proper costs whatever it cost the contractor to terminate and settle his subcontracts, and would pay these costs. Finally, in specific instances the Government would pay money in amortization of the cost of machinery and tools bought especially for war use, the sum to be proportioned to the amount of work completed. And whatever else the contractor was out of pocket legitimately, the Government would pay. When the various costs were brought together as a lump, to this sum the Government would add 10 per cent as profit. It would, moreover, allow 6 per cent interest on money which the contractor had invested in materials, reckoning from the average time of purchase to the date of the settlement; but it would not allow 10 per cent profit on this investment in addition.

These terms received widespread acceptance, although they allowed no prospective profits, and thereupon the various districts became scenes of great activity as the ordnance officers worked with the contractors to expedite the presentation of settlement claims by the latter. Inspectors and agents employed by the district boards checked manufacturers' inventories, and boxed and set aside materials to be delivered to the Government, while district accountants audited the costs statements. Each field agent of a district board was made responsible for a few specific claims. He stood at the contractor's elbow and helped him rough out his claim into proper form. A spirit of amiability prevailed. For many reasons the contractor wished to make his settlement as quickly as possible, and the district agent was there to tell him what items in his claim were indisputable, and what ones were likely to be contested, thereby holding up the final settlement. When the district agent and the contractor had agreed as to a claim, they submitted it informally to one of the members of the district claims board for his opinion. If he thought his board would be unlikely to allow certain items, the contractor could usually be persuaded to omit such items. Claims prepared under such conditions presented little difficulty to the various claims boards, and most of them went through to settlement without a hitch in the proceedings.

Most contractors were willing to forego their technical rights in order to save the Government from paying for useless production, but a few were obdurate. One man, working under a contract with a thirty-day termination clause, deliberately increased his rate of production five times in order to collect a maximum amount from the Government. When the Ordnance Department discovered his plan, it breached the contract outright and allowed the producer to take his grievance, if he continued to nurse one, into the courts. A rare instance of this sort, however, is cited only to show by contrast the prevalent attitude of industrial coöperation with the Government. Numerous producers omitted from their claims many items the validity of which could probably have been sustained in the future negotiations, but which were, however, subject to close scrutiny and therefore a factor of delay in the settlements.

The wheels of war industry had not ceased to turn before the Government began to make advance payments in settlement of the industrial claims. If the contractors were generous, so was the Government. The first settlement made illustrated the War Department's attitude right through. A New York contractor had submitted a claim for about $15,000. On January 20, 1919, he informed the New York District Claims Board that two days later he had to meet a note for $10,000, a debt incurred in prosecution of his war contract. A member of the New York Claims Board took this claim in person to Washington and next day secured its approval by the Ordnance Claims Board, together with an authorization to advance $10,000 to the contractor pending the final approval and settlement by the War Department Claims Board. The New York district finance officer paid over the $10,000 in time to save the note from going to protest.

As the weeks went on the New York manufacturer's plight was duplicated over and over again. The producers of ordnance supplies, after the termination of their contracts, faced enormous financial obligations which they would have to meet long before the machinery of liquidation could act upon their claims. To such producers the system of advance partial payments afforded great relief. The policy of advance payments not only saved numerous concerns from financial ruin, but it stimulated the general commercial reconstruction and resumption of normal business by releasing large sums of money and putting it again into circulation. And, it should not be forgotten, the system greatly aided the Government to secure favorable settlement terms from the contractors by offering the reward of early payments to those whose war business was quickly liquidated.

Since the prime contractors' subcontract settlements were acknowledged costs which the Government was bound to pay in the prime settlements, it was vitally important that the Ordnance Department intervene to obtain for the prime contractors the most favorable terms possible in the settlement of their subcontracts. Every subcontractor, of course, had the legal right to insist upon the full performance of his contract, and he was not to be coerced by the bogey of the Court of Claims and its long-drawn-out procedure. He could go into the state courts and enforce his rights within reasonable time. Therefore, it is indicative of the spirit of war industry that the ordance district claims boards found little difficulty in settling with the subcontractors on favorable terms. The prime contractors had no such interest in these terms as did the Government, since, whatever the subcontract settlement costs might be, the Government would have to pay them. The agents of the district boards readily persuaded the subcontractors, as a sporting proposition, to surrender their prospective profits voluntarily and accept the profit of 10 per cent on work actually done, even as the prime contractors, who had assumed the chief risk in the first place, had been willing to do. The efforts of the ordnance field agents in this direction saved the Government many millions.

The first complete claim received by the Ordnance Claims Board came from the Detroit district on January 10, 1919. The first claim to go through to final settlement by the Ordnance Claims Board was passed on February 20. The district claims boards sent the bulky and valuable settlement papers to Washington by courier rather than entrust them to the mails. When the system settled into its routine the Ordnance Claims

Board passed upon the average claim within a week after its arrival in Washington. On the average the Government paid in the settlement of ordnance contractors' claims an amount equal to about 12 per cent of the face value of the uncompleted portions of the contracts. The average ordnance contract entailed a government obligation somewhere between $100,000 and $250,000 in amount, but many were much larger. The Marlin-Rockwell Corporation of New Haven, Connecticut, one of the chief producers of machine guns and small arms, presented a claim for nearly $14,000,000. One of the largest war contracts was that with the American Car & Foundry Company, of a face value of over $100,000,000. In contrast, the New York Ordnance District Claims Board, which settled that contract, settled another (a subcontract) for $1.50. The claim of the DuPont Powder Company against the Ordnance Department was for about $3,280,000—this in settlement of contracts with a value of $50,000,000. The New York Air Brake Company presented to the Rochester Ordnance Claims Board claims aggregating $9,000,000. The New York District board settled 206 claims for $1.00 each, the contractors voluntarily refraining from presenting any claims above the statutory dollar which had to be paid to make the settlement legal.

Many were the interesting episodes which occurred during the ordnance liquidation. The St. Louis district was the chief source of black walnut timber secured during the war. Walnut was used in making gunstocks and airplane propellers. In hunting for walnut in this district we discovered that we were gleaning where Germany had reaped before us. The former solid stands of walnut in this district had been cleaned out in recent years, much of the timber having been shipped to Germany *via* the Gulf ports. Yet our gleaning was successful. Walnut trees, growing as individuals or in small groups, were still to be found along the country lanes, in farm lots, at the edges of orchards, and shading the grounds of the farmsteads. Nowhere were more than thirty trees in a group discovered. Consequently an adequate supply of walnut for the munitions plants depended upon a foot-by-foot search of the entire American countryside in the walnut regions. In this work the Government was assisted by tens of thousands of volunteers aroused to the need by the widespread publicity. The Boy Scouts turned their hikes into walnut-hunting expeditions. The country doctor, the circuit-riding clergyman, the bee hunter, and the muskrat trapper all made it their business to locate and report stands of walnut timber. As a result unexpectedly ample quantities of the wood were secured from regions supposedly denuded of it. On the day of the armistice the timber dealers found themselves stocked up with enough black walnut to meet all commercial demands for five years ahead.

One of the Ordnance Department's timber cruisers located a grove of black walnut trees shading the farm home of a woman living in Missouri. She hated to sacrifice her trees, but listened to the appeal of patriotism and accepted an offer of $1,100 for them. Then, when the agent had left with her signed agreement in his pocket, she repented of her bargain and grieved so much at her forthcoming loss that the village minister suggested a remedy. He told her that the anticipated proceeds of the sale would pay for an automobile in which she could ride about the country and, amid the pleasant rural scenes, forget about the devastation soon to be staged in her own front yard. She acted on this suggestion, bought a car for $1,080, and in payment gave a note which she agreed to lift when the Government took the trees and paid her the money. The armistice intervened before the timber cutters appeared, and the Ordnance Department canceled the contract with the timber dealer. That left the woman with a half-used car, a note maturing in the bank to meet which she had no funds, and a clump of walnut trees for which the Government had no use. The St. Louis District Claims Board could not relieve her distress, but a member of the board brought the case to the attention of a meeting of war contractors; and it was arranged for the Missouri lady to keep both her automobile and her walnut trees.

The New York District Claims Board settled for $275,000 the claim of the Wah Chang Trading Corporation, of China, which supplied a large amount of antimony used in making shrapnel bullets. In the New York district also there had been a contract with the Japan Paper Company to supply paper parachutes for carrying floating signal lights. The contract was not a large one; yet in its settlement it was disclosed that there were about 10,000 subcontractors—individual Japanese families working in their own homes in Japan. Under the circumstances the board waived the usual rule that with every prime contract claim must be filed statements of settlement certified by every subcontractor.

Each of the district claims boards maintained in its quarters a progress chart which showed graphically each day the amount of industrial liquidation accomplished and the amount remaining to be done. In eleven of the districts this chart took the form of a thermometer, the rising mercury showing the amount of completed work. In the twelfth—at Cleveland—the chart was a representation of a bottle containing a celebrated beverage that does duty in these dry days for beer, and the task of the board was to empty this container.

On the first anniversary of the armistice the Ordnance Department's system of industrial demobilization had cleared up a large part of the war business. The district boards had passed upon 94 per cent of all contractors' claims presented, and the Ordnance Claims Board in Washington had disposed of 73 per cent of the ordnance claims. The settlements at this time had cost the United States nearly $131,000,000, but that sum had settled uncompleted portions of contracts to the value of approximately $1,000,000,000; and, in finding the net cost of the liquidation to the United States, from the sum paid out in these settlements there was still to be subtracted the receipts from the sale of materials taken over in the settlements. By the end of 1919 the district boards had passed 97 per cent of all claims and the Ordnance Claims Board 81 per cent. By that time the total amount approved for payment in adjusting the claims was more than $166,000,000.

In the latter part of 1919, however, a different system of settlement went into effect. By that time about three-fourths of the ordnance claims had been settled, in a spirit essentially of bargain and compromise, the Government yielding points and the contractors yielding them in order to reach swift agreements. Those who did the bargaining for the Government were for the most part the original members of the district organizations, the men who had been in touch with the industry from the start. As the unfinished business diminished in quantity, however, the members of the district claims boards one by one left the government service and returned to their own affairs, until by the autumn of 1919 the boards were made up largely of new members, most of them uniformed army officers who bore no such intimate relationship to the contractors. Within the Government, too, there was a growing spirit of criticism of the bargaining method of settling the contracts, even though the bargains had been highly advantageous to the Government. It was felt that more conventional methods should be employed. The result was a marked slowing down in the rate of industrial demobilization in the Ordnance Department.

It seems fitting here to say a word for the men who manufactured our ordnance during the war. The popular picture of a war contractor is that of a man swollen with new wealth and spending his money in riotous extravagances. This indictment, at any rate, cannot hold against the ordnance maker. Instead of profiting, the average ordnance contractor was glad enough to get out of the enterprise with a whole financial skin. Many were not so fortunate. An impartial investigation made by the Ordnance Department over its entire war manufacturing field showed that not more than one contractor in three or four, when the business was closed up, had anything to show for his war experience except the self-satisfying sense of having served his country.

In the light of the fact that so few of them profited at all and so many incurred actual loss, it is remarkable that they were not more grasping in the demobilization settlements; but the eternal fact remains that they were inclined to ask for less, rather than more, than was coming to them under their legal rights. This attitude was consistent with their whole attitude during the war. In the history of American industry there is no chapter more creditable to it than that of the attitude and accomplishments of the producers of ordnance during the World War. These men entered the undertaking with a zeal unsurpassed in any other part of the war organization. Working under an urgency such as American industry had never before experienced, they accepted the handicaps that had been placed upon the nation by its own peace-loving traditions and worked together as a unit to overcome the handicaps. They transformed their manufacturing plants with never a thought for the business they would one day have to resume. They undertook to produce, in quantities never before even projected, intricate materials of warfare the very names of which were unfamiliar to them. Despite the mounting costs of materials and labor, they managed to hammer down the prices of rifles, machine guns, explosives, shrapnel, and other important commodities, delivering to the Government not only a superior product, but a product costing the Government less than other nations at war paid for the same things. To accomplish this result they threw their normal rivalries on the scrap heap, opened up their trade secrets to each other, and virtually became partners in the single enterprise of supplying the American troops with the best munitions which American industry could produce.

As a rule, the profit-making war contractor was one who supplied commodities essentially like those produced in normal times. But supplies of this sort were almost unknown in the whole range of ordnance. The typical thing was to find on the day of the armistice the ordnance plant which had not yet come into full production under the original contract. This was because of the difficulties encountered in producing the more important items of ordnance. The months of the war had been marked by the heavy expenditure of money in the expansion of plants and the development of processes, and the armistice cut off the development before it had reached the profitable stage.

The producers did not attempt to recoup in the business liquidation that followed. These sentences are not intended to give a clean bill of health to the whole body of ordnance producers—some few of them sought to get more than they were morally entitled to get; some few, like the country horse trader, adopted the age-old procedure of barter by asking more than they expected to get. But where one man held out for the last penny of his rights, there could be found half a dozen others who put in no claims at all for money to which they were justly entitled. The great steel-producing industry, in particular, showed an aristocratic contempt of requiring its full due. Many steel producers pocketed their losses without a word: in fact, the Government settled a surprising number of ordnance contracts for the statutory one dollar apiece and thus saved itself millions for which it was legally liable. When the curious ordnance officers asked some of these contractors why they did not claim their full rights, they responded that the victory over Germany was compensation enough for them. As one of them expressed it, the achievements of the American boys in France had given him his run for his money.

In the Pittsburg district two steel producers had been engaged on contracts for essentially the same sort of material and on about the same scale. One was a small concern which had been kept at its wits' end most of the time to finance its war enterprise. The other was one of the largest corporations in the United States, with ample financial resources. Into the Ordnance Claims Board came two claims terminating contracts of approximately identical characteristics. One of the claims was several times larger than the other, and naturally the Washington authorities questioned the larger claim. They found that the latter was a just claim in every particular. The discovery was made that the smaller of the two claims had asked for an amount in settlement much below what the producer was entitled to receive. The larger claim had been submitted by the producer whose finances could not stand any loss; the smaller by the great corporation referred to above. Both were allowed in full.

Of the 317 large ordnance contracts in the Pittsburg district, the Government settled 149, involving a total obligation of more than $23,000,000, for $1.00 each. In this and other districts thousands of subcontractors forgave the prime contractors their legal obligations without the transfer of a penny. In the Philadelphia district the prime contractors cleared up thousands of their subcontracts and said nothing about them in their liquidation claims. These instances of generosity were discovered only when the Ordnance Department checked up to find out why the final settlement costs were so much lower than the preliminary estimate of those costs, made in the first hurried days after the armistice.

The record of American ordnance production was not a flawless one—it was too large to be that—but in view of the general attitude of the producers, it is submitted that to have participated in that war industry was a distinguished honor.

CHAPTER XI

ARTILLERY

THERE was a great deal more to the demobilization of the war ordnance industry than the mere office operation of settling with the contractors. It included an immense field activity of utmost practical interest both to the War Department and to the public. The armistice found the United States in a state of industrial preparation for war that would have been unattainable under any other circumstances. The world situation had forced us to turn American industry into a vast munitions plant which, at the cessation of hostilities, was just beginning to get into production with some of the most essential materials of warfare. That plant had been acquired only at the cost of heavy mortgage (in the form of government war bonds) placed upon the future, and hence it would have been folly to close out the business entirely with nothing to show for the whole effort but debts and the realization that the existence of the business had had a psychological effect in winning the war and protecting the United States. The sensible thing to do was to save out of the dismantling of war industry a material equipment which should afford national military insurance for years to come; and that was what the Ordnance Department did.

In building up this equipment the Ordnance Department was confronted with the three major questions of (1) what quantities of materials to allow the industry to go on and produce before closing down finally, (2) what to do with the buildings and machinery which the Government had provided for the enterprise, and (3) what disposition to make of surpluses of both materials and facilities beyond the Government's future needs.

Artillery constitutes the most important of all war supplies. Upon the production of artillery and its ammunition the Government expended more money than upon any other single class of materials. From a manufacturing standpoint, a unit of artillery consists of three principal parts—the gun tube itself, the recuperator (or recoil mechanism), and the carriage with its attending caissons. Each of these manufacturing phases called into existence during 1917-1918 huge industries. On the day of the armistice nineteen mills, built new from the ground up, were turning out gun and howitzer tubes at the rate of nearly 800 a month, a figure that may be contrasted with the annual American production of seventy-five guns before 1917. Five great plants, built new at a cost of many millions, were engaged in building recuperators of French design, and other producers were manufacturing American- and British-type recoil mechanisms. The carriages, limbers, and caissons, being, after all, wheeled vehicles, offered no particular manufacturing problem, and it was therefore unnecessary to create a new industry to produce them. Nevertheless, the carriage contracts engaged a large section of the car- and truck-building industries of the United States. Yet, for the reason that the vehicle builders could come quickly into the production of artillery carriages, the physical demobilization of this branch of the industry offered little difficulty, the chief problems centering around the termination of the production of gun tubes and recuperators. These problems involved questions of reserves to be produced before the industries were dissolved and the storage afterwards of the manufacturing facilities to give the United States a potential producing capacity that could be quickly utilized in the event of another war.

Several important considerations influenced the responses to these questions. In the first place our whole artillery manufacturing project had been aimed at the year 1919, and in the interim the American Expeditionary Forces purchased heavy quantities of artillery in France and England—in all, nearly 5,500 field guns of the latest and best designs. Including cap-

Photo by Howard E. Coffin

HAVOC WROUGHT BY GERMAN GUNS AT FORT NEAR RHEIMS

Photo by Howard E. Coffin

"WIPERS" READY FOR TOURISTS

Photo by Howard E. Coffin

FRENCH AND GERMAN AIRPLANE ENGINES AFTER COMBAT

Photo by Howard E. Coffin

RUINED TANKS NEAR CAMBRAI

tured *matériel*, the A. E. F. sent back to the United States after the armistice about 6,000 guns, with their full equipment of limbers, caissons, and supply vehicles. This in itself was a quantity sufficient to arm a large field force; and, on the face of it, this reserve seemed to make unnecessary any post-armistice production at all from our own ordnance plants. As a counterbalance, however, there was the industrial situation. The gun plants were heavy employers of labor. To close them all down forthwith might have created a serious amount of unemployment, to the detriment of the national prosperity. Then, too, it was good business to order the completion of *matériel* almost complete on the day of the armistice, and this procedure was adopted as a general policy.

General rules and policies could at best serve the field men of the Ordnance Department only as rough guides. Each of the nineteen gun factories supplied its own special problems in demobilization. The process of closing down the factories may be shown by the example of what went on after the armistice at the plant of the Bullard Engineering Works at Bridgeport, Connecticut.

This was a plant producing 155-millimeter guns—the tubes only. The 155, a French weapon, was the highest-powered fieldpiece used by the A. E. F., the railroad guns not being considered to be field guns. The supply of the useful 155 was never equal to the demand. The French factories could not deliver as many as the A. E. F. needed; and, because of the difficulty of producing the recuperator, our own industry did not succeed in turning out a single completely assembled unit before the armistice, although all parts had been successfully produced ready for assembling. Here, then, was an important class of artillery in which a shortage existed, and therefore the Ordnance Department was liberal in allowing production after the armistice.

The Bullard Engineering Works held contracts calling for the production of 1,400 155-millimeter gun tubes. On the first day of the armistice it had delivered forty-five finished tubes, and 500 others were progressing through the plant in various stages of completion. Many of these incomplete units had passed through the difficult shrinking process. Guns are built up in layers of steel, each one heated, superimposed upon the adjoining one, and then shrunk on in various cooling processes, thus putting into the steel strata a compression that enables the gun to sustain tremendous interior pressures without distortion. The ordnance officers looked at the status of work at the Bullard plant and ordered the completion of the 500 units in process, terminating the rest of the great contract.

This action was taken on the eleventh day of the armistice. The company expected to be able to complete the remaining 500 guns in six months, a course that would enable the manufacture to taper off and the gunmakers to find other employment. Two months later it was found that other industry was readily absorbing the excess labor of the gun plant, and therefore another cut was made in the contemplated production, the number of completions ordered being reduced to 262 in number. These were to be finished by April 15, 1919, after which war work at the plant was to cease entirely.

Note, now, the measures adopted in terminating the work. It is evident that the post-armistice operation was going to deliver to the Government 262 finished guns and 238 unfinished ones. The latter would stand for a government expenditure of millions of dollars. As an industrial commodity these unfinished tubes would have value only as scrap steel, to be melted up and made into other things. Yet to the Government they possessed a real military value. In the event of another war occurring before the present-day types of artillery become obsolete, the Army would need not only reserves of guns ready for use, but also another great gunmaking industry, to produce for an indefinitely expanding field force. Therefore proper war reserves should consist not only of guns, but also of reserve facilities for manufacturing guns—machinery and tools, designs, plans, and instructions, and, especially, the rough forgings of gun elements, so that, the moment a new gun factory was organized and equipped, it could start working, without having to wait weeks and months until the raw materials came up from the forging plants. The Bullard Works were instructed to stop work on the incompleted units at such points as would enable future gunmakers, if necessary, to resume the work without difficulty. All incomplete units, however, were to be carried through the shrinking process before being dropped. The various hoops and jackets which are shrunk upon gun tubes are machined to a precision expressed in thousandths of an inch. In heavy metal working, such exactness is ordinarily unknown. It is evident that only a little rusting would destroy the fit of the contact surfaces and ruin the unassembled jackets and hoops, and therefore the company was instructed to assemble these otherwise perishable elements before stopping the work. After the shrinking, all uncompleted pieces were slushed in grease, packed for protection, and stored away, to be used, according to the plan, in the manufacture which will be necessary in the peace-time maintenance of the artillery equipment. Some of the incomplete Bullard tubes of the 155's were later transferred to the Watervliet Arsenal and finished with the machinery there. The arsenal completed 300 guns of this size after the armistice.

This, essentially, so far as the partially finished units were concerned, was the procedure followed by the Ordnance Department in all nineteen emergency gun plants. Although the mills turning out rough forgings for the gun plants were taken from this branch of war work immediately after the armistice, the Ordnance Department reserved and stored a supply of forgings in order to keep the future gun plants in operation until new forging mills can come into production.

Seventeen of the emergency gun plants were closed out altogether after the armistice. Two remain among the war assets of the United States, held "in ordinary," as the phrase goes, meaning that they are closed, but ready with machinery and materials in all stages of completion to start up in full operation as soon as the workmen can be recruited and the fires started. These two additions to our arsenal system were named the Rochester Gun Plant and the Erie Howitzer Plant; and at these two plants and at the government arsenals the Ordnance Department concentrated the great equipment of machinery, tools, plans, and materials left on its hands after the dissolution of the gunmaking industry created by the war, all stored so systematically that the War Department, at any time for years to come, can, in theory, at any rate, quickly reëstablish a gun industry on the scale known in 1918. Recently it has been proposed to transfer the facilities at Rochester to some other place.

The existence of this manufacturing equipment in the possession of the Ordnance Department gives the United States a stronger military potentiality than the nation ever possessed before. For the first time in our history the Government itself during peace is in possession of extensive facilities for the manufacture of light and medium-heavy artillery. Before the war the Army procured all its field guns (and those only in negligible quantities) principally from private makers. Its two gunmaking arsenals, Watertown and Watervliet, turned out principally large guns for fixed mounting at the coastal forts. Before showing what was done at the Rochester and Erie plants, it is worth while pausing to note the legacy received from the war industry of 1917-1918 by the two established gunmaking arsenals.

The Watertown Arsenal is to-day the War Department's chief permanent establishment for the production of gun forgings. Watervliet is the great gun-finishing plant. At a cost of many millions these two institutions were built up and expanded on a vast scale during the war. After the armistice these two arsenals received the reserve supply of machinery and materials used in making the heavier field guns—principally 155-millimeter guns and 240-millimeter howitzers—forging machinery at Watertown, finishing machinery at Watervliet. For the manufacture of lighter guns, the machinery has been stored principally at the new Rochester and Erie plants.

With the new equipment installed at the Watervliet Arsenal during the war, that institution reached a productive capacity of sixty 155-millimeter guns a month and sixty 240-

millimeter howitzers. These facilities to-day are set up and ready for immediate operation. But in addition to the arsenal's own proper plant, the Ordnance Department has stored at Watervliet reserve machinery sufficient to manufacture fifty-two 155-millimeter howitzers, seventeen 4.7-inch guns, and forty-nine 75-millimeter guns every month. This machinery, in the event of another war, is to be shipped to emergency war plants and set up in them. Besides this, all the war-time equipment for producing anti-aircraft guns has been stored at Watervliet. One of the later inventive developments of the World War was to increase the power of the already powerful 155-millimeter gun by increasing its caliber to 194 millimeters and adding to its length, making an entirely new weapon, but one of the same type as the 155. None of these guns was actually built during the war, but machinery able to produce twenty of them every month is included within the equipment at Watervliet, one-third of this machinery set up and needing only slight rearrangement and modification to be ready for immediate operation.

All this equipment at Watervliet for the production of medium-weight field guns is idle and probably will remain so as long as the great reserve of finished artillery accumulated during the war continues to have military value. Unless another great war comes to upset the plans, the only production of light field artillery in this country for many years henceforth will be that resulting from the operation of a small experimental gun plant at Watervliet, to be maintained in operation to the sole end that the United States may keep pace with the progress of artillery manufacture. Whenever improvements are devised, the necessary changes will, if Congress provides the funds and present ambitions are realized, be made in the reserve machinery to enable it to turn out the improved models from the start of operation.

Meanwhile Watervliet and Watertown will continue to be what they were before 1917—the main reliance of the Army for its guns of the largest calibers for use at the coastal forts and on railway mounts. At best, the production of such weapons is a slow and intricate process, and the only way to procure a supply of them is to keep producing them all the time. Watertown makes the forgings for these guns, and Watervliet, with its own great equipment augmented by machinery from the dismantled war plants, can now manufacture guns up to 16 inches in caliber and howitzers from 12 to 16 inches. At Watervliet, too, has been stored some of the machinery from the American Ordnance Base Depot in France for relining big guns and restoring them to use.

Now let us look at the two chief auxiliaries to the two gun-making arsenals, the Rochester Gun Plant and the Erie Howitzer Plant, which are now "stand-by" factories for the production of field artillery of the smaller sizes—75-millimeter and 4.7-inch guns and 155-millimeter howitzers. The Rochester Gun Plant, with its own war tools and with the equipment concentrated there during the demobilization, is now equipped to turn out 360 75-millimeter guns every month. Its equipment includes not only the elaborate finishing machinery, but also a shop capable of heat-treating and rough-machining 200 sets of black forgings for the gun every month. This plant alone can produce 75's to keep pace with the needs of a great army, including its battle wastage, until a new gun industry can come into existence. All the buildings are new steel and concrete structures. The plant was built on twelve and a half acres of ground at Rochester during the war by the Symington-Anderson Company for the Government. This site is now leased by the Government. Its purchase would guarantee the continued existence of this important military asset.

The Rochester plant is held entirely in ordinary: machinery slushed in grease and boxed, and materials at hand in every department ready for machining, but watchmen the only occupants of the buildings. Not the least important part of the plant's equipment is a book containing a detailed mechanical description of every one of the 521 manufacturing operations in the production of a 75-millimeter gun, and including even a chart showing the correct organization of the working forces at the plant. Even such complete plans, however, cannot be made to include the small kinks and short cuts of shop practice, which must be developed and learned by actual experience at the machines. Any future force of plant operatives, therefore, would have to learn the obscure secrets of manufacture before the plant could reach great efficiency.

At the Erie Howitzer Plant a similar procedure was followed. Here, on eleven acres of what had been vacant ground in August, 1917, the American Brake Shoe & Foundry Company six months later turned out finished 155-millimeter howitzers and reached a productive capacity of twelve howitzers daily before the armistice. The plant stands to-day as a complete gun factory, although all its equipment is greased and housed up, and its bays echo only to the steps of watchmen. While it was selected chiefly to be the stand-by plant for the production of 155-millimeter howitzers, at the shop has been concentrated the machinery and tooling used by the Northwestern Ordnance Company to produce 4.7-inch guns at its war plant at Madison, Wisconsin. This machinery had a capacity of four such guns daily. The howitzer shop and the gun shop occupy separate buildings. In the third building has been installed machinery for producing shell for 155-millimeter guns.

The machinery set up at Erie is designed to allow for increases in the powers of the two weapons to be made there. The howitzer can be increased in length (thereby increasing its range), and the 4.7-inch gun can be increased to 5 inches in caliber, without requiring fundamental changes in the machinery.

The present industrial position of the United States with respect to the manufacture of mobile field artillery may be seen in the following tabular summing up of the preceding paragraphs:

Place of Manufacture	*Type of Weapon*	*Monthly Production Capacity*
Rochester Gun Plant	75-millimeter gun	360
Watervliet Arsenal	75-millimeter gun	49
Erie Howitzer Plant	4.7-inch gun	100
Watervliet Arsenal	4.7-inch gun	17
Erie Howitzer Plant	155-millimeter howitzer	200
Watervliet Arsenal	155-millimeter howitzer	52
Watervliet Arsenal	155-millimeter gun	60
Watervliet Arsenal	240-millimeter howitzer	60
	Total monthly gunmaking capacity	898

These fine weapons, all but one of which were designed by the French, the builders of the finest field artillery known, and manufactured only in France before the war, would be useless without recuperators, the recoil-absorbing mechanisms which make modern quick firing possible. Along with the guns there came to us the designs for the four French hydropneumatic recuperators. The French hesitated in the beginning about giving us their recuperator plans—not because they did not desire us to have the best in artillery, but because they thought, with much justification, that we should never be able to build them in time to be of service in the World War, although it was possible that after the war, by long and determined effort, we might be able to train mechanics who could make them. Only the sudden termination of the war, however, kept American-built French recuperators from serving at the front, for every one was successfully produced in this country before the armistice, including a single specimen of the perplexing 75-millimeter recuperator. Three immense, specially equipped plants and two government arsenals produced them.

Millions of dollars were spent in preparing to build French recuperators. The Singer Manufacturing Company built a great plant at Elizabethport, New Jersey, to make 75-millimeter recuperators. The Rock Island Arsenal equipped a new department to build this same mechanism. Dodge Brothers spent $11,000,000 on an immense plant at Detroit for the manufacture of the recuperators for 155-millimeter guns and howitzers, separate designs, and separate manufacturing propositions. The fourth type, the 240, was put in production at a plant equipped for the purpose at Chicago by the Otis Elevator Company. Only one of the mechanisms, the 155-millimeter howitzer recuperator, reached the stage of quantity production before the armistice. For the millions spent on the others the Government had only the experience and a quantity of forgings and semi-finished recuperators possessing only scrap value as they existed on the day of the armistice. Therefore the Ordnance Department did not stop this vital production at once after the armistice.

The Singer Company was working on orders for 2,500 75-millimeter recuperators. Although it had not succeeded in turning out a single acceptable recuperator by November 11, 1918, its processes had been refined almost to the point where they could begin producing these beautiful pieces of metallic sculpture in quantity. The Willys-Overland Company had built about 300 carriages for the French 75 by the date of the armistice, and it was decided to allow the Singer Company to build recuperators for these carriages and an additional 450 as a reserve. Considerations of economy later held the Singer Company to a total production of 247 recuperators, resulting in a shortage as compared with the carriages.

Meanwhile, be it remembered, the Rock Island Arsenal was working on 75-millimeter recuperators. It was decided to retain the recuperator department as an active branch of the arsenal. The arsenal was a little ahead of the Singer Company in the development, for it had actually produced an acceptable recuperator before the armistice; and it had 542 others in process in the shop. The arsenal's production proper was therefore limited to this number, but the incomplete units from Elizabethport were later transferred to Rock Island, and the arsenal eventually completed 555 75-millimeter recuperators before closing down the department. These were pronounced to be in every way the equal of the French product.

The War Department provided no arsenal facilities for the production of recuperators for the 155-millimeter guns and howitzers, but centered its entire program for both mechanisms in the Dodge plant at Detroit. After the armistice it was first decided to retain the Dodge factory as a stand-by recuperator plant. All machinery and materials were protected against deterioration, and the plant, under guard, was added to the arsenal system, ranking as a subsidiary to the Rock Island Arsenal. Later the Dodge plant was sold, and nearly half of its machinery was moved to Rock Island.

The plan of artillery demobilization and industrial preparedness in this direction is now evident. Watertown Arsenal is the development center for the raw materials of artillery manufacture. Watervliet Arsenal, with its stand-by plants at Rochester and Erie, is the gun-producing center. Rock Island Arsenal is the center for gun carriages and recuperators.

One exception to this scheme is to be noted. The war-time producers of the 240-millimeter recuperators were two—the Otis Elevator Company at Chicago and the Watertown Arsenal. The Otis plant, originally having orders for 1,000 recuperators, was ordered to finish 250 of them after the armistice. Thereafter some of its machinery was transferred and stored at the Watertown Arsenal, which thus remains as the manufacturing center for this heavy mechanism.

There was no need for the Ordnance Department during the demobilization to exercise so much care looking to the future production of artillery carriages, and for the reason mentioned, that the manufacture of carriages was easier than the manufacture of guns and recuperators. Carriages can be produced with machinery essentially the same as that used in making motor trucks, street cars, and other heavy vehicles. Consequently, the War Department contented itself with reserving enough machinery to equip at Rock Island Arsenal a model carriage-building department large enough to maintain the existing reserves of artillery and to experiment with new designs. This plant can now manufacture every month one hundred carriages for the lighter field artillery—for the 75's, the 4.7's, and the 155's, both howitzers and guns. In addition, at Rock Island have been concentrated jigs, fixtures, gauges, and special tools used by the war factories, this equipment being boxed, catalogued, and ready for instant shipment to commercial factories that may be called upon to build artillery carriages in a hurry. No machine tools used in carriage building, however, have been retained.

The same economic, military, and business reasons that influenced the post-armistice production of guns and recuperators, controlled also the closing down of the carriage plants. There was a considerable production of field artillery carriages after the immediate military need for them had passed.

The artillery war orders called for the production of about 20,000 complete units, a unit being a gun, recuperator, carriage, and accompanying limbers and caissons. The total production attributable to the war was 6,663 complete units, produced about half before the armistice and half afterwards. The value of this *matériel*, together with the semi-finished components retained, was about $300,000,000.

After the armistice the General Staff adopted the policy that in the demobilization sufficient mobile field artillery should be retained to equip an army of twenty divisions—800,000 men—with reserves to take care of battle wastage over a period of six months, during which interval a new artillery industry would be brought into existence. It is interesting to note how completely the Ordnance Department met this policy. Including the 6,000 field guns brought back by the American Expeditionary Forces (this figure not including captured *matériel*), the Army now has an equipment of about 10,000 artillery units.* The staff plan indicates 2,583 as the proper number of 75-millimeter guns to be in reserve: the Army actually possesses 6,000. The projected army of twenty divisions needs 986 155-millimeter howitzers: the War Department owns 2,171. The projected force should have 976 155-millimeter guns: the Army to-day owns 993. These liberal margins obtain throughout the range of mobile field guns.

* The A. E. F. importations include all American-made guns shipped to France, these same guns also being included among the 6,663 units noted as built in the United States.

On the theory (and it is a correct theory) that all the money put into artillery before the armistice should be charged off as part of the cost of victory, the post-armistice production of field artillery was a prudent transaction for the War Department. By spending $6,000,000 on the completion of 75-millimeter *matériel* after the armistice, the Government obtained property worth over $14,500,000. By spending $11,000,000 in the 155-millimeter gun project after the armistice, the Government secured artillery worth $18,000,000. By spending $9,000,000 for 155-millimeter howitzers after the armistice, the Government obtained *matériel* valued at $15,000,000.

The storage of the vast reserves of field artillery presented a special problem to the Ordnance Department after the armistice. Not only the guns themselves, but also the accessory vehicles, had to be stored, and the latter outnumbered the guns several times. For example, the American factories built 18,000 caissons and 20,000 caisson limbers for 75-millimeter guns alone, and accessory vehicles in like proportions were brought back from France by the A. E. F. It required about 5,000,000 square feet of storage space to house all the *matériel*. The Rock Island Arsenal was selected as the storage center for field artillery, augmented by storage facilities created at the Savanna Proving Ground in Illinois, the Erie Proving Ground in Ohio, and the Aberdeen Proving Ground in Maryland. Some of the artillery was stored at Raritan Arsenal in New Jersey and at Fort D. A. Russell in Wyoming. For storing the artillery the Ordnance Department used brick warehouses and also portable steel storehouses built originally to protect the reserve American artillery in France. The Ordnance Department retained a complete engineering collection of the captured enemy artillery, one example of every type, and this has been set up as an exhibit at Aberdeen. The collection includes a complete unit of the famous German 42-centimeter howitzer used against the fortifications of Liège and Verdun.

In demobilizing the industry which was producing our railway artillery, the Ordnance Department again availed itself of the opportunity to provide for the future defense of the United States; and in this branch of war industry, too, we find the same tapering-off process after the armistice, the completion of some materials which were nearing completion at the time of the armistice, and the retention of machinery to provide for a possible future industry. As a result of these measures, the Atlantic seaboard is now defended by a system of powerful guns mounted on railway cars and capable of being moved on the regular railroad tracks, supplemented by new tracks laid both during and since the war by the Coast Artillery Corps, to any point which may be in need of defense. Before 1917 all our coast-defense guns were mounted on fixed emplacements at the forts. Camp Abraham Eustis, which sprang into existence during the war as the embarkation camp for artillery at Newport News, has been turned over permanently to the Coast Artillery Corps and is now the headquarters for the Coast Artillery Railway Brigade. Fortunately the railway units nearest completion on the day of the armistice were those best suited for use along the seacoast.

The project to build railway artillery, it should be understood, was one of producing mounts for guns most of which were already in existence. These guns came principally from the fixed mounts in the coastal defenses, but some of them from the Navy and other sources. The guns ranged in size from the 7-inch rifles, procured from the Navy, to 16-inch howitzers, one of which had been built experimentally by the Ordnance Department before 1917. Two or three of the railway projects—such as that of the 7-inch navy guns and that of the three 12-inch guns originally manufactured for Chile, but commandeered at the gun plant by the United States—were complete on the day of the armistice. When the Ordnance Department faced the task of terminating the industry, there were eight incomplete projects in railway artillery. Two were canceled outright; in three others partial production after the armistice was permitted; and the final three were carried through completely.

One of the projects completed after the armistice was that providing for railway mounts for forty-seven 8-inch, 35 calibers, seacoast rifles. The two contractors—the Morgan Engineering Company of Alliance, Ohio, and the Harrisburg Manufacturing & Boiler Company of Harrisburg, Pennsylvania—had built eighteen complete units, each consisting of a gun car and numerous accessory ammunition and repair cars, a whole train in itself, and had manufactured all the parts for the rest. These parts were ordered assembled. This purely American mount possesses the advantage of permitting the gun to fire at any angle, the mount revolving upon a barbette carriage, and the disadvantage that in traveling on narrow-gauge track (such as is being laid at isolated places along the coast) its gun must be transferred to a special gun car—a transfer, however, quickly effected by the machinery which the gun train itself carries. Seventy-seven ammunition cars for these guns, built as they were for operation in French railway trains and therefore useless in this country, were sold to the French Government for about $250,000, a price which covered every cent spent in their production.

A second project completed after the armistice placed twelve 12-inch guns on French Batignolle railway mounts. This mount absorbs the gun recoil in an enormous hydropneumatic recuperator, permitting rapid fire and the fastening of the gun car to the track to avoid any retrograde movement. (Several of the railway mounts slid backward and had to be restored to aim after each shot.) The 12-inch mount, however, permits only a small traverse swing to the gun, which, for correct aiming, has, therefore, to run upon curved tracks, or epis, as they are called. These mounts were built by the Marion Steam Shovel Company with machinery partly the property of the Government. At the completion of the work this machinery was shipped to the Watertown Arsenal.

The final completed project was the mounting of ninety 12-inch mortars (seacoast weapons) upon railway cars. The Morgan Engineering Company built a special plant costing $3,500,000 for this one job, providing mount-building capacity twelve times that of the Watertown Arsenal before 1917 —and that arsenal had been the Army's sole source of big-gun mounts. On November 11, 1918, this plant had manufactured all the parts for all ninety mounts, and the assembling of these mounts was therefore ordered. About 100 ammunition cars of French design were sold to the French Government for about $350,000, thus returning most of the money put into them. The Alliance plant itself was too large and expensive to maintain as a stand-by plant; and, after shipping most of the special-purpose machinery to the Watertown Arsenal, the Ordnance Department disposed of the building to a private buyer.*

The armistice cut short the joint Franco-American project to mount thirty-six American seacoast 10-inch guns upon the Schneider railway mount, a French design, America to produce the parts for the mounts and France to assemble them. Four complete sets of parts had been sent to France before the armistice. The contractors were three: the Harrisburg Manufacturing & Boiler Company (mounts), the Pullman Car Company (trucks for the gun cars), and the American Car & Foundry Company (ammunition cars). The weapon is not ideal for coastal defense, because the mount allows no traverse aiming, and the car therefore must be used on curved track. The contractors were permitted to finish eighteen of these mounts in all.

A gigantic piece of ordnance was the 16-inch howitzer mounted on a railway truck during the war. In a project to build sixty-one such weapons by the year 1920 the Government spent $6,000,000 on a special plant at the mill of the Midvale Steel Company near Philadelphia. The whole project was abandoned after the armistice, but one building had been erected and the structural steel for the rest of the plant was on the ground. Meanwhile the toolmakers of the country were working on the vast projected manufacturing equipment for

* This and other special artillery plants since sold to private buyers are regarded as military assets. In the event of another great war they would undoubtedly be used once more for the work their walls encompassed in 1918.

this plant; and a small amount of this machinery was completed after the armistice and sent to Watervliet and Watertown arsenals.

The Neville Island Gun Plant was projected in 1918 as a source of supply for guns of the largest size for mounting upon railway cars. The plant, which was to cost $150,000,000, a sum which would have made it by far the largest gun plant in the world, was expected to manufacture over 450 guns of the biggest sizes during 1919 and 1920—more railway guns than the Germans owned altogether. The enterprise, which was entirely abandoned after the armistice, cost the Government about $9,000,000. Every ordnance officer, however, believes that the mere project, actively started, had its effect in ending the war by depressing the enemy morale. The war cost us about $50,000,000 a day. If, therefore, the Neville project shortened the war by as much as three days, it wrote off its entire estimated cost.

The project, immature though it was when terminated, placed in the war reserves certain steel-working machinery of the heaviest sort. One 6,500-ton forging press, costing $500,000, was completed and turned over to the Navy Department for installation in the navy gun-forging plant at Charleston, West Virginia. Certain costly shell-making machinery was completed after the armistice and either sold to private buyers (at favorable prices, as compared with what the Ordnance Department could have obtained for the unfinished machines) or else stored at the Watertown Arsenal.

Watertown has thus become the producing center for railway artillery of the future. The liquidation of war industry enormously expanded that institution. Before 1917 the government investment in the Watertown Arsenal was less than $4,000,000. After the concentration there of the special-purpose gunmaking machinery acquired by the Government during the war, the arsenal was worth, at a conservative valuation, $20,000,000.

Photo by Howard E. Coffin

AMERICAN FIELD GUNS ON THE RHINE

Photo by Howard E. Coffin

AMERICAN GUN ON EHRENBREITSTEIN, COBLENZ

Photo by Signal Corps

DESTROYING CAPTURED GERMAN AMMUNITION

Photo by Signal Corps

A CAPTURED AMMUNITION DUMP

CHAPTER XII

AMMUNITION AND OTHER ORDNANCE

THE armistice found in the United States an enormous industry devoted to the production of ammunition for the artillery. Including its powder-making plants and its plants for the production of the raw materials of powder, its scores of shell-making factories, and its loading establishments, this industry overshadowed, in money invested and operatives employed, even the artillery-manufacturing project. The demobilization of this vast enterprise, therefore, afforded the Ordnance Department one of its major problems after the armistice.

The production of powders, both high-explosive and propellant, in which about 70,000 persons were engaged at the time of the armistice, was terminated in a remarkably brief time. When the armistice was six weeks old all manufacture of high explosives on war contracts had ceased, and two weeks after that the last of the war-time propellant (smokeless) powder was made. This termination left on the hands of the Ordnance Department a considerable amount of special-purpose machinery which had little or no market value. This machinery was therefore retained and stored at various arsenals, particularly at the Frankford and Picatinny arsenals, the permanent army ammunition production centers.

For a while the Old Hickory Powder Plant at Nashville, Tennessee,—its daily capacity of 900,000 pounds of smokeless powder making it the largest powder factory in the world,—was retained as a stand-by plant, but later it was sold. The Nitro (West Virginia) Powder Plant, another government institution nearly as large as Old Hickory, was sold after the armistice, with the result that a new industrial city is developing on its site. The War Department's enormous ammonium nitrate plant at Perryville, Maryland (ammonium nitrate being used in the manufacture of the widely used war explosive amatol), the equipment of which included several hundred model dwellings, was, after the armistice, turned over to the Public Health Service to be used as a hospital for ex-service men. The three government picric acid plants—at Little Rock, Arkansas, Grand Rapids, Michigan, and Savannah, Georgia—were sold. Briggs & Turivas, Chicago steel manufacturers, bought the plant built by the Government at Senter, Michigan, for the production of tetryl, an explosive used as the charge in boosters in high-explosive shell. The Ordnance Department also closed out and sold the facilities provided at Bound Brook, New Jersey, for the production of tetranitroaniline, another booster charge.

In general, plants and machinery used in making powder could be used also to some extent to make the commodities of peaceful commerce, and therefore the Ordnance Department had little difficulty in disposing of these surplus facilities at good prices. The powder-making facilities created during the war by the DuPont Powder Company near Wilmington, for instance, almost at once after the armistice turned to the manufacture of dyestuffs. Another war powder plant, with practically the same machinery, is to-day producing artificial silk, a cellulose commodity similar in chemical composition to smokeless powder. A third is making celluloid and artificial ivory; a fourth, paper.

Since trinitrotoluol (T. N. T.) was the most widely used of all war explosives, the Ordnance Department was forced to go into the production of the basic toluol itself as well as into the manufacture of its nitrated compound. One war source of toluol was coal gas, and to secure the chemical from this source the Ordnance Department set up stripping plants in the gas works of thirteen American cities. Nine of the gas companies bought this equipment after the armistice. The other four plants were sold on the market, the machinery eventually finding its way into the new industry which is taking gasoline from natural gas. The Government sold out completely its two T. N. T. plants, which were located respectively at Racine, Wisconsin, and Giant, California.

One of the most notable enterprises in all the liquidation of war industry was that of closing up the war project for the fixation of atmospheric nitrogen and the placing of that undertaking upon a permanent peace footing. In order to conduct this enterprise intelligently the Secretary of War selected certain scientists and men of business experience to study every phase of the subject of the military and commercial fixation of nitrogen and to recommend to the War Department what disposition to make of the war fixation plants. This board was known as the Fixed Nitrogen Administration.

In 1916 the United States, almost entirely dependent upon foreign sources for its supply of commercial nitrogen, took the first step toward independence by appropriating $20,000,000 for the work of developing a domestic fixation industry. With this money the Corps of Engineers began, about the time we declared war against Germany, the construction of a great dam to arrest the power of the Tennessee River at Muscle Shoals, Alabama. This project, including a hydroelectric power house, was set for completion in 1923. The head of water at Muscle Shoals is expected to provide from 100,000 to 200,000 horsepower continuously, and during nine months of the year high water will produce a secondary power almost as great.

Aware that this development would in all probability not come through in time to serve the war explosives program, soon after the declaration of war the Government entered upon an enormous project to fix atmospheric nitrogen with power developed from coal. Five fixation plants of this sort were from first to last authorized. Three of these were completely built, and the other two were partially constructed before their projects were canceled.

In the fall of 1917 the War Department began the construction of a nitrogen plant at Sheffield, Alabama, and in 1918 completed it, at a cost of about $13,000,000. This plant produced usable nitrogen in the form of ammonium nitrate, a product used with trinitrotoluol in the production of the important shell-explosive amatol. It used the modified German Haber process, combining hydrogen and nitrogen to form ammonia, which is oxidized into nitric acid, which in turn is combined with ammonia to form ammonium nitrate. This plant produced its first ammonia in September, 1918, and its first ammonium nitrate on the second day of the armistice. The process, however, was never satisfactorily developed in this plant.

The second fixation-plant project was inaugurated in the autumn of 1917 about the time the Interallied Ordnance Agreement put upon the United States the burden of producing most of the powder and explosives used by the Allies, thus tremendously increasing our need of nitrogen. It was no time to be experimenting with processes. The one fixation process of proved success known in the United States was the cyanamid process, used by the American Cyanamid Company at its plant at Niagara Falls. The Government therefore engaged this concern to build an enormous fixation plant at Muscle Shoals, a plant which was to use steam power until the hydroelectric power from the river should become available. On the day of the armistice this plant, known as the No. 2 Nitrate Plant, was nearly complete: it turned out its first ammonium nitrate within two weeks thereafter. It cost $70,000,000 and had a capacity of 110,000 tons of ammonium nitrate a year. The test runs indicated that the plant could fix nitrogen at a cost commercially practicable.

Two other plants, both to use the cyanamid process, were projected in 1918, and the Government began the construction of both of them. One was at Toledo, Ohio, and the other at Cincinnati. Their combined capacity was to equal the capacity of the Muscle Shoals plant. At the armistice the construction of these plants was well under way, but the Government terminated both projects, at a net cost of $12,000,000.

The fifth plant was built by the Bureau of Mines for the Chemical Warfare Service at Saltville, Virginia. It used the

Bucher process, producing fixed atmospheric nitrogen in the form of sodium cyanide, a chemical used in the manufacture of toxic war gases. It was about complete at the time of the armistice, having cost the Government $2,500,000. A test run indicated that the Bucher process was too costly to be practicable in normal times.

The Fixed Nitrogen Administration, in its report, recommended that the Saltville plant be abandoned, but that the plant at Sheffield and the one at Muscle Shoals be retained permanently, the modified Haber process at the No. 1 Plant to be developed by further research. No. 2 Plant at Muscle Shoals was designated as the principal peace-time source of nitrates within the United States, and the report advised the United States to remain in the nitrates business as a commercial producer of fertilizer material, the Government to operate through a corporation similar to that which operates the Panama Railroad and its related steamship line. This report was based upon research which sent a commission of experts to Europe to study fixation processes there, and which even cultivated experimental farms in the United States to determine by practical tests upon growing crops the fertilizing value of various forms of fixed atmospheric nitrogen.

The armistice found dozens upon dozens of American factories and machine shops, both large and small, engaged exclusively in producing the metallic shell used by the field artillery. This in itself was an industry of great size. The industry had not yet attained its production peak, but it was rapidly nearing that point; so nearly so that, during the tapering-off process, the factories working only eight hours of each twenty-four (as compared with the pre-armistice three-shift, twenty-four-hour day), the output was enormous. Take, as an example, the 75-millimeter size alone. In sixteen months before the armistice the mills, working continuously twenty-four hours a day, produced about 10,000,000 forgings for 75-millimeter shell. The same mills after the armistice, working now only eight hours each day and tapering off their work as rapidly as possible, in the two months before the wheels stopped, produced 5,000,000 additional forgings.

The total production of the metallic elements of artillery shell, both before and after the armistice, recorded some totals of fantastic size. It should be remembered that for the most part our war shell were of the European nose-fuse type and therefore unlike any shell which the War Department had ever produced before. An apparently simple manufacturing proposition turned out to be a most difficult one, particularly in the production of two small but important elements of the nose-fuse shell, the booster, which accelerates the rate of explosion, and the adapter, which holds the booster in place. It was months before our manufacturers could produce boosters and adapters successfully, but then the effort came along with a rush. When production ceased the Ordnance Department had 26,000,000 boosters and adapters to dispose of. Other surpluses for salvage were 60,000,000 shell forgings, 60,000,000 shell machinings, 60,000,000 cannon cartridge cases, nearly 70,000,000 metal parts for grenades, and over 6,000,000 metal parts for trench mortar shell.

The demobilization policy was to store reserves of shell sufficient to meet the consumption of an army of 1,000,000 men during six months of active field service. In the 75-millimeter size, for instance, such a reserve meant 2,500,000 shell. Since we had produced 15,000,000 75-millimeter shell, it is evident that the Ordnance Department found on its hands 12,500,000 such shell to be disposed of in some way. Surpluses in other sizes were also large. The steel strike of the autumn of 1919 occurred opportunely for those disposing of the excess shell, for it enabled the surplus metal to be sold at good prices as melting scrap. A brisk demand for shell and cartridge cases as souvenirs also absorbed a surprisingly large quantity of the excess materials.

As in the demobilization of the artillery industry, here in the shell-making industry we see at work the same preparedness policy of designating established arsenals and retained stand-by plants to be a manufacturing reserve against some future war emergency. Frankford and Picatinny arsenals were selected to inherit the shell-making facilities created in private plants during the war. At Frankford Arsenal was concentrated an equipment able to manufacture daily 6,000 shell, ranging from 75 millimeters to 240 millimeters. The Frankford shell plant was made a complete unit, capable of taking billet steel, forging out the shell blanks, machining them, and turning out shell ready for loading. At Picatinny Arsenal was created an experimental shell plant with a daily capacity of 300 shell of all sizes.

As an addition to the two arsenals, but as a subsidiary to the Frankford Arsenal, the Ordnance Department retained the 155-millimeter shell factory of the Symington-Anderson Company at Chicago and equipped it as an enormous stand-by shell factory with facilities for producing simultaneously 155-millimeter and 240-millimeter shell. This plant has been named the Chicago Storage Depot. Here was concentrated most of the special-purpose shell-making machinery acquired by the Ordnance Department during the war. It consists to-day of two departments. The active manufacturing department exists in ordinary, all machinery ready for immediate operation. In the storage department exists special machinery with a capacity for producing nearly 70,000 shell daily. This machinery is catalogued and assembled in factory layouts, virtually complete except for the ordinary commercial machinery used in the manufacturing processes, so that on short notice the Ordnance Department can ship from the depot shell-making units up to whatever capacity any future war contractor may wish to undertake. The installed equipment of the active manufacturing department has a daily capacity of 12,000 shell. In 1917 the shell-making capacity of the United States was small, and it was a year before facilities could be created and production started on a quantity basis. The reserve industrial equipment to-day gives us a daily manufacturing capacity of nearly 90,000 shell, a sufficient supply for a field army of 1,000,000 men until a new shell-making industry can come into existence.

Powder and shell after manufacture went to the various sorts of loading plants, the propellant powder to be loaded into cartridge cases (for field guns of smaller calibers) or bags (for the bigger guns) and the high explosive to be poured or packed into the shell, boosters, or fuses. In carrying on this enterprise the Government either built or fostered the creation of seventeen great loading plants, eight of them—employing 35,000 persons, most of whom were women—being owned entirely by the Government. These had cost from $5,000,000 to $12,000,000 apiece. A few of these government institutions were retained by the War Department after the armistice. The shell-loading plant at Amatol, New Jersey, was added to the arsenal system under the name of the Amatol Arsenal, but the machinery was condemned for salvage. The Amatol Arsenal is being used principally as a depot for the storage of reserve shell-loading machinery acquired during the war. A fire in October, 1918, destroyed the government shell-loading plant at Morgan, New Jersey, and a temporary storage depot was erected on the site. The two bag-loading plants at Woodbury, New Jersey, and Seven Pines, Virginia, were disposed of after the armistice; but the third, at Tullytown, Pennsylvania, as the Tullytown Arsenal, was retained as an ammunition storage depot. Four other shell-loading plants were retained as storage depots, and at these several points exist the great reserves of loaded ammunition and of ammunition components left by the war.

Nearly all the loading machinery was concentrated at Amatol and Picatinny arsenals. At Picatinny also was set up an experimental plant for the development of processes in loading powder and explosives. This plant also contains machinery for loaded pyrotechnics in rockets, star shell, and signal-pistol cartridges. One piece of equipment is a dark tunnel in which the candle power of field illuminants can be tested. The plant includes facilities for loading grenades, fuses, and boosters.

The American Expeditionary Forces after the armistice had on their hands some 65,000 tons of field ammunition, mostly of French manufacture, besides several thousand tons of German ammunition taken in the advance to the Rhine under the terms of the armistice agreement. At first it was thought that the French ammunition, shipped to the United States, would be a military asset for several years to come; but as the months went on it became evident that, instead of being an asset, this ammunition was an embarrassment and a liability, and finally the War Department was glad enough to pay various foreign governments to take it off its hands.

Gas shell, for instance, it was thought, could not be stored, because the contained chemicals would soon destroy the metal, and the shell would begin to leak their lethal contents. Later experience, however, showed that there was no sound basis for such an apprehension. In the advance through Belgium, Alsace-Lorraine, Luxemburg, and the German Rhine country, the American forces collected about 7,000 tons of German ammunition, none of which would fit our own guns and much of which consisted of gas shell. The gas shell could not be destroyed in dumps because of the danger to civilians in the neighborhood. The only safe method of destruction was to transport it to sea and sink it in deep water; but the A. E. F. had no labor to spare for this work, and, besides, the French Government refused to allow the gas shell to be shipped on the French railroads. Finally, for a price, the French themselves undertook to dispose of this German gas ammunition.

In Belgium we had 6,000 tons of captured German ammunition. The Belgians could not use it, forbade its destruction in dumps because these dumps were in territory which had not been devastated by the war, and would not permit it to be moved by rail to the devastated districts, because of the supposed danger from the gas shell. The A. E. F. therefore had 6,000 tons of ammunition which it could not use, give away, destroy, or move. Finally, by agreeing to give the Belgians a large quantity of German engineering and construction material found in this area, the American authorities induced the Belgian Government to accept responsibility for this ammunition.

The German ammunition found in Germany was sold to German contractors, and, under the eyes of American inspectors, changed into useful commercial products.

As to the A. E. F.'s own 65,000 tons of loaded shell, it was decided to destroy all gas shell and all explosive shell and cartridges loaded with explosives of doubtful stability and to return the rest to the United States. The work of shipping the serviceable ammunition home actually started, but it went on slowly because of the lack both of labor and of ammunition ships. A fire destroyed one of the three collection dumps in the Château-Thierry area. As the ships repatriated the A. E. F. at a faster and faster rate, the various army areas were evacuated one by one, but it was necessary to leave guards behind at the various ammunition dumps. Then the War Department began studying the problem with a practical eye. Nearly all this ammunition was "war quality": good enough for rapid consumption on the field, but made hurriedly by inexperienced labor under conditions that made its permanent stability questionable. It was found to be impossible to separate the better ammunition from that of doubtful stability. It was conceded that under ideal conditions this ammunition might be stored safely for five years. Some of it had already been stored for eighteen months; it would take at least a year to transport it all to the United States; and therefore in this country it would be good for only a brief time. Accordingly the A. E. F. authorities negotiated with the French to assume liability for the ammunition, and it all went into the general settlement of 1919 with the French, but as an American liability reducing the financial liability of the French under the agreement.

The chief permanent benefits accruing to the United States from its extensive war industry engaged in the manufacture of instruments for sighting and controlling the fire of field guns were (1) a reserve of optical instruments of the most advanced types, some of which had previously been produced only by the French, (2) a large collection of machinery for making these and similar instruments, and (3) an optical glass industry more than sufficient to the normal needs of the country. Before

1914 little, if any, optical glass had been produced in the United States. In demobilizing this industry, the Ordnance Department took care that all these military assets were properly fitted into the preparedness plan.

Again we see at work the policy of centering future production in an arsenal. Frankford Arsenal was designated as the military center for fire-control instruments, and here were brought the reserves of materials and tools acquired by the Government in the course of the enterprise.

The production of some of the artillery sights proved to be almost beyond the mechanical ability of American workmen. It took three skilled organizations to produce the panoramic sights. Warner & Swasey, of Cleveland, built these sights, but had to turn to the J. A. Brashear Company, of Pittsburg, for the optical-glass prisms to go into them. That company, in turn, did not have a skilled force large enough to correct the roof angles of all the prisms required. The Ordnance Department found a man who understood the correction of optical plane surfaces in the person of Dr. G. W. Ritchey of the Mt. Wilson Observatory, Pasadena, California. He trained a number of men in this recondite craft, and they staffed an important department of the extensive optical shop which the Carnegie Institution built at government expense at Pasadena.

An extensive production of military optical instruments was permitted after the armistice and before the contracts were terminated. The work of producing some of these instruments was long and difficult, the instruments themselves would not deteriorate in storage, and the evolution and improvement of such instruments is slow. Moreover, the labor cost is by far the greatest cost in making optical instruments. The value of the unfinished components as scrap, even from an industry as large as that created in 1917-1918, with its eighty-three factories at work on contracts of a value of $50,000,000, was almost negligible. As a result of this permission to proceed, the industry reached its peak of production late in January, 1919. The only contracts terminated were those under which no production had begun before the armistice, those the holders of which asked for termination, and those which had already produced undue excesses of easily made articles.

The largest producer of army optical instruments, the Bausch & Lomb Optical Company, of Rochester, held contracts amounting to more than $6,000,000 in value and produced before the armistice materials worth over $3,000,000. The War Department obtained no machinery from this plant when the contracts were terminated, but it received and shipped to Frankford Arsenal large quantities of finished parts of instruments. The present optical shop at Frankford was largely equipped with machinery originally procured by the Recording & Computing Machines Company of Dayton. This company, which had never built optical instruments before the war, took contracts worth $4,000,000, built and equipped a complete optical plant, and became a producer, among other things developing a mechanical method of milling glass for prisms. Similar methods of demobilization were followed at all the war factories making sights and fire-control instruments: desirable machinery and unfinished components were collected at Frankford Arsenal, and the excess materials were sold. This plan put thousands of instruments into the war reserves, enough of some sorts to maintain the military establishment for years to come. Of certain important classes of instruments the quantities obtained from the war industry are deficient.

Between the year 1914, when war broke out, shutting off the export of optical glass from Germany, and 1917, when the United States went into the war, five American organizations—the Bureau of Standards, the Pittsburg Plate Glass Company, Keuffel & Esser, the Spencer Lens Company, and Bausch & Lomb—developed the manufacture of optical glass on a small scale, but in quality the glass was not up to the European standard. In the spring of 1917, scientists of the Carnegie Institution of Washington stepped in to help the manufacturers with their glass problems, and complete cooperation all along the line resulted in a successful industry before many months had gone by. The four commercial producers eventually turned out optical glass more rapidly than both the Army and Navy could use it. Some of this glass was the equal of any ever made in Germany, and much of it, though of "war quality," was still good enough for many uses. The army ordnance contracts were entirely with Bausch & Lomb and the Pittsburg Plate Glass Company at its Charleroi (Pennsylvania) plant. The production of glass on the war contracts was terminated immediately after the armistice. A large quantity of glass not yet formed into sets of optics was stored at Frankford. The Pittsburg Plate Glass Company did not resume any production, but Bausch & Lomb continued to make optical glass for their own uses.

Those who assume that, because we created an ample optical glass industry during the war, the United States is to be forever free of dependence upon foreign sources of this commodity, probably are too optimistic. There are numerous reasons why an optical glass industry is not likely to survive in the United States, at least on any large scale. The total normal American consumption of optical glass amounts to less than $1,000,000 a year—not enough to support many glass-making establishments. Secondly, nearly all the Allies developed war glass industries of their own, and the result is that the world has a large surplus of optical glass, which, if of good quality, does not deteriorate in storage. Thirdly, the war expansion of the world industry has created facilities above the present normal world requirements. In the fourth place, the industry is a precarious one, subject to heavy losses from carelessness or ineptitude in the mill. In the fifth, there is no tariff protection for American glass, the law permitting the free importation of precision optics for scientific purposes. Finally, there is a long-standing prejudice in favor of European-made scientific instruments, a prejudice against which an American industry would have to fight. Three American producers, however, are said to be making optical glass for their trade.

In anticipation of a possible collapse of the industry, the Bureau of Standards has brought to Washington the glass-making facilities which it set up in a special war plant at

Pittsburg. This plant can make two tons of optical glass a month. It is to be operated by the Government with the view both of improving processes and of creating within the Government an expert knowledge of this vital war industry.

The United States carried further than any other nation in the war the substitution of mechanical power for the power of draft animals in the movement of field artillery. Nothing in our army equipment in France did the French, themselves the premier artillerists of the world, admire more than our motorization of artillery. The total contracts for ordnance vehicles represented an expenditure of $400,000,000. The program actually delivered 13,000 vehicles to the A. E. F., produced before the armistice an equal number ready for shipment abroad, and had 60,000 other vehicles under construction when the halt came. The Maxwell-Chalmers plant at Detroit and the Reo plant at Lansing, working in coöperation, were producing 1,100 5-ton tractors a month, and this production represented the military power of 12,000 draft animals and 4,000 men.

The demobilization of this industry was accomplished rapidly. Orders were cut to the bone, merely enough post-armistice production being allowed to enable the plants to dovetail their war business into the resumption of their commercial businesses. Since little special-purpose machinery was required in producing war tractors, the Ordnance Department created no manufacturing center after the armistice as a source of future supply. The war left the Army, however, with a number of engineers who had gained experience in adapting mechanical power to military uses in the field, and these men are continuing a development which, doubtless, will in time eliminate the horse from our artillery regiments.

One of the innovations of the war was the motor-driven mobile repair shop for repairing artillery in the field. Each shop consisted of two sections, with fifteen trucks and fourteen trailers in each section—nearly sixty vehicles to the entire shop. On the trailers were installed the heavy machine tools, and one trailer of each section was equipped with an electric generator for light and power. When the shop was set up for business it presented the spectacle of two rings of vehicles ranged around the two power plants and hooked up with electric cables. The manufacturing program, both before and after the armistice, produced sixteen such shops, consisting of 600 vehicles. Six of these shops have been stored; ten are in use by the permanent establishments. In addition, in terminating the contracts the Ordnance Department came into possession of the unassembled but finished components of eight additional shops. Thousands of jigs, fixtures, and small tools used in this manufacturing project have been stored away and catalogued.

Tank production was drastically curtailed immediately after the armistice. The tank contracts involved the expenditure of $175,000,000. The total production of 6-ton Renault tanks was limited to 950, of which sixty-four were produced before the armistice. The contracts with the Ford Motor Company to build 15,000 3-ton tanks were terminated at once after the armistice, production being limited to the fifteen trial machines produced before November 11, 1918. Of the great 36-ton tanks, Anglo-American design, the Ordnance Department built 100 at Rock Island Arsenal after the armistice, procuring from the British for the purpose the hulls and guns. The tank assembly plant at Châteauroux, France, went to the French Government in the general settlement of 1919 and is now being used as a car repair shop.

No considerations of future reserves of finished materials affected the demobilization of the extensive war industry which was manufacturing our rifles, machine guns, pistols, and the ammunition for them. The production of these articles had been so successful that the moment the war ended the supplies on hand were sufficient for the permanent Army for years to come, with reserve supplies heavy enough to arm a large field force. The interests of the Army, considered alone, therefore, demanded the immediate cessation after the armistice of all this manufacture; but economic considerations and the dictates of good business practice made it expedient to taper off this production gradually, even at the cost of producing more materials than the War Department could possibly use.

Special problems arose in the liquidation of this great industry. In the first place, the factories which made rifles and machine guns were sharply specialized for just this work, making it difficult for them to turn to any commercial production with the same equipment. Several of these plants were specially created for the war work, and therefore had no prewar occupation to which they could turn. It was necessary for them either to close out entirely (as the Eddystone rifle plant of the Midvale Steel & Ordnance Company near Philadelphia actually did do) or to develop some new product. Two of the small-arms plants after the armistice added departments for the manufacture of ball bearings, one went into the production of automobile accessories and sporting arms, and a fourth (which had made bayonets) took up the manufacture of cutlery. It was necessary to give these concerns time to work out these conversions, if an acute problem in unemployment were to be avoided.

The sharp centralization of the small-arms industry in the East was another factor which influenced the Government to permit an unwelcome production after the armistice. Most of the rifles, for instance, were manufactured within a small area in the state of Connecticut. The Winchester plant at New Haven employed 20,000 operatives, the Remington plant at Bridgeport 12,000, and there were several others of this size. To close them all up forthwith would have created a bad industrial situation in this busy and prosperous section of New England.

The policy adopted, therefore, was to taper off the production of such materials. Upon the signing of the armistice ten American plants were engaged exclusively in the production of automatic arms. They employed 20,000 persons. They had reached a daily output of more than 1,100 machine guns and automatic rifles on contracts calling for the delivery of 650,000 such weapons, at a projected cost of $193,000,000, of which 465,000 guns were as yet undelivered. The final cancellations stopped the production of 382,000 guns, making the total war production 268,000 guns. In the various plants the Government had invested $11,000,000 in machinery.

By January 15, 1919, the rate of producing machine guns had been cut in two. By June 28, all production of machine guns had stopped. The Springfield and Rock Island arsenals, always the Army's development and manufacturing centers for small arms, were selected to receive the reserve manufacturing equipment acquired by the Ordnance Department in the prosecution of the machine-gun project. One unit of machinery sufficient for the daily manufacture of 100 Browning heavy machine guns, and another unit for the daily manufacture of 200 Browning automatic rifles were stored at Rock Island Arsenal. This reserve machinery was worth about $4,275,000.

Similar measures were taken in the demobilization of the war rifle industry. Production was curtailed gradually, ceasing entirely in March, 1919. Three great private plants and two government factories (Springfield Armory and Rock Island Arsenal) built our war rifles. The War Department invested over $22,000,000 in machinery. With this machinery the rifle-making departments of the Springfield Armory and the Rock Island Arsenal were practically reëquipped to produce the Model of 1903 (Springfield) rifle. The Springfield Armory (the chief future manufacturing center for this arm) was equipped to make 1,000 of these rifles in an 8-hour day, and Rock Island, 600. Working at full speed, both centers can produce 3,500 Springfield rifles every twenty-four hours. In addition special small tools, jigs, and fixtures sufficient for the production of 1,000 Model of 1917 (Enfield) rifles daily were stored at the Springfield Armory, and a unit of manufacturing equipment for producing 500 automatic pistols daily was also stored at Springfield.

Four-fifths of the outstanding orders for 5,250,000,000 rounds of rifle and pistol cartridges were terminated after the armistice. The policy adopted was to permit the small-arms ammunition factories to operate until September 1, 1919, if they so elected; but their production in that time could not exceed a quantity equal to what they might have produced if they had operated twenty-four hours a day from the armistice to February 1, 1919. This policy enabled the factories to dispense with their war labor slowly. About 1,600,000,000 rounds of small-arms ammunition were stored as a future reserve. The War Department had purchased machinery with a total producing capacity of about 3,000,000 rounds of ammunition in an 8-hour day. All the single-purpose special machinery and all special tools, jigs, and fixtures were retained, and with them the Frankford Arsenal was built up as a great center for the manufacture of small-arms ammunition. Before 1917 the annual productive capacity of the arsenal was not more than 100,000,000 rounds of rifle and pistol ammunition. The Ordnance Department has increased this capacity to 750,000 rounds in an 8-hour day. Immense quantities of bandoleers, cartridge clips, cartridge cases, metal, and other ammunition components acquired in the liquidation have been stored for future use.

CHAPTER XIII

AIRCRAFT

NEXT to the manufacture of ordnance, the production of airplanes and balloons and their accessories was the largest war enterprise of American industry. A hundred thousand workmen toiled in the aircraft factories, the business of which was represented by over 5,000 war contracts with a face value of several hundred million dollars. For the airplanes themselves, the contracts involved the War Department in the sum of $196,000,000, but this branch of the industry was but a small part of the entire air program. Merely for motor trucks the Air Service entered upon commitments reaching a value of $45,000,000. The investment in flying fields, balloon schools, and other physical installations erected during the war in the United States was, on November 11, 1918, approximately $75,000,000. Nearly 20,000 men had been trained to fly, and the Air Service numbered all its officers and men at 175,000—an organization larger than the regular army establishment in 1916. On Armistice Day the Air Service had spent $43,000,000 in the production of spruce for our own airplane factories and those of the Allies. For this investment it had to show a great logging equipment, including sawmills, three railroad systems (with 130 miles of trackage), hotels, and the housing for thousands of woodsmen. It was heavily involved also in plans for the production of other raw materials used in the manufacture of airplanes—$30,000,000 invested or obligated in the development of a chain of chemical plants for producing "dope," the varnish that stretches and waterproofs the fabric of airplane wings; and $8,000,000 tied up in the fabric itself or in raw cotton for weaving into fabric. The Service spent over $25,000,000 for gasoline and oil. The largest enterprise of all was the production of airplane engines, the contracts for which reached a total value of $450,000,000.

These figures are cited to show the enormous size of our air project, to show, also, how small a part of a balanced air program is the manufacture of the airplanes themselves, and, finally, to controvert and refute the widespread, the almost universal, impression to-day that the whole air program of America in the war was a failure, a scandal, and a blot on the fair name of our war industry.

The average American, if he has not examined the record of our war aircraft program, probably holds the opinion that a billion dollars or more appropriated for aircraft vanished into thin air during the war, and that all we had to show for the enormous expenditure was a few hundred airplanes of inferior design. To this day such statements are still being made by irresponsible journalists and other careless critics of the conduct of the war. Against such assertions we oppose the statement that the production of aëronautical materials during the war was as successful as any other great branch of war industry, that we got value received for our money—"war value," that is—and that the losses incurred were the natural and inevitable losses to be expected by any nation unprepared for war. The general charge of shocking waste and failure reposes upon nothing more substantial than rumor and muddy impression. Behind the rejoinder we are able to marshal the facts, which are, with the demobilization of the industry virtually complete, now to be evaluated as a whole.

In the first place, how much money did we actually spend in the prosecution of the great aircraft program? A billion and a half? A billion? Not at all. The war appropriations for the air were widely advertised; the acts of Congress covering back into the Treasury the unexpended balances, the transfers of air service funds to other purposes, and the recoveries and reimbursements from the sales of surplus materials were not so well advertised. The well-advertised appropriations came to a total of $1,691,854,758. But the greater part of these appropriations was made when the Air Service was a branch of the

Photo from Packard Motor Car Co.

PREPARING LIBERTY ENGINES FOR STORAGE

Photo by Signal Corps

ASSEMBLING PLANT AT ROMORANTIN

Signal Corps Photo from drawing by J. André Smith

FLYING FIELD AT ISSOUDUN

Signal Corps Photo from drawing by J. André Smith

LAME DUCKS

Signal Corps, and a considerable sum went for the procurement of signaling materials not connected with aircraft at all. Moreover, when the armistice came, several hundred million dollars of these authorizations were as yet untouched by those procuring the aircraft, and Congress revoked all such appropriations. When the subtractions are made on account of the Signal Corps' proper business and on account of revoked appropriations, we find that the net appropriation on account of the air program was $1,158,070,773.

But this vast sum is still far above the sum actually spent. On the day of the armistice there were great unexpended balances in practically all the appropriations granted to the Air Service, and these balances remained great after the liquidation of the industry. Since the unexpended balances eventually will be recovered into the general funds of the Treasury, it is proper to subtract them here; and by making the subtraction, we find that the war expenditure for the aircraft program was approximately $868,000,000. Yet even this was not net expenditure. From this amount there is still to be subtracted the millions received from the sale and transfer of surplus materials, the reimbursements on account of overpayments to contractors, and other items. The full subtraction of these credits leaves us with a net war expenditure for aircraft of approximately $720,000,000.

This figure, indeed, is an estimate; but it is a close estimate. It is an estimate because, at the time this is written (July, 1921), the liquidation of the war aircraft industry is not yet quite complete. Four contractors' claims are still unsettled, and surplus worth less than $18,000,000 remains unsold. Therefore, even if the estimated cost of settling the claims and the estimated recovery from the sale of surplus are grossly inaccurate, such errors cannot greatly affect the total estimate. The last official financial statement on the war business of the Air Service, dated April 23, 1921, showed that the net cost then was $738,133,972.28, leaving in the Treasury at that time an unexpended balance of $419,936,801.20, and this cost was still to be reduced by recoveries from the sale of surplus and by reimbursements of overpayments made to contractors in the settlements.

Thus we have, as the cost of the war air program, the figure $720,000,000—not half the billion and a half alleged by the critics to have been wasted. But what happened to the $720,000,000? Was it wasted? What did we get for it? The answers to these questions may be a revelation to those who have accepted the common misstatement that the whole project ended in a colossal failure.

First, airplanes. For the money spent the Army received, not a few hundred airplanes, but approximately 19,000. When the money was appropriated, those in charge of the air program, and the public, too, expected these funds to produce airplanes in numbers sufficient to darken the skies. Well, here was the sky-darkening cloud of them—19,000 planes, produced and delivered to the Army. And at least half this number consisted of "service" planes, as distinguished from training machines. The average value of an airplane without engine may be conservatively placed at $6,000. Thus, the planes delivered on the war orders were worth $114,000,000, a sum which accounts for nearly one-sixth of the total war expenditure made by the Air Service. In round numbers, the American industry produced 12,000 of these planes before the armistice, and afterwards, during the termination of the work, completed production on 1,500 that were unfinished. The remaining 5,500 were purchased from the French, British, and Italian industries. Those who criticize the administration of this branch of our war industry commonly lose sight of the fact that all the foreign airplanes procured by us were bought with the funds appropriated for the Air Service.

Planes, however, are a small item compared with some of the other materials procured with the $720,000,000. The American industry produced 30,000 aviation engines before the armistice and more than 11,000 afterwards on war orders during the termination of the industry—the exact figure, representing the total war production, being 41,590. Of these, 20,478 were Liberty engines, 15,572 of which were produced before November 30, 1918. The Liberty engines alone represented over 8,000,000 horsepower. In addition, from the $720,000,000 spent, we bought several thousand aviation engines in Europe. In all we received approximately 45,000 engines for our money. At $6,000 apiece—a fair average price—this procurement accounted for $270,000,000 of the money. Planes and engines together accounted for $384,000,000, or more than half the total expenditure.

This was all value received. But we have still to consider many important items of expense necessary to the prosecution of an air project such as ours was. It took, for instance, $190,000,000 to maintain the Air Service of the American Expeditionary Forces. The appropriation procured 1,100 balloons both before and after the armistice, at a cost, say, of $11,000,000. As we have noted above, $75,000,000 went into buildings for the Air Service in this country, another great sum into motor trucks, still another into fuel and lubricating oils, and upwards of $80,000,000 into the development of raw materials for airplane manufacture—spruce, dope, and fabric. This last was a necessary and justifiable expenditure, in that it sustained the airplane industry, not only of the United States, but of the principal Allies as well. Too, the development of raw materials was on a scale which anticipated great expansion of the manufacture of airplanes in 1919 and 1920. And so we can go, item by item, through the list of sub-enterprises in the aviation project and find that we received great value for our money and that almost the only wastes were the to-be-expected war wastes, largely due to our unpreparedness for war. These wastes were represented in the high prices paid for materials produced in such a hurry on such a scale. These high unit prices, of course, took care of the cost of creating almost the whole manufacturing equipment of the industry. However, we secured the materials.

We may pause here, too, to correct another misapprehension which has had some currency: namely, that not only was a billion shamefully wasted on aircraft but it was wasted by the so-called dollar-a-year men called to Washington and placed in charge of the aircraft program. The only dollar-a-year men connected with that program in a conspicuous capacity were the civilian members of the Aircraft Board—Mr. Howard E. Coffin, chairman, and Messrs. Richard F. Howe and Harry B. Thayer, the other two members. But the Aircraft Board was advisory only in function and possessed absolutely no administrative or executive powers. It acted as a clearing house in the effort to coördinate the aircraft production of the War and Navy departments. The actual work of procuring aircraft—designing, contracting for, inspecting, and receiving materials—was always in the hands of the uniformed services. The Aircraft Board had no control of the spending of appropriations, except that of the relatively insignificant appropriation of $100,000 granted to it by Congress to cover its office expenses.

The industry which wrote the records of aircraft production was attaining great momentum when the armistice was signed, although it had not yet reached capacity production. It had, however, in the final thirty-one days of active hostilities, produced 1,582 airplanes (1,081 of which were De Haviland service planes for use in France), 5,177 engines (of which 3,034 were Liberty engines), and 249 kite balloons. The business of terminating this industry was difficult. The liquidation plan adopted was essentially like that used by the Ordnance Department. Before the armistice the production branch of the Air Service was organized into eight manufacturing districts, with headquarters respectively at Boston, Buffalo, Chicago, Dayton, Detroit, New York, Pittsburg, and San Francisco. Five thousand persons were employed by the district organizations. After the armistice the district production boards became district claims boards for the Air Service, and they conducted most of the actual work of terminating production and arranging settlements with the contractors. Their settlements went up for approval, first, to the Air Service Claims Board and, finally, to the War Department Claims Board.

The air service contracts outstanding on the first day of the armistice obligated the Government to accept completed materials to the value of $767,423,308.50. Completed materials and raw and semi-finished materials accepted by the Government in the settlement with the contractors after the armistice reached a value of $259,733,874.30. Thus the contracts and parts of contracts terminated in the liquidation accounted for a cancellation of work to the value of $509,689,434.20. In addition to accepting and paying for the materials, the Government paid in cash to the producers in settlement of their claims the sum of $94,013,776.51. Hundreds of contractors accepted the statutory $1.00 and relieved the Government of all financial obligation.

For the sole or leading purpose of creating reserves for future use by the Army, there was little or no production of air supplies after the armistice. Leaving aside all questions of the obsolescence of design, no major class of military supplies is less durable in storage than aircraft materials. Like an egg, an airplane or a balloon cannot be slightly bad and still be usable. It must be 100-per-cent perfect, or it is dangerous. The life of rubber is short even under the most favorable conditions. The rubber in balloon fabric does not escape this swift impairment. The rubber tires of airplanes deteriorate with equal rapidity. The laminated and glued joints of the wooden wing beams of airplanes expand, contract, and work loose in the varying humidity of the surrounding air and are soon weakened below the safety point. Propellers are also highly sensitive to changes in humidity and temperature. Storage batteries, when stacked together in storage, wear out in a few months, each cell apparently working upon and adversely affecting its neighbors. Bolted wing cloth, when left folded, becomes weak along the creases. Of all aviation supplies, engines are the least susceptible to deterioration in storage.

In view of these considerations, such production of aircraft and aviation supplies as was permitted after the armistice was undertaken almost solely in the interest of the contractors and their employees. Most of the factories were allowed to continue in operation under war contracts only until they had used up materials in process of manufacture when the armistice was signed. Even this operation was conducted at a reduced rate.

The airplane contracts had called for a delivery of 27,000 planes in all. The production under these contracts, in exact figures, amounted to 11,754 planes before the armistice and 1,732 afterwards, a total of 13,486 airplanes produced by the American factories. Contract terminations canceled the production of about an equal number.

The post-armistice production of airplane engines was somewhat greater, both proportionately and in numbers of units delivered. This was due partly to the greater momentum acquired by the engine project, partly to the fact that engines could be stored safely and would retain good military value for years to come, and partly to the necessity of keeping the engine makers at work while their factories were turning to normal production. The total American production of aviation engines on the war contracts was as follows: deliveries to October 31, 1918, 28,509; deliveries thereafter, 13,081; total war production, 41,590. Of these engines 20,493 were Liberty engines, of which about 5,000 were produced after the armistice.

About 300 observation balloons were produced after the armistice before the manufacture could be terminated.

In one important particular the policy adopted in the demobilization of the war aircraft industry was exactly the opposite of that used in demobilizing the ordnance industry. In working back to a peace footing, it was the policy of the Ordnance Department to reserve complete manufacturing equipments and to set up stand-by plants for the manufacture of some of the most important materials in ordnance supply. On the other hand, in demobilizing the airplane industry it was the policy for the Government not to retain any manufacturing facilities whatsoever. There were strong strategic reasons behind both these policies. For field guns, for recuperators, for shell, and for other important ordnance, there is little or no normal commercial demand; and the only way the Ordnance Department could guarantee the future existence of facilities for producing these materials was to retain the equipment created during the war. But there is, or can be, some commercial demand for airplanes, and some day there will undoubtedly be a great commercial demand for them. It is important to the military welfare of the United States that this country take a foremost place in the improvement of designs and in the production of flying machines for commercial use. Only through the development of a great independent aircraft industry in this country can the Government be assured of the existence of facilities upon which it can rely to give this nation great power in the air. As conditions now are, the Government itself must be the chief customer of the airplane industry, and on the government orders the industry must live until commercial flying begins to develop on a scale comparable at least to the early development of railway transportation in the United States. If the Air Service were to have retained the war manufacturing facilities as government producing and stand-by plants, that act would have dealt a staggering blow to the infant commercial industry in the most uncertain period of its existence.

Only one exception was made. During the war the Wright-Martin Aircraft Corporation developed a plant in Long Island City for the production of Hispano-Suiza engines. This plant was purchased by the War Department and is being retained as a stand-by plant under the name of the United States Aëronautical Engine Plant. The future of this establishment, however, is uncertain.

Although it ruthlessly dispensed with the war manufacturing facilities, the Air Service retained in the demobilization a considerable part of the physical plant created for it during the war. Of the twenty-six flying fields used in the training of the war aviators, six have been retained as flying fields. These are the Bolling, Langley, Mather, and Kelly flying fields and the Carlstrom and March pilot training fields. The present equipment also includes three balloon schools, three balloon fields, one mechanics school (Chanute Field), one observation school, various stations for the defense of our island possessions and for the patrol of the Mexican border, nineteen supply, storage, and repair depots, and various other stations.

The storage of reserve supplies retained by the Air Service afforded some interesting problems, since nearly every class of supplies required special treatment in storage. Engines, for instance, were thoroughly covered inside and out with a heavy rust-preventing grease compound before being stored away in dry, cool concrete warehouses. Reserve balloons were dusted with talc, rolled carefully so as to put as little weight as possible on creases and folds, enclosed in sealed rubber envelopes, packed in wooden chests, which were then sealed up so as to be practically waterproof and air-tight, and then stacked in dry rooms in which air at a medium temperature circulates constantly among the chests. Even so, no long life for the balloons is expected. Wing fabric, both cotton and linen, was unbolted, rolled upon cardboard tubes, wrapped in paper, and suspended on racks in rooms heated in winter. Aviators' fur and woolen clothing was stored in fly-proof and moth-proof tar-paper-lined rooms, the floors of which were thickly covered with naphthaline. Fabric was stripped from airplane wings before storage in order to permit the free ventilation of the wood; glued joints were given an extra coat of varnish; all metal parts were painted with red lead or white lead; and the wings were stored in racks designed to keep their edges straight. Thousands of propellers were stored at the aviation supply depot at Middletown, Pennsylvania, in a room in which moisture sprayers maintain a constant humidity and a thermostat a constant temperature.

The aircraft contractors' claims proved to be fairly easy to adjust except one, the so-called castor bean case. This proved to be one of the most vexing settlements which came before the War Department Claims Board. From its humble position as an unwelcome medicament of the nursery, castor oil jumped during the war to the eminence of being an indispensable lubricant for the rotary engines used in driving airplanes. The prospective demand in 1918 for castor oil far outstripped the world supply. We needed 6,000,000 gallons by July, 1919. The Air Service therefore took the unprecedented step of attempting to grow castor beans in America, although castor beans, in merchantable quantities, had never been grown here before. Still, in the Southern States we had the correct climate, and no obstacle seemed to stand in the way of a successful crop.

Accordingly, through twenty-three prime contractors, the Air Service arranged with some 12,000 southern farmers to plant castor beans in 100,000 acres of land. Glittering prospects were held forth: thirty bushels an acre was only an average yield, and the Government would pay handsomely for the beans. Thus castor beans won 100,000 acres of good American soil away from rice, cotton, and corn, even at the war prices of these commodities. About planting-time in 1918 all was ready—fields, husbandmen, and tools—all except seed. After all, the farmers had to have seed; and to get seed the Government seized a cargo of castor beans from India, originally committed to a more sinister purpose. These beans the Government distributed among the 12,000 prospective producers, who planted them; and then, as the cartoonist so aptly says, the fun began.

Certain of the growers, like suburban gardeners, watched for bean shoots that never appeared. Some of these alien beans seemed to derive a sort of floral madness from the heady gulf loam and sent up veritable trunks twenty, thirty, and forty feet in air. But never a bean pod crowned such luxuriant growth. Whether because of the growers' lack of experience, unfavorable climate, or, more likely, defective seed, there has seldom been an American crop failure more nearly total than this. By gleaning every bean, the producers managed to gather 181,000 bushels, or 1.8 bushels to the acre.

As soon as the fell result was known, 12,000 angry farmers besieged the Government with demands for reparation. The claims aggregated millions. Not only did the farmers hold the Government responsible for the crop loss, but they also, dozens of them, put in claims for property damage and restoration costs, maintaining that in clearing their lands after the bean crop they had had to use stump pullers and dynamite to rout out the enormous stalks. One farmer sarcastically credited the

War Department with his winter's supply of firewood, which he said he had been able to cut from his bean patch. The War Department finally settled the claims for a total of $1,540,-638, which was at the rate of $8.50 a bushel for the beans received. Thus ended the first lesson in the American cultivation of the castor bean. It will be some time yet before the Department of Agriculture will have to create a branch to gather statistics on the domestic castor bean crop.

The work of demobilizing the Air Service of the American Expeditionary Forces ramified into several main branches: the cancellation of our foreign contracts and the settlement of our accounts with the governments of the Allies arising from the mutual purchases of materials; the sale of the installations and surplus movable property acquired by the Service during the war; the salvaging of worn-out equipment; and the shipment to the United States of airplanes and other equipment retained by the Air Service for future use. Most of the surplus property of the Air Service abroad went to France in the bulk sale of all surplus A. E. F. property, although some was taken by other governments in Europe in smaller purchases. These sales were consummated by the United States Liquidation Commission, which also concluded the financial settlements of our air service accounts with the Allied governments. These transactions are to be explained in some detail in a later chapter. The disposition of all aircraft materials retained by the A. E. F. was accomplished by the Air Service itself.

The A. E. F.'s production center before the armistice had been at the great flying field at Romorantin, near Tours. Here all new airplanes acquired by the A. E. F., either from the American industry or from the factories in Europe, had been received, assembled, equipped, and dispatched to the front. It had taken more than 10,000 officers and enlisted men to do this work. After the armistice Romorantin was made the concentration depot for all American air service supplies in France, and here all materials for return to the United States were boxed and forwarded to the ports. About 1,000 airplane engines were shipped to the United States and 2,097 planes, of which 347 were German, 1,139 British and French, and 611 American De Havilands.

Merely the packing of this equipment was a work of great size. It required, for instance, 7,500,000 board feet of seasoned lumber for the crates, besides large quantities of nails, bolts, clamps, wire cable, paint, and roofing paper, and also tools for the packers. A lumber mill employing 195 operatives was set up merely to resaw, tongue, and groove the lumber for boxes and crates.

The 2,000 airplanes returned to the United States represented practically all of the great aërial equipment of the A. E. F. which was saved for use after the war. The sales of our used airplanes abroad after the armistice, to either governments or individuals, were practically nothing. The remaining thousands of airplanes which had once borne the American insignia aloft were stripped of their salvageable materials and burned in great bonfires, the pyres of original investments running up into millions of dollars. This seeming profligacy was harshly criticized by those in this country who did not understand the conditions; but, when those responsible for the destruction had put in their defense, the criticism ceased.

The life of airplanes in use or in storage is short at best. Thousands of the A. E. F. planes had given considerable service, either at the training fields or at the front. The average life expectancy of these ships was probably less than three months. There was no sale for them abroad—France already owned many more airplanes than she could possibly use up, and the attempts of the Air Service to sell used planes to individuals ended in complete failure. To knock down these machines, box them, subject them once more to the deteriorating effects of the salt humidity of a transatlantic voyage, and to reassemble them in the United States, would still further impair their condition and still further abbreviate their average life. There was also to be considered the expense of maintaining soldiers in France to protect this *matériel* for several months, the expense of preparing it for shipment, and finally, —the chief cost,—the expense of transporting it to the United

States. The question was whether it was good business to spend all this money for the sake of returning to the United States materials which at best would have a useful life of only a few weeks, and which, because of the surpluses of new or little used airplanes already on hand, might never be used at all. The War Department did not hesitate in its answer. It ordered the sale or destruction of all A. E. F. airplanes of this class; and, since sale proved to be impossible, the order meant their destruction.

Those in charge of the work, realizing that criticism would be likely to follow, proceeded most carefully. Only the newest, least used, and best conditioned planes were reserved for shipment home. The air squadrons with the Army of Occupation were given a plentiful supply of airplanes. The rest, destined for destruction, were given several inspections by different committees and boards of survey, in order that the Chief of the Air Service might have a plentitude of expert opinion on which to base his condemnation orders.

The Class D material, as this condemned property was called, was concentrated in three centers—Romorantin, Issoudun (where the A. E. F. had operated the largest flying school in the world), and Colombey-les-Belles (the demobilization depot for the zone of advance). Here were conducted the final inspections. Many of the condemned planes presented, to the unpracticed eye, a perfect appearance. Storage space in the zone of advance after the armistice had always been short, and these apparently good machines had suffered from exposure to the weather. They were water-soaked; glued joints had given away, wooden parts were warped, and so on. They would have had to be completely rebuilt to be safe. Others had broken struts and cross braces and other damaged parts. All such machines were set aside for salvage.

The condemned airplanes then passed from crew to crew, who dismantled them. All miscellaneous metal parts were stripped out and sent to the quartermaster depots for sale as junk metal. Engines were removed and saved, as were also propellers, landing gears, wheels, tires, axles, cowls, gas tanks and oil tanks, controls, instruments, radio apparatus, machine guns,

Photo from Air Service

AMERICAN AIRPLANE WRECKAGE

Photo from Air Service

FUEL FOR THE BONFIRE

Photo by Signal Corps

GERMAN LOCOMOTIVE TAKEN OVER BY A. E. F. ENGINEERS

Photo by Signal Corps

ENGINEERS CONSTRUCTING BEAUNE UNIVERSITY

bomb racks, and many other serviceable articles. Even complete wings, when in good condition, were removed and packed for shipment to the United States. The remaining débris, consisting of little more than the highly inflammable wooden construction members and dope-covered wing fabric, was piled in great heaps and burned. More than 2,300 airplanes were thus disposed of.

One hundred observation balloons were ripped up and used for tarpaulins, wagon covers, and the like. The rest of the A. E. F. balloons were returned to the United States.

Airdromes on leased lands, occupied by small aviation units of the A. E. F., were turned back to the owners of the property after troops had dismantled all the war structures. With the exception of these, the entire plant equipment of the Air Service in France, consisting of training stations, observation schools, supply depots, and the like, was taken over by the French Government. The American surplus of aircraft in England was disposed of by the British Government, acting as agent for the United States.

CHAPTER XIV

TECHNICAL SUPPLIES

THE demobilization problem of the Corps of Engineers was a two-branched one in that, while the Engineers had purchased heavily of supplies in the United States, they had used those supplies principally in France, where also they had placed contracts for the delivery of large quantities of engineering materials which it was not expedient to ship to the A. E. F. from the United States. When the armistice came, it found great engineering production projects well advanced both in this country and abroad, large surpluses of materials on hand on both sides of the ocean, and in France an enormous activity in the construction of buildings and other more or less permanently installed facilities for the expedition. In France the Engineer Corps was charged with the duty of building docks, port terminal facilities, storage depots, hospitals, barracks, railroads, and other equipment for the Army, as well as that of building roads and bridges, tunneling out mines, and stringing wire for the troops at the front. It was the job of the Engineers after the armistice to terminate this whole vast business, closing out the contracts, settling with the contractors, disposing of surplus supplies, and storing reserves for possible use by a future army of large size.

At the time of the armistice the Engineers were engaged on more than 600 separate construction projects in France. The work on 246 of these was stopped immediately, and the only permitted post-armistice construction was that of facilities to be used during the demobilization of the A. E. F. These cancellations accounted for a saving of $135,000,000. The cancellations included projects for the construction of 450 miles of railroad. Contracts with French producers of engineering materials were canceled to the value of $30,000,000. In settling with the contractors the Engineers followed the principle that the American Government would compensate the foreign producers for all losses sustained by them, but would pay no anticipated profits. Eventually the French contractors' claims were settled by the payment of less than $1,500,000. Purchase orders placed with French producers, calling for the delivery of materials worth about $13,000,000, were canceled and settled for less than $90,000, of which sum about $60,000 was paid for supplies accepted in the settlement.

The Engineers in France found considerable constructive work to do after the armistice. There were camps to be built at the American ports of embarkation in France, nearly 10,000 miles of roads to be repaired, and schools, theatres, and athletic fields, including the Pershing Stadium near Paris, to be constructed. These, and the installations put in before the armistice, constituted for the A. E. F. a physical equipment on which the American Government had spent hundreds of millions of dollars; yet after the return of the Expeditionary Forces, the physical installation in France, taken as a whole, was more of an embarrassment to the United States than an asset. Some of the railroads, docks, and other great pieces of construction work undoubtedly possessed great inherent future value to the French, and we could expect to be well paid for turning them over to the French Government; but as an offset there were scores of installations of no peace-time value at all —roads, military railroads, and vast camps of flimsy construction built upon fertile farm lands. The obligation was upon the A. E. F. to restore these occupied French lands to their original condition; but there were approximately 50,000 acres of French farms so occupied, and to have restored this land would have taken the time of 30,000 men for several years.

The great reserves of engineering supplies in France, as contrasted with permanent installations, were indeed an asset, but not so much of an asset as one would think. In the first place, to sell them to private buyers in the European markets would have been a work of several years, during which time the American Government would have had to maintain in France a force of perhaps 5,000 men. Moreover, all that time the engineering stores would have been constantly deteriorating, so that their average value would not have been nearly so great as their value at the time of the armistice.

These were the considerations which led to the decision to dispose of all American engineering facilities in France, both supplies and permanent or semi-permanent installations, in one blanket, lump-sum deal with the French Government. The installations went to the French at a price difficult to fix exactly, because in this same bargain was included all other A. E. F. property not returned to the United States and not sold to other foreign countries, the French paying the flat price of $400,000,000 for the whole lot. It is estimated that the American army installations in France accounted for $32,000,-000 of the total sum paid. If we accept that figure, then we must call it a good bargain; for the French Government also assumed our obligations to the French property owners, thus relieving us of the work of restoring their farms to usable condition, ripping out the plumbing and other modern conveniences with which we had profaned some of their most ancient chateaux and monasteries, and doing a thousand similar tasks, or, in lieu of such work, paying to the owners the cost of the restoration in cash.

The few engineering supplies accumulated by the Americans in England were sold to individual buyers. Enemy engineering *matériel* captured in France by the A. E. F. went to France in the lump-sum sale. In Belgium the captured *matériel* consisted principally of lumber and sawmill equipment, worth about $250,000, and this went to Belgium to pay that country for assuming the liability for the German ammunition captured by our forces in Belgium.

It was the policy, because of the scarcity of shipping, to return no heavy engineering supplies to the United States, but to bring back such light technical equipment as searchlights, flash-ranging and sound-ranging devices, instruments, and the like. It was, however, expedient to return large quantities of steel rails and beams, because these could serve as ballast in ships; and the Government also ordered the return of a large quantity of road-building machinery for the use of the Bureau of Public Roads. The Engineers saw to it that samples of most of the engineering equipment used by other armies in the World War were shipped to the United States for study here.

The property bargain with France disposed of everything except two large claims against the United States: one for the American use of the French railroads, and the other for the damage wrought by the A. E. F.'s lumbering operations in the French forests. The railroad claim was most intricate and complicated because of the inaccuracy of the records and for other reasons, but it was finally settled in full by allowing the French Government a credit of about $61,000,000 (435,000,000 francs valued at seven to the dollar). The forestry claim was settled by allowing the French a credit of $10,000,000.

The claims of French contractors who had supplied us with engineering materials were settled, along with nearly all other French contractors' claims, by the United States Liquidation Commission in a blanket negotiation with the French Government. One engineering claim, however, remained unsettled. The contractor had agreed to supply 6,000 demountable barracks to the A. E. F., but he had delivered no buildings by the beginning of the armistice and had made little progress in his contract. Nevertheless, he presented a claim for damages amounting to $600,000. The Liquidation Commission offered him $1,200, and he refused it. His itemized costs included purchases of liquors, ladies' dressing tables, and oriental rugs, and he even admitted orally that one of his "costs" was a mysterious payment of $4,000 to a French interpreter in the office of the American engineer purchasing officer in France.

On the first day of the armistice there were nearly 200,000 tons of engineering war materials produced and on hand in the United States and awaiting shipment to France. This accumulation was worth $31,000,000. It included hundreds of locomotives, thousands of cars, and tens of thousands of tons of track materials, building materials, general machinery, and tools. Meanwhile the American contracts for the production of such supplies had reached a value of upwards of $365,000,000, and production had reached such rates as 300 locomotives and 1,800 railway cars a month. This business was terminated with the utmost rapidity which was consistent with the manufacturer's need to convert his factory to other work without undue disturbance to his labor force, and with the Government's need to acquire adequate military reserves of such supplies and to realize most on the money which it had invested in the enterprise.

When the war industry came to an end, the War Department thus found on its hands great quantities of engineering supplies. Some of these supplies, such as cranes and road-building supplies, were turned over to other departments of the Government for use in public works. Up to May 15, 1920, engineering equipment and supplies had been sold on the market with a gross cash return of over $110,000,000. Since the cost of these materials had been about $128,000,000, the sales return was about 85 per cent of the cost, an extraordinarily high recovery rate. Foreign governments were heavy purchasers, particularly of railroad locomotives and cars. The Engineers reserved from sale and stored in various interior depots an immense reserve of supplies for possible future military use. The principal items in this reserve are as follows:

*197	Consolidation-type locomotives.
*12,750	Cars, including gondolas, flat, box, tank, and dump cars.
736	Track-miles of standard-gauge railway materials.
353	Track-miles of light railway materials.
35	Divisions of heavy ponton bridge equipment.
6	Divisions of light ponton bridge equipment.
†67	Divisions of unit equipment.
81	60-inch open-type searchlight units (Cadillac trucks).
154	36-inch barrel-type searchlight units (Mack trucks).
1	Sound-ranging set.
10	Bull-Tucker recording sets.
25	Flash-ranging sets.
35	Ground-ranging sets.

* Includes surplus for sale.
† Sufficient to equip engineer troops with army of 825,000 men.

The financial liquidation of the American war business of the Engineers was unusually satisfactory, both because of the celerity with which it was carried out and because of the low cost of its termination to the Government. Shortly before the armistice many of the most important purchasing activities of the Engineers were transferred to the Director of Purchase, Storage, and Traffic, except that the Chief of Engineers continued to buy railroad equipment and several other sorts of heavy materials and also searchlights and ranging apparatus. After the armistice the engineering contracts were consequently terminated and settled by two agencies—the Engineers themselves and the Division of Purchase, Storage, and Traffic. The Engineer Claims Board was created to liquidate the war engineering industry for the Corps of Engineers, acting, however, as subsidiary to the War Department Claims Board. By May 15, 1920, the Engineer Claims Board had settled up finally 168 of its total of 171 war claims. These claims accounted for a total war business amounting to $238,000,000. Production after the armistice resulted in the delivery of supplies worth $17,000,000, which the War Department paid for at the contract prices. The terminations equaled $218,500,000 in amount, and for this termination the Government had to pay in cancellation costs only a little more than $1,850,000, or less than 1 per cent of the original obligation.

The orders for engineering supplies taken over by the Director of Purchase, Storage, and Traffic amounted to $138,000,000. A considerable part of this production was allowed to go through to completion, and some of the business was transferred to other branches of the War Department for settlement. The Director of Purchase and Storage terminated entirely business amounting to $29,600,000 and paid in termination charges $2,800,000—about 9 per cent of the original obligation.

One engineer contractor, a builder of locomotives, whose contracts were $55,000,000 in amount, canceled the entire business without cost to the Government.

CHEMICAL WARFARE MATERIALS

The armistice and the order to begin demobilization played havoc for a time with the Chemical Warfare Service, for the first assumption was that the use of poisonous gases in warfare had originated and been developed in, and would end with, the World War. On November 29, 1918, the Director of the Chemical Warfare Service received an official notice that "the amount of such [chemical warfare] equipment for the needs of the Army after the passing of the present emergency will be zero." The gas-mask production division of the Chemical Warfare Service was a highly organized and highly efficient body, and so rapidly did it work after the armistice that it succeeded in dismantling its gas-mask manufacturing plants and selling almost all the machinery before Congress blocked the plan and, with new legislation, made the Chemical Warfare Service a permanent branch of the regular military establishment. The gas production division of the Service, however, was not so precipitate, and it retained the facilities acquired during the war for the production of poison gases and chemicals.

The Gas Defense Division, which produced the gas masks and other defensive equipment, largely did its own manufacturing; but it contracted extensively for the materials used in the manufacture. On the day of the armistice its outstanding contracts amounted to $5,000,000. By the end of the year 1918, or less than eight weeks later, these contracts had been reduced by terminations to about $150,000. The sales of surplus materials brought in about $8,000,000. The termination of the production of gas masks at the two great plants on Long Island was guided entirely by the best interests of the thousands of employees, not one of whom was discharged until one of the official employment agencies had found a place for him in commercial life. In six months the demobilization of this branch of the Chemical Warfare Service was complete.

So far as the employees were concerned, the demobilization of the gas-making industry was not a difficult problem. All the plants were owned by the Government, and most of the operatives were enlisted men in uniform. Moreover, for nearly a month before the armistice there had been almost a complete suspension of the manufacture of war gas, due to a shortage of shell to be filled with gas.

The War Department's equipment for making gas consisted of the Edgewood Arsenal and a number of subsidiary plants located in various parts of the country. The Edgewood Arsenal was retained, at first in stand-by condition, with all machinery cleaned and oiled, all outdoor equipment housed in safe storage, and all surfaces subject to deterioration painted. The subsidiary plants, buildings, and equipment, were sold, principally to manufacturers of chemicals and dyes. The sales were conducted by the auction method, and the Government received good prices.

Even some of the experts in the Chemical Warfare Service accepted the common, but, as it proved, erroneous, opinion after the armistice that the great quantities of war gases accumulated by this nation and others during the war would be a dangerous menace as long as they were in storage, and that they would have to be destroyed, presumably by being dumped into the sea. These poisons were supposed to be so corrosive in their action that no metal containers would hold them long. Since large quantities of the war gases on hand after the armistice were loaded into steel shell, it was assumed that these shell and their contents would be a dead loss, except, perhaps, for some slight salvage value.

Events after the armistice seemed to strengthen this impression. Leakage, for instance, was undoubtedly occurring in the gas shell stored in our shell dumps in France; and it was dangerous for unmasked men to work around some of these dumps. An even more convincing demonstration of the instability of loaded gas projectiles was given accidentally at Edgewood Arsenal after the armistice. Among the war stocks there declared surplus was one consignment of 500,000 hand grenades loaded with stannic chloride, a smoke-producing chemical. These had been returned from France, and they were undoubtedly in poor condition. On the voyage from France the chemical had begun to eat holes through the metal of the grenades, and several thousand of the grenades had had to be thrown overboard. The Chemical Warfare Service sold these grenades to a chemical company. When a locomotive backed down to couple to the cars containing the grenades, the slight jar exploded fully half the missiles, and nobody could go near that sidetrack for two or three days.

This incident apparently showed the impermanency of war gases. Actually it demonstrated the impermanency only of stannic chloride, which is highly corrosive to metal; and stannic chloride, in the quantities produced, was a relatively unimportant war chemical. Nevertheless, in the fear that other more highly toxic gases would also corrode and eat through their containers, the Chemical Warfare Service dumped into the ocean some twenty tons of phosgene and a large quantity of mustard-gas shell. This was probably sheer waste, as it proved, because subsequent experimentation established the fact that the most deadly of the war gases could be safely stored for years if all water moisture were driven from the chemicals themselves and all air exhausted from the containers, leaving only the pure chemicals in contact with the metal of the containers. Corrosion was found to be due to the presence of moisture within the containers.

Nearly 1,400 tons of phosgene, chlorpicrin, mustard, and other deadly gases made during the war are now stored at Edgewood; and to-day, nearly three years after the armistice, their containers are still in almost perfect condition. It is estimated that they will not deteriorate in storage for at least ten years, a fact indicating that poison gases are as durable in storage as smokeless powder. There are also stored at Edgewood large quantities of loaded gas shell manufactured during the war. These are frequently inspected and tested, and the tests show that they are keeping well. The experts now estimate that loaded gas shell will exist in good condition as long as a battleship can give service, from the time of commissioning the ship to the time when it is declared obsolete.

Other reserves of chemical warfare equipment now stored at Edgewood include 51,000 Livens projectors, 88 trench mortars, 3,000,000 unfilled gas shell, and 700,000 unfilled hand grenades. There are also in storage over 2,000,000 gas masks and 1,000 tons of activated charcoal for use as a gas absorbent in the mask canisters. The masks are stored in hermetically sealed boxes, a method of preservation which, it is hoped, will protect the rubberized fabric from deterioration for years to come. Other stored supplies include protective suits, protective ointment, and gas alarm devices.

Such chemicals as the Chemical Warfare Service did sell after the armistice brought good prices. The prices of many chemicals went up after the armistice, and the Chemical Warfare Service profited accordingly. The Service made a profit of 100 per cent on the phosgene it sold and also found a good market for its chlorine.

Among the reserves stored at Edgewood was a considerable quantity of the felt which was developed by Americans as a protection against arsenical smoke, a deadly chemical never given a trial in the field of battle, but regarded as an inevitable development in the expected campaign in 1919. The production of toxic smoke was one of the most interesting phases of the history of chemical warfare in the World War. The candles which projected this smoke were perhaps the most appalling weapon devised by any of the belligerents during the conflict, and the armistice interrupted an Anglo-American project, well under way, to asphyxiate the Germany Army with them in the spring of 1919. This development was one of the deepest military secrets both in England and the United States. Except for the French, not even the other Allies were admitted to the secret.

The smoke candles employed an arsenical compound known as diphenolchlorarsine. In the laboratory this was not a new substance—in fact, none of the war gases actually used in the field was a new development; and of projected poisons, so far as is known, only the deadly Lewisite, the invention of Captain W. Lee Lewis in the Chemical Warfare Service's laboratory in Washington, was a new chemical creation evolved specifically for use in war.* The other war gases had all been known to organic chemistry, some of them for many years. So with diphenolchlorarsine. It was first produced in Germany in the last century, and the Germans also originated its use as a military weapon.

The Germans produced and used diphenolchlorarsine as a solid. The substance was put into glass bottles, which, in turn, were inserted in the T. N. T. filler of shell. The explosion pulverized the chemical into a fog which had the advantage of being able to pass through the cotton baffles in the canister of an ordinary gas mask. This fog was highly irritating to the membrane of the nose and throat and caused sneezing, which prevented a soldier gassed with it from putting on his mask, so that he was left a victim to more lethal gases fired simultaneously.

The British secured "dud" shell containing diphenolchlorarsine and at once recognized this chemical as potentially much the most fatal substance yet brought out in chemical warfare. But it was evident that the German was not using it properly, in such a way as to release its full toxic effect. The question was how to atomize diphenolchlorarsine much more finely. British chemists and mechanical engineers eventually succeeded in producing the substance in candles which burned and cast out dense smoke. This smoke was diphenolchlorarsine so finely divided that the American gas mask, the most effective mask of all, was utterly powerless against it. The smoke particles passed freely through the baffles; and, since the particles were minute solids and not true gas at all, they were unaffected by the gas-absorbing charcoal and lime of the mask canister.

Every masked experimenter gassed by this smoke declared that a mask was worse than no protection at all. It is notable, too, that every one gassed, without knowing that he was merely reiterating what others before him had said, declared that, if he had not been able to escape quickly from the concentration, he would have shot himself rather than endure the agony

* *Chemical Warfare.* By Fries and West; the McGraw-Hill Company.

longer. As to the persistence and diffusibility of the smoke, at one demonstration when two candles were burned in a desolate spot in England, civilians were slightly gassed in a village several miles away.

So much for the substance which outdid any of the horrors of the most horrible of all wars. But the weapon was useless unless protection against it could also be developed. America invented the protection—thick felt which was a textile triumph in that it absolutely caught and held the smoke particles, yet permitted fairly easy breathing through itself. The plan was to issue this felt in small pieces which the soldiers could wrap around their canisters, in order that all inhalation should be through the felt. The felt-wrapped canister would then be placed back in its knapsack. In the joint project, we were to produce the protective felt and the British the candles. The British had ordered several million of these and were actually producing them in large quantities at the time of the armistice. By that date the American mills were turning out the felt by thousands of yards, and our Chemical Warfare Service was also planning a factory in which to produce diphenolchlorarsine candles. All this activity was an intense secret in both countries. The program was being directed at a certain week in the spring of 1919, when, at a favorable hour, the troops on our side having quietly been protected against the smoke, it was proposed to fire the candles everywhere along the front. The gas warfare organizations of Great Britain and America confidently expected that when that lethal infusion had disappeared, the German Army would practically have ceased to exist, and the war would be over.

There is reason to believe that the German also realized the inefficiency of diphenolchlorarsine when fired in shell and had followed an independent line of development which led him to the production of candles. It is asserted that such candles were made in Germany before the armistice. It is doubtful, however, whether the German succeeded in developing a protection against the smoke.

After the armistice our Chemical Warfare Service continued

an independent development of arsenical smoke. The problem was a mechanical one. The chemical is driven off as smoke by means of heat. If the heat is too great, the substance will burn and be changed into non-toxic compounds. If the heat is too mild, the smoke will not be thrown off efficiently. This problem we have solved.

Mention should be made also of that other chemical secret of the war, Lewisite. In one sense Lewisite can be termed a development of mustard gas, for the laboratory process of making mustard suggested to Captain Lewis certain analogous chemical reactions, out of one of which came the hitherto unknown liquid which was named after him. Like mustard, Lewisite is a so-called vesicant, a substance which blisters the skin, but it is much more powerful; for, whereas mustard gas merely burns, Lewisite is absorbed through the skin into the system. Three drops of this chemical placed on the belly of a rat will kill the animal in two or three hours, and it is believed that this would be the effect of a similar quantity sprinkled on the skin of a man. Like mustard, too, Lewisite gives off fumes slowly, and these fumes have a burning, deadly effect.

Before and since the armistice there have been other developments of war gases in this country, and for some of these, as well as for some of the better known gases, there is, or can be, civilian use. Believing that chemical warfare has come to stay as long as there shall be wars, the Chemical Warfare Service has sought since the armistice to develop peace-time uses for war gases in order that there may be a continuous production of them, with a simultaneous training of chemists on whom the Government can rely in time of war. A new tear gas which has been developed is called chloracetophenone. The presence of a minute quantity of this gas in the air has a blinding lachrymatory effect upon the eyes of one caught in it; yet the gas is non-toxic. Various metropolitan police forces are experimenting with this gas to determine its effect in dispersing mobs. Another distressing, but not dangerous, gas bears the staggering chemical name of diphenylaminechlorarsine. It is temporarily blinding and causes nausea and vomiting, but it is not regarded as a lethal gas. It is proposed to use this in protecting vaults in which valuables are stored. Phosgene is used in making brilliant dyes, and it can also be used to exterminate rats. Chlorine is a widely used disinfectant. With other war gases it is proposed to exterminate numerous sorts of weevil and other insect pests which annually cause great damage to American crops.*

SIGNAL SUPPLIES

SIGNAL corps contracts on the day of the armistice were 1,244 in number. They contemplated a production of supplies worth upwards of $45,000,000. Telephones, telegraph equipment, radio, field glasses, photographic cameras, pigeons, wrist watches—these were the sorts of things the Signal Corps procured.

The termination of this industry was guided almost solely by industrial conditions. With most signaling supplies it was impracticable to build up large war reserves. There is perhaps no branch of modern mechanical development to which applied science pays more attention than it does to perfecting the means of communication. Progress is rapid, and therefore any large reserves of supplies set aside by the Signal Corps were likely to become obsolete and without value after a few years. Moreover, although the war industry of the Signal Corps scored its greatest production records with such common things as telephone and telegraph instruments and wire, all this equipment was of special design unknown in ordinary commercial use and therefore without value to it. Consequently there was not the usual good business reason to continue production under the well-advanced signal corps contracts—namely, that a greater cash recovery could be obtained from the sale of finished products than from the junk sale of semi-finished materials. Finally, many of the signal corps supplies—and this applies particularly to radio—were heavily protected by valid patents. These patents the Government made free with during

* Abridged from the discussion in *Chemical Warfare*. By Fries and West; the McGraw-Hill Company.

the war, but the existence of the patents virtually precluded the Government from selling its excess radio equipment after the war. For these and other reasons the signal corps war business was terminated at precisely the rate at which the manufacturing equipment and its operatives could be diverted to other work.

Unlike the Ordnance Department and the Air Service, the Signal Corps was not organized before the armistice by manufacturing districts, but conducted all its business from the central office in Washington. The Washington headquarters, however, maintained intimate contact with the contractors through its so-called flying squadron, an organization of officers who visited the war factories, inspected their work, and co-operated with the producers in the solution of their shop problems. This same organization after the armistice conducted the field work of the industrial liquidation, acting under the direction of the Signal Corps Board of Contract Termination, which, in turn, was subsidiary to the War Department Claims Board.

The new and unused materials acquired before the industry could be terminated were disposed of in various ways. Adequate war reserves of supplies were placed in safe storage. During the war the Signal Corps had built up a large training school at Camp Alfred Vail in New Jersey. This camp has been retained as a permanent adjunct to the Signal Corps. To the warehouses of Camp Vail were sent large quantities of surplus signal corps supplies, both finished articles and partially manufactured apparatus, there to be studied and developed in the laboratories of the camp. The Post Office Department took a certain amount of radio telephone and telegraph apparatus for use on its mail planes. The Forest Service took radio and also some of the homing pigeons for use in its fire-protection service in the national forests. Other supplies were sold to the public.

The Signal Corps, as one of its duties, created and compiled a photographic history of America's participation in the World War, both in motion pictures and in "still" views. The hundreds of thousands of negatives in this history were collected in Washington after the armistice and stored in a specially constructed building which is not only fireproof, but which provides air of uniform temperature and dryness, to prevent rapid deterioration of the negatives. A complete catalogue of views was prepared, and the sale of duplicates to the public was authorized. Many of the illustrations in these volumes are taken from that collection.

The disposal of surplus A. E. F. signaling equipment was notable in that it included a large sale to the French Government of equipment not embraced by the general bulk sale of 1919. When the armistice came the A. E. F. was provided with hundreds of miles of main-line telephone and telegraph cables, hooking up a complete net of branch lines, wires, and exchanges, all of it American-made and American-operated. The question was whether to rip it all out, after which it would be represented by some thousands of tons of junk, or to sell it intact as it was; and there was but one possible customer, the French Government, which monopolizes telegraph and telephone communication in France. Signal corps officers in France took up with the French Government, directly after the armistice, the question of the sale of these installations to France, and the negotiations were so well advanced in the spring of 1919, when the United States Liquidation Commission (which conducted the blanket sale) arrived, that the signal corps sale was specifically exempted from the bulk sale. France paid $6,400,000 for the installations. France and England jointly paid $130,000 for the American cross-Channel cable, laid with great difficulty (and at an approximate cost of $238,000) between Cackmere, England, and Cap d'Antifer, France.* Negotiations were also under way for the purchase by the French Government of a large quantity of American wire-system construction material, but this was finally included in the supplies delivered under the terms of the bulk sale. Sales to other governments and to individuals were small.

* Under the contract France and England must at any time lease this or some other cross-Channel cable to the United States upon the request of this country.

MOTOR VEHICLES

All of the A. E. F.'s surplus motor vehicles (a classification including bicycles and trailers as well as trucks, automobiles, motorcycles, and sidecars), as this surplus existed in August, 1919, went to the French Government under the terms of the bulk sale. The sale value of these vehicles was estimated by our appraisers at $100,000,000, an estimate arrived at as follows: the original purchase cost had been $310,000,000. Wear and tear, however, had reduced the usable value to the Army to $220,000,000. A second-hand machine, however, must be sold at a second-hand price, which will not represent the value of the machine to the owner disposing of it. A fair second-hand sale value of this equipment (assuming that the vehicles would be sold to private purchasers) was estimated at $132,000,000. But sale in bulk to the French Government relieved the United States of the cost of disposing of the vehicles in various sized lots to private purchasers. It was estimated that the overhead expense of selling the vehicles to individuals would be approximately $32,000,000. As one item in this sales expense, it would require the services of 3,000 troops for one year to take care of the unsold vehicles. In that interval there would be a further depreciation in the value of the vehicles. Therefore, the A. E. F. was willing to throw off $32,000,000 and make to the French Government a flat price of $100,000,000 for the equipment.

Before this sale, however, there had been sales to others, both governments and speculators. The Poles and some of the new Slavic nations bought nearly 3,000 vehicles from the A. E. F. American motor vehicles in England (they were not many) were sold at auction. The Italian Government bought about 200 trucks, ambulances, and motorcycles. As our troops were demobilized from the Army of Occupation in Germany, they left a surplus of over 14,000 motor vehicles. These were sold to a British syndicate for $25,000,000. Over 1,200 trucks of German make, acquired by the A. E. F. under the armistice terms, were sold to a German dealer.

The war orders for motor vehicles (including bicycles and

Photo from Engineer Department

AIR VIEW OF A. E. F. ORDNANCE DOCKS

Photo by Air Service

A GAS DEMONSTRATION

Photo by Signal Corps

MOTOR TRANSPORT IN FRANCE

Photo by Signal Corps

PART OF A. E. F.'S SURPLUS MOTOR EQUIPMENT

trailers) of all sorts from American factories called for the production of 434,000 of them. Of this number approximately 110,000 were bicycles and trailers, the rest being motor vehicles proper. The war industry had produced great numbers of these vehicles before the armistice, 118,000 having been shipped to the A. E. F., while thousands of others were either in use by the Army within the United States or were awaiting shipment overseas on the day of the armistice. By the fourth day of the armistice, termination requests had stopped the production of 178,000 vehicles under the war orders. The rest were allowed to go through to completion. Adding to the reserves on hand at the signing of the armistice the production after the armistice, we find that the results of the war industry were to provide the Army in this country with 138,000 motor vehicles, none of which had crossed the ocean.

The continuation of production after the armistice was allowed for numerous reasons. A motor truck is an article readily salable at a good price. Its fabricated parts, however, have little value other than that of scrap metal. Moreover, to permit the completion of contracts saved the Government from the payment of cancellation charges. For example, as a result of these business considerations one order for 8,000 Standard B trucks, under which order production had started about November 1, 1918, was allowed to go through to completion. The Standard B truck was an assemblage of standard parts. Many factories made the parts, and a few, under contract with the Government, assembled the parts and turned out the completed chassis. To have terminated the contracts would have left on the Government's hands a mass of parts of doubtful sales value and an obligation to pay heavy cancellation charges besides. The completed trucks could be sold for nearly all, if not all, the money the Government had put into them. The same was true of some of the other standardized trucks.

Production was continued in some instances to place in the Army's hands certain sorts of trucks of which the Army was short even after the great production ending with the armistice. Finally, many of the truck factories were working exclusively on government contracts, and to have ended this work forthwith would have thrown tens of thousands of men out of work. It is notable, however, that two of the largest contractors, the Ford Motor Company and the Dodge Motor Company, both of Detroit, agreed to accept termination of all work uncompleted on November 16, 1918, at no cost to the Government except the cost of uncompleted materials which they would be unable to use in their commercial enterprises.

The whole vast war business of building motor vehicles for the Army was terminated at a cost of $12,300,000 to the Government. As an offset to this cost, the Government took in materials worth $4,100,000, making the net cost of termination about $8,200,000.

MEDICAL SUPPLIES

The armistice turned what had been an insufficient quantity of medical supplies for the expanding, fighting American Army into an enormous surplus for the demobilizing Army and the future permanent military establishment. The total purchases by the Medical Corps had reached a value of nearly $250,000,000. Of these purchases, supplies to the value of about $11,000,000 had been procured in Europe, principally in France. The supplies on hand on the day of the armistice and delivered on contract afterwards were worth $110,000,000.

With the warehouses filled with hospital equipment, medicines, ambulances, and the other articles which the military surgeons used, the war industry producing these things was terminated expeditiously after the armistice. In the United States over 1,400 contracts and purchase orders, calling for the production of supplies worth $60,000,000, were terminated at a net cancellation cost of $3,000,000. Deliveries after the armistice from American factories gave to the Medical Corps supplies worth $32,000,000. In France and England the contract cancellations saved $3,500,000. These cancellations terminated, among other things, a project which would in time have delivered to the A. E. F. twenty-nine complete ambulance trains, each with sixteen coaches. Nineteen such trains had been delivered to the A. E. F. before the armistice.

In the general bulk sale of A. E. F. property to the French Government went American medical supplies worth $34,000,000. The Medical Corps turned over to the American Red Cross in France supplies worth $9,000,000 for use in the relief of the stricken populations of Europe. To other governments the A. E. F. sold medical supplies worth $6,000,000. The rest of the medical supplies in Europe were returned to the United States. In this country the surplus medical supplies were distributed in various ways—to the Public Health Service, into the army reserves, and (by sale) to the public.

CHAPTER XV

QUARTERMASTER SUPPLIES

THE quartermaster does not loom large against the heroic background of war. The Army's victualer and clothier collects few *croix de guerre*, and his interest in the Congressional Medal of Honor is impersonal. So long as his work is going well, you hear little about him; but let him once supply some tainted beef to the troops in the field or fail to deliver on time the Army's winter underwear, and then the country takes notice of the quartermaster.

God nowadays is on the side of the army with the best business organization, as even Napoleon himself might admit if he were to look over the cash balances of the late war. By that token the Quartermaster Service was the chief factor in the victory, because that organization became approximately the business office of the Army. For purely the creature comforts—food, clothing, and shelter—the Army spent far more money than it did for its weapons and ammunition; but the activities of the army quartermasters embraced a much wider range of supplies than these. Theorize as you will about the evolution of the Army's purchasing offices during the war until they were brought together into a single centralized purchasing agency, the fact remains that the ultimate purchasing agency was essentially the Quartermaster Service, magnified and expanded in power. General George W. Goethals was Quartermaster General when the General Staff Division of Purchase, Storage, and Traffic (which unified all army buying and brought order into the supply situation) was built around his personality and ability, and thereafter his chief assistant bore the title of "Quartermaster General, Director of Purchase and Storage." The new Division retained all the duties of buying quartermaster supplies and assumed also the duty of buying all other supplies except the strictly technical ones. And even these were purchased by the older supply bureaus under the complete supervision of the Division of Purchase, Storage, and Traffic.

When we approach the subject of the demobilization of the war industry which produced quartermaster supplies, we confront what was, measured in tons and in dollars and cents, the greatest business undertaking of the war. These pages have been filled by the story of the spectacular contest of American industrial genius with the inanimate resources which it fabricated into airplanes, artillery, and ammunition; but what filled the freight trains and the holds of the transatlantic cargo transports and the fleets of roaring trucks on the roads of France was not arms and the machinery of destruction to the degree that it was eatables and wearables, tentage, stoves and ranges, pots and pans—quartermaster supplies. There was the main weight and bulk; into them went the most money.

The war business of the Director of Purchase was represented by nearly 16,000 contracts. The total face value of these contracts came to nearly $8,000,000,000. They represented all food procured by the Army during the war and afterwards, all forage for the Army's animals, all clothing, all textile supplies of every sort, all shoes, harness, and other leather goods, all animals purchased, all motor vehicles, all wagons of every sort, all carts hand-drawn, engineering supplies of many kinds, all coal, oil, gasoline, paints, hospital equipment, medical and surgical supplies, hardware of all sorts, tools, tentage and other camp equipment, rope, office supplies, and many less conspicuous things. Several of these classes, it will be noted, consisted of munitions formerly procured by the separate technical supply bureaus, but the mass of them were the traditional quartermaster supplies.

To get a comprehensive and clear-cut picture of the demobilization of this branch of war industry, let us start in France and follow back the home-bound expedition after it had closed up its business abroad.

In the first place, the A. E. F. became a heavy purchaser of quartermaster supplies abroad. The purchasing office of the expedition became a great business organization. It bought supplies in almost every accessible country of Europe, and its agents even went to Africa and made purchases in Algeria and Morocco. These supplies were bought, not because America could not furnish them, but for the familiar sake of saving the use of the precious ocean tonnage. And a great deal of tonnage was saved by these foreign purchases. The Quartermaster Corps with the A. E. F. purchased 400,000 tons of miscellaneous supplies, but chiefly food and clothing, at the cost of $150,000,000. In addition, many horses were procured in Europe. The greatest tonnage saving of all, however, was brought about by the arrangement which permitted the A. E. F. to purchase coal at the Welsh mines. The cross-Channel fleet freighted more than 1,000,000 tons of coal from England. This not only relieved the transatlantic fleet of the necessity of lifting that amount of cargo, but it also permitted the employment in the Channel of vessels not well adapted to the transoceanic convoying. It is a moderate estimate that the American quartermaster purchases abroad saved the transatlantic shipment of 1,500,000 tons of cargo, a lading that would fill 300 large ships.

Naturally the armistice found France, principally, and the other nations of western Europe to a slighter extent, liberally sprinkled with A. E. F. contracts for the production of quartermaster supplies. Sixty-six French factories, for instance, were working exclusively for the Americans in producing bread, biscuits, macaroni, and candy. The question immediately arose as to the best method of stopping all European production for the A. E. F. The expedition's warehouses and depots were crammed to their capacities, and additional supplies were on the ocean in transports bound for France. A month, even a week, earlier it had not seemed possible that the industries of America and Europe put together, could produce an oversupply of these munitions, for the A. E. F. was looking forward to a strength of 4,500,000 men in 1919. But with the sudden armistice the expedition found itself with a stock of supplies on hand which it could not possibly consume.

For that reason its European war industry was terminated abruptly. There was little of the tapering-off of production that was characteristic of the demobilization in the United States. The military authorities were not nearly so considerate of the welfare of their foreign contractors as they were of those at home. The American business abroad was so small, compared with the whole war industry of the countries of the Allies, that the outright abrogation of the American contracts could not cause a general industrial slump. But there were other considerations. The War Department could make use of much of the domestic post-armistice production, either as war reserves or as goods for sale. In Europe every pound of quartermaster supplies produced after the armistice was likely to prove a dead loss to the United States. Such supplies were not needed for military reserves, of which there was an abundance already within the United States. They could not be sold advantageously abroad, because there was no market for them, with the Allied armies dumping their enormous surpluses on that same market. They could not be shipped in reasonable time to the United States for sale, because of the lack of ocean tonnage. Consequently, whereas it was the policy within the United States to terminate war industry gradually, the keynote of our industrial demobilization abroad was outright cancellation. It was cheaper to pay cancellation indemnities than to accept the supplies that would otherwise have been produced; and this was the general policy adopted in terminating all our foreign contracts, with such exceptions, notably in some of the airplane and artillery contracts, as are noted elsewhere in this volume.

To investigate claims and negotiate settlements with the European contractors the A. E. F. created its Board of Contracts and Adjustments, which for several months served as the liquidating agency for the war business. Later the unsettled cases were turned over for final disposal by the United States Liquidation Commission.

The termination of the foreign production for the A. E. F. was not nearly so puzzling a problem as the disposition of the excess military stores with the expedition. We had shipped from the United States to the A. E. F. over 6,000,000 tons of military supplies, and those shipments now crowded the warehouses in the American areas. After the armistice the first step looking to the disposition of these stocks was a rough, but fairly comprehensive, inventory of all military property stored in our bases and depots. This inventory gave basis for an estimate of a surplus valued at $1,500,000,000 over and above what the diminishing forces abroad could possibly use. Nearly half these excess stores were quartermaster supplies, therefore goods more or less perishable. Long before the American cargo ships could transport these supplies back to America they would have lost value to the amount of untold millions of dollars. The Government faced an enormous loss. Whatever was to be done about it had to be done quickly. The one way out was to sell the surplus in Europe, but it was a grave question whether that could be done successfully at all.

In the first place, all our army supplies had been placed in France without the payment of any import duties. So long as these supplies were being consumed by the American soldiers, well and good; but, when it was proposed to sell them to private purchasers outside the A. E. F., the French Government insisted upon its right to collect import taxes upon such supplies as were to be sold. When the United States was not ready to concede this point, then the French Government offered the alternative of permitting the United States to sell its surplus in France without payment of import duties, provided the sales were made exclusively to the French Government itself. The United States felt obliged to accept this condition.

Thus, in selling our surplus in France we were limited to a single customer; and when you can sell your product to only one buyer you must prepare to accept the buyer's scale of prices. Of course, the inhibition upon sales did not apply to sales to other foreign governments; for in that event the

American goods were regarded as being in France in bond, and it was not incumbent upon the United States to pay the French import duties upon them. On the other hand, a physical reason operated against the sale of stores to European countries outside France—the run-down and almost wrecked condition of the French railroads. The delivery of locomotives and cars by the Germans under the armistice terms virtually rehabilitated the rolling stock of the French railways, but the trackage had deteriorated during the war, and the incursions of military conscription had left the operating *personnel* poor in quality and deficient in quantity. It was next to impossible to ship anything out of France. During the early months after the armistice America sold surplus supplies to various countries of Europe outside France—particularly to Belgium and the liberated nations of southeastern Europe—to the value of many millions; but, up to August 1, 1919, it had been able to deliver less than one-fifth of these supplies.

Another advantage accruing to France as the principal buyer of the American surplus was that the A. E. F. was making what amounted to a forced sale. If anything was evident in the attitude of the French people after the armistice, it was that they earnestly desired to speed their departing military guests out of France. The American troops no less ardently wished to go, and it was the policy of the American Government to repatriate them as rapidly as the shipping could be provided. The disposal of the supplies was a secondary consideration. If the Americans had attempted to hold out for favorable markets and good prices for their surpluses in piecemeal sales, they would have had to keep from 20,000 to 30,000 troops in France for several years to guard the unsold stocks. The alternative of hiring civilian guards was out of the question, from the standpoint of expense alone. There was nothing else to do except sell out quickly for the best prices obtainable under the circumstances.

These obvious advantages to the French in striking a bargain price for the bulk of the American surplus property in France was largely counterbalanced by the fact that, of the

American quartermaster stores for sale, nearly half consisted of food supplies, and the highest-quality food then in Europe. There was no oversupply of food in Europe, but the very contrary. England had surplus army property estimated to be worth more than $3,000,000,000; France herself had almost as much to dispose of; and Italy was to be a heavy seller; but the food stocks in all these Allied surpluses were not enough to satisfy the hunger of the undernourished or actually famine-stricken populations of Europe. The much-desired food was used by the American authorities to induce the French not only to pay good prices for materials they did not need, and of which indeed they had surpluses of their own, but also to accept responsibility for such liabilities as the American stores of unstable and dangerous ammunition and our accumulations of junk.

Such were some of the conditions surrounding the bulk sale of A. E. F. surplus property to the French Government in the summer of 1919. This sale, as we have said, was consummated by the United States Liquidation Commission, the activities of which are to be discussed in greater detail farther on. Meanwhile a sporadic and piecemeal sale of A. E. F. property in Europe had been going on under the direction of the General Sales Agent and General Sales Board of the A. E. F. The General Sales Agent took up his work on January 1, 1919. He was assisted by the General Sales Board, which was made up of representatives of all the army organizations that had anything to sell. Under this organization the sales of surplus materials reached a total of approximately $175,000,000 by the end of July, 1919, just before the general bulk sale was closed. Of these receipts the sales of quartermaster supplies accounted for $122,000,000. The supplies were sold almost exclusively to governments and relief and welfare commissions. The sales to commercial firms and individuals were insignificant.

Almost as soon as the armistice was signed the needy nations of Europe opened negotiations for the purchase of excess quartermaster supplies of the A. E. F., particularly food.

Semi-starvation was chronic in most of the newly liberated countries of southeastern Europe. The Poles were still fighting and needed supplies for their soldiers. Belgium and northern France were impoverished by the German occupation. Austria was in the grip of actual famine, and the hungry mobs were rioting in Vienna. In fact, some of the first surplus A. E. F. food to be sold was shipped into Austria. It was a situation which demanded scientific study, since, no matter how much the American officials individually might sympathize with the European civilians, their first duty was to safeguard the interests of the taxpayers of the United States; and that meant to discover what ones of the needy were willing and able to pay the best prices. Consequently the General Sales Board of the A. E. F. created its information bureau, which investigated the conditions throughout Europe and reported to the Board. These investigations enabled the A. E. F. to distribute its surpluses intelligently.

Before the general sales organization took hold, the Quartermaster Corps itself in France had been disposing of surplus stores during the first weeks of the armistice. Many of these early sales were made to Mr. Herbert Hoover for the Belgian Relief Commission. When, in January, 1919, Congress appropriated $100,000,000 for the relief of starving Europe, Mr. Hoover, who had the spending of the money, was urged to make use of the excess A. E. F. supplies as much as possible. The largest single sale of A. E. F. surplus food was made to the Belgian Relief Commission. About $30,000,000 changed hands in the transaction, and the food sold included such items as 60,000,000 pounds of army issue bacon, 122,000,000 pounds of flour, 6,000,000 pounds of rice, and 600,000,000 cans of evaporated milk. All this time, too, the General Sales Board was selling directly to the Belgian Government; and the Relief Commission coöperated with the Army to make sure that Belgium, through these two channels of supply, did not receive an undue portion of the army stores. There was always danger that Belgian speculators might acquire stocks of such surplus products as fats and soap and sell them into Germany at famine prices. Twice this coöperation was able to checkmate the plans of cold-blooded profiteers. Next to making advantageous sales, the chief concern of the General Sales Board was to distribute its products fairly among the countries in direst need.

The Government of Portugal bought a large number of American army shoes. Czecho-Slovakia took 10,000 army overcoats, much other clothing, and several hundred tons of food supplies. The Polish Relief Corporation bought quartermaster supplies to the value of $1,500,000. Roumania took a consignment of food and clothing at $7,150,000. Portugal took a shipload of potatoes f. o. b. Ireland. These nations, Serbia, Esthonia, and several others, were constantly in the market for American supplies. Esthonia bought 3,000 tons of army bacon. The French Government, too, was a large purchaser during this piecemeal selling, on one occasion buying American suspenders to the value of $22,000, as well as large quantities of food and clothing.

For the most part the United States accepted debentures rather than cash in payment for these supplies. It was obviously impossible to secure cash, for the small nations did not have any, and even France was skipping the interest payments on her five-billion-dollar debt to the United States. The American Government accepted treasury notes or other official securities at par, payable in three to five years with interest at 5 per cent. And, although such credits would have been heavily discounted in commercial centers, nevertheless America did not try to cover by charging high prices for the surplus stores or by exacting profits of any sort. The greater part of our supplies were sold at the cost of manufacture in the United States plus the cost of transportation to Europe, and plus nothing else. Consequently the sales proved to be a great stroke of advertising for the fair name of the United States.

Trainload after trainload of supplies sold in this fashion left the American depots during the spring and early summer of 1919; but still, when the bulk sale to France went through, these shipments had seemed to make scarcely any impression upon the mass of the surplus, so great had been the reserves created in France by American industry. The utilization value of the surplus army property in France was estimated at $1,000,000,000. Of this quantity, quartermaster stocks (not including animals) were valued at $670,000,000. Of this surplus an amount worth $87,000,000 (consisting principally of new clothing) was returned to the United States, and the rest, except what had been disposed of by individual sale, was turned over to the French Government, the final delivery being made on November 15, 1919.

None of these sales included the used supplies repaired and restored in the army salvage shops in France. Salvage was a new note amid the age-old wastefulness of war. After the great battles of the Civil War the countryside was littered with the débris of warfare. The bodies of men and animals were buried, and the soldiers did what they could to clean up by burning the refuse they could collect; but for the most part the disposition of muskets, sabers, cannon, harness, and clothing was left to the souvenir hunter and to the slow action of the elements. After our battles in the World War far more materials were left abandoned on the field than after any conflict of the Civil War, but these materials were picked up and reclaimed for such value as the Army could still get out of them. And the Army found that it could make valuable use of salvaged materials, and particularly of salvaged clothing. The savings wrought by salvage ran close to $150,000,000 in cash value, besides representing a great economy in the use of shipping space in the ocean transports.

Whereas, before the armistice, many of the recovered supplies went into the army stores for reissue, in 1919, when the A. E. F. was rapidly dwindling in size, the salvaged articles were sold, and principally to the French. All through France one could see peasants of both sexes wearing articles once of American army issue. Paris might dictate women's styles to America; but Paris, Kentucky, where dwelt some of the seamstresses doing home work for the great army shirt factory at Jeffersonville, Indiana, had something to say about what

French women wore. The French peasant woman wearing an American army shirt, with a bit of ribbon for a collar, was a common enough sight in some of the former American areas. Another familiar makeshift was the skirt made of an ex-army blanket. Even the dumps, on which were thrown materials of which the salvage shops could make no use, were carefully sorted over by the peasants, who sometimes trudged for miles with their carts in order to avail themselves of these opportunities.

Extensive commercial sales of salvaged materials were also made. Crushed tin cans sold by the ton as metal scrap. Rags went to the French paper makers and waste wool to the English textile mills. Grease, damaged oats, damaged flour, and worn rubber tires also went by sale. The Polish Army bought reclaimed American harness by weight. A large number of outer uniforms, having shrunk in sterilization so as to be too small for reissue, were dyed black and sold to the Belgian Relief Commission for wear by destitute civilians. Germans paid record prices for grease and other kitchen waste products. The salvage sales in 1919 brought in more than $4,000,000.

The horses and mules used by the A. E. F. were not included in the bulk sale of property to the French Government. The disposition of them (for few, if any, A. E. F. animals were returned to the United States) was a separate transaction, conducted almost entirely by the Remount Service of the A. E. F., a branch of the Quartermaster Corps. The A. E. F. acquired in all some 243,000 animals at a cost of $82,500,000. More than two-thirds of them were purchased abroad by the Americans. The mules numbered 61,000, and of these approximately half came from the United States, the rest principally from southern France and Spain. About 64,000 animals died in the service, and the rest were sold in Europe either to various governments or to civilians, the recovery from these sales being slightly more than $33,000,000. Thus the net war cost of the animals used by our forces in Europe was approximately $50,000,000.

With Americans the horse is (or is supposed to be) a single-purpose animal, used exclusively for his power of motivity, whether that power be exerted for speed or for pulling a load. To many Europeans he also possesses gastronomic value, and this fact enabled the Remount Service to get good prices for condemned horses from the expeditionary corrals. About 11,000 horses, broken down by service, were sold by the A. E. F. to French and German butchers, at an average price of $50 a head.

Because of the dearth of farm animals in France, the French Government offered no objection to the sale of the surplus horses and mules directly to private buyers. The chief condition made was that the animals must first be offered (at auction) to farmers whose horses had been requisitioned during the war. If these men would not offer satisfactory prices, then anyone was to be allowed to bid. Then the French Government arranged to take over 15,000 A. E. F. animals and dispose of them for the expedition. The prices obtained from the French Government under this arrangement were so much below what the A. E. F. was obtaining from its auctions that the United States Liquidation Commission sought and received authority to dispose of all the animals at auction. Because of the high taxes and auctioneers' commissions, even the auction sale was not satisfactory; and the Remount Service asked permission to sell animals at private sale. This permission was never formally granted, but nevertheless the Remount Service went ahead and sold thousands of animals directly to buyers. The average price received from the French Government was $77.58 a head, whereas from the auction and direct sales to private purchasers the average price received was $201.65.

The French Government itself, by direct purchases from the A. E. F., took 50,000 animals at an average price of $190.21 a head. Thousands of surplus animals at good prices went to the governments of Belgium, Poland, Czecho-Slovakia, and Bavaria. To civilians in France and Germany went 85,000 A. E. F. animals. Approximately the last of the original 243,000 had been sold when the final troops of the A. E. F. departed for the United States in the late summer of 1919.

Although we sent to France some of the finest mules in America (and, therefore, in the world), there was at first some difficulty in disposing of them to the French buyers. The farmers of southern France knew the mule and justly valued it, and during the early months of the demobilization a constant stream of American army mules went into that region for sale. Finally the southern French mule market became glutted, and then it became necessary to "sell" the mule to the farmers in the American areas in northern France. The French peasants did not hold the mule's clouded ancestry against him, but what their thriftiness did object to was his dearth of hope of posterity. However, after a few of the peasants had bought and worked the army mules, the good qualities of the animal became widely advertised, and thousands of them thereafter were bought at good prices.

After the armistice the first step in the liquidation of the quartermaster war business and of the other enterprises conducted by the Director of Purchase in the United States was to terminate the industry and to settle with the contractors, of whom, as is indicated above, there were approximately 15,900 —parties to agreements which committed the United States to purchase supplies to the value of more than $7,800,000,000. A large part of these were quartermaster supplies, but they also included motor vehicles and engineering, medical, signal corps, and general supplies, the procurement of which, under the reorganization of the War Department, was placed in the hands of the Director of Purchase.

The immediate result of the armistice was to silence the activity in these thousands of factories. The Director of Purchase sent broadcast by telegraph a general request to suspend all production while the War Department could estimate its position. After a few days the mills were permitted to resume production. Subsequently about 5,000 of the contracts were allowed to go through to completion. The remaining 11,000 were terminated either abruptly, as with those under which no production had started, or by graduation, when that was

Photo by Signal Corps

A. E. F. SUPPLY TRAIN ON WAY TO RATION DUMP

Photo by Signal Corps

A. E. F. FLOUR ON WAY TO STARVING AUSTRIA

Photo by Signal Corps

A. E. F. HORSES TO BE SOLD

Photo from Quartermaster Department

STORAGE WAREHOUSES AT JEFFERSONVILLE DEPOT

advantageous either to the Government or to the industrial situation.

Like the Ordnance Department and the Air Service, the Quartermaster Corps decentralized the supervision of its war industry into manufacturing districts—thirteen of them—which were called zones. When most of the purchasing activities of the War Department were brought together under the Director of Purchase, these zones came along with the transferred organization, as did also seven procurement divisions taken over from the other supply bureaus. During the demobilization, claims boards were established in all the zones and procurement divisions. These twenty primary boards were subsidiary to the general Purchase Claims Board, which in turn was responsible to the War Department Claims Board through the representative of the latter attached to the Purchase Claims Board. This was the organization which settled the vast war business conducted under the Director of Purchase.

The general policies, the application of which to the termination of the ordnance contracts we have already described, were followed in closing out the industry which manufactured our quartermaster supplies. The Government paid no prospective profits, but stood all the legitimate expenses which the manufacturer had incurred looking to future production of finished supplies.

But it was not all termination and no buying for the Director of Purchase after the armistice. There was still an enormous army in the field and camps which had to be sustained; and, while great surpluses existed in some branches of supply, in others, such as immediately perishable supplies, the stocks on hand were sufficient for only a few weeks ahead. The purchases between the date of the armistice and January 24, 1920, by which date the demobilization of troops was about complete, came to $611,000,000, of which food purchases accounted for $420,000,000.

One national inheritance from the war experience in buying quartermaster supplies has been the creation at Chicago of a permanent subsistence school to which the Army sends officers and enlisted men for training as inspectors and buyers of food supplies. Another is the creation within the War Department of a division which studies the sources and supplies of the raw materials used by war industry and also determines the priority of access to these materials by the various consuming branches of the War Department. When the war came, the United States was sadly lacking in the very knowledge which these studies will develop. During the war the development of raw materials and the determination of priorities were administered by the Council of National Defense and, later and more successfully, by the War Industries Board, which became perhaps the most powerful and important of all the emergency war organizations. The War Department is thus retaining a nucleus around which another such organization might be built in a future emergency.

No outline of the demobilization of the quartermaster war enterprises portrays an adequate picture of what happened unless it tells something about the termination of the Government's wool business. To protect its war interests the Government requisitioned all the raw wool in the United States in 1917 and 1918. Uncle Sam himself became the wool trade, the sole dealer, the sole market. Although the Navy and several other government branches used wool, the control over the commodity was exercised by the War Department through its Wool Administrator at Boston, who reported to the Quartermaster General in Washington.

On the first day of the armistice the Government had on its hands, or was obligated to accept delivery of, about 525,000,000 pounds of wool, a quantity which may be visualized by comparing it with the total annual American production of wool, which is less than 300,000,000 pounds. About one-fifth of this quantity was Australasian wool which had been purchased by the Foreign Mission of the War Industries Board. About 100,000 bales (33,000,000 pounds) of the Australasian wool had been shipped to the United States. We were left, therefore, with a binding contract to accept 200,000 bales from the Antipodes, this to come piling in on top of an accumulation which comprised a huge surplus over and above the normal national consumption. By some clever business jockeying (the British having various American contracts which they also wished to terminate) the British Government was induced to cancel the unfulfilled portion of the wool contract.

Even with this deduction, the Wool Administrator had, in the late autumn of 1918, about 460,000,000 pounds of wool to dispose of. The normal textile industry had never before been called upon to absorb such a visible supply, and there was some question if it would be able to do so. The manufacturers naturally began at once to urge the Government to dump its wool on the market. The 700,000 American wool growers, on the other hand, who had been receiving a high and stable price for wool (the price adopted on July 30, 1917) urged the Government to stay in the business for another year at least and take the 1919 clip at the war price.

The decision in Washington was to sell the wool and get out of the wool business at once. This was displeasing to the farmers; but, to prevent any drastic slump in wool prices, the War Department decided to sell its wool in auction sales, in which the Government itself would set minimum prices below which no wool would be sold. This action guaranteed that the growers would get a fair price for the 1919 clip.

Within approximately a month after the armistice the wool auctions began—first at Boston, where in three days (December 18, 19, and 20, 1918) the buyers bid in over 10,000,000 pounds of wool, out of 17,000,000 pounds offered for sale. The unsold offerings, of course, were lots for which no buyers bid up to the minimum fixed prices. Although prices were fixed, only in a sense were they sustained artificially. For each sort of wool the Government fixed a minimum price which equaled what it would cost to import the same quantity and grade of wool and deliver it to the American market. Thus the world prices actually prevailed, except that the huge American surplus was artificially kept from being a depressing factor in the world price. To sustain prices higher than these would have attracted large importations and thus injured the growers. To allow prices to go lower than the importation prices would also have worked injury to the wool growers of the United States.

As a further concession to the farmers, the Government announced that it would stay out of the wool market when the 1919 American clip began reaching the market in quantities sufficient to supply the mills. In accordance with this promise, the government wool sales ceased on July 1, 1919, and did not resume again until the following November.

When the auctions suspended on July 1, more that 316,000,000 pounds of the Government's wool had been sold. Auctions had been held twice a month in Boston and once a month in Philadelphia, and three sales had been conducted at Portland, Oregon, for the benefit of the western woolen mills. Upon the resumption of the sales in November the wool continued to sell well, with the result that by the end of 1919 the sales had disposed of 365,000,000 pounds, and the success of the complete liquidation was assured. The sale of this wool was a triumph of merchandizing. The wool trade had never known such sales before, not even in England, the world center of wool, nor had the American trade ever before absorbed such a quantity of wool in such a short time.

Like the storied mill which ground salt until it swamped the ship of the thieving merchant, the mill producing quartermaster supplies before the armistice was hard to stop afterwards, and its output embarrassed the War Department for want of space in which to store the excess supplies. As long as the home Army and the A. E. F. were expanding in size and the convoys grew in size and frequency, there was no critical backing-up of supplies. Immediately after the armistice, however, the order came to ship no more freight to France, except food and other necessaries specifically requested. At the time of the armistice there were 600,000 tons of supplies on the docks in this country and 400,000 other tons moving toward the seaboard. Since the mills kept right on producing more, the flood of new materials inundated the supply service in this country. In December, 1918, the Storage Service was operating 65,000,000 square feet of warehouse space in the United States. A year later it was occupying nearly 400,000,000 square feet, three-fourths of which was leased. A large quantity of this space was open storage, unprotected from the elements. These figures are exclusive of the quantities of warehousing and open storage occupied by the various technical bureaus, such as the Ordnance Department, the Air Service, and the Signal Corps. The operation of the general storage facilities was the charge of the Director of Storage, one of the chief functionaries of the Division of Purchase, Storage, and Traffic.

An even greater problem than storage was the disposition of the enormous surpluses of goods which accumulated after the armistice. The first concern of the War Department in approaching this question was the military future of the United States. In 1914 much was made of the thoroughness of German military preparation, which had been such that, when the fatal hour struck and the conscripts by hundreds of thousands left their homes and poured into the German barracks, for every man there was waiting ready a uniform, shoes, a helmet, underclothing, and everything needed to prepare him immediately for service in the field. What Germany had been able to accomplish by premeditated, long, and expensive effort, the United States now derives as a by-product of the war Germany forced it to fight. America, too, is now prepared in these minute details. Before any of the surplus quartermaster stocks were set aside for sale or other disposition, a complete and balanced selection of uniforms, overcoats, underclothing, socks, caps, shoes, and other nonperishable articles in the individual equipment of troops, in quantities sufficient to outfit an army of approximately 1,000,000 men, was set aside and placed in indefinite storage. In addition, stores of such supplies were retained for the future consumption of the regular standing Army, of the National Guard, and of the Reserve Officers' Training Corps.

The war construction provided for the War Department three enormous interior reserve depots located respectively at Schenectady, New York, New Cumberland, Pennsylvania, and Columbus, Ohio. In these many of the reserve quartermaster supplies are stored. These installations are all of permanent and spacious construction. The warehouses are nearly all one story high, built of hollow tile and concrete, and divided into sections by fire walls. For additional storage the War Department is also using numerous wooden warehouses built at the retained cantonments. These buildings, though well constructed, are not fireproof and have to be guarded carefully to prevent their destruction.

It was found further that various branches of the Government could make good use of supplies originally procured for the Army. Many of the army hospitals were turned over to the Public Health Service, and with the hospitals the War Department delivered large quantities of medical supplies. Incidentally it may be noted here that the Army has retained and stored sufficient field medical equipment for an army of 1,000,000 men. Large lots of such general supplies as hardware, tools, rope, brushes, and office furniture went to the Bureau of Public Roads, the Interior Department, the Panama Canal, and other federal agencies.

Then, several foreign governments were allowed to purchase from our excess supplies. Clothing, textiles, medical equipment, and other supplies, all to the value of $20,000,000, went to various Russian societies. The French Government took machine tools and other machinery originally built for the Engineers, to the value of $25,000,000. Belgium bought a large quantity of construction materials.

In selling surplus materials to consumers in the United States, the preference went to charitable and welfare organizations. Hospital equipment, for instance, was offered first to state and municipal hospitals, free clinics, and similar institutions. Prices for medical supplies were fixed far below the prevailing market prices; and yet the Government had manufactured this equipment at such low cost that the financial recovery from the sales represented practically every penny which the War Department had put into the supplies. General supplies were offered first to welfare organizations, the Young

Men's Christian Association, the Boy Scouts, hospitals, sanitariums, and relief societies.

After that came the public. Private dealers were permitted to bid on lots of supplies. Regular days were set apart for the sale of various classes of commodities: Monday, textiles and leather goods; Tuesday, raw materials, machinery, and engineering supplies; Wednesday, general supplies; Thursday, medical supplies and motor vehicles; Friday, clothing; and Saturday, food supplies. These bidding sales were widely advertised, in advance, and bids could be submitted either to the War Department in Washington or to any of the zone, or district, supply offices. The private consumer could buy army food, clothing, textiles, tools, and other commodities of household utility either by parcel post (through the coöperation of the Post Office Department) or at any of the Army's retail stores, a great chain of which was set up throughout the country.

By sales and transfers the Army, at the end of the first year of effort, had disposed of supplies originally procured under the administration of the Director of Purchase to the value of $357,000,000. The transfers and sales brought back to the War Department more than seventy-seven cents of every dollar originally expended in the production of these goods. The story of the ingenuity displayed by the Government's officers in selling these and other surplus supplies (particularly the surpluses in the hands of the Ordnance Department and the Air Service after the armistice) is left for another chapter.

Before dropping the subject of the demobilization of the quartermaster war business, however, we should not overlook the disposition of the horses and mules acquired by the Army, but not shipped to France. The Remount Service purchased about 308,000 animals during the war. It started the war with about 90,000 animals on hand. The war losses amounted to 33,000 animals. Approximately 68,000 were shipped to France. Thus, at the time of the armistice the Remount Service had in its stables and corrals nearly 300,000 horses and mules.

About 215,000 of these were declared surplus and sold, and the rest were retained for the permanent Army.

The decision of the Remount Service to sell 200,000 animals on the market as rapidly as the market could absorb them was roundly criticized by horsemen, who pointed out that normally the American market had never absorbed more than 60,000 horses and mules in a year. The result would be, the critics declared, that the Government would get fair prices for the first 50,000 or 60,000 animals offered, and after that the surplus animals would be a drug on the market, not only forcing the Government to stand a great financial loss, but so depressing prices that dealers everywhere would suffer. On the other hand, it was costing the Government a dollar a day to feed and care for each of these animals. By retarding the sales the Government might be able to get better prices, but the gain would be more than absorbed by the cost of maintaining the establishment in the meantime.

And so it worked out. The market, indeed, proved itself to be able to absorb the surplus animals, and prices even grew better as the sales progressed. The average price paid was $111 a head, or about 57 per cent of the original average cost of $192. On the other hand, the Government escaped paying heavy maintenance charges.

All the animals were sold at public auctions, 189 of which were held at thirty-nine different places. Great crowds of buyers attended the sales, most of which were held at camps where the animals were quartered. The local post exchanges sold sandwiches and other refreshments to the buyers. Although the Government guaranteed no animals, all of them were carefully examined for blemishes and defects before the sales, and their demerits were noted in the lists read by the auctioneers. The Government could not afford to gain a David Harum reputation as a horse trader, for it had too many animals to sell. If dissatisfaction arose from the earlier sales, it would adversely affect the later ones. Only five complaints from buyers were made after the sales. These were referred to the Purchase Claims Board for settlement.

The Government invested $74,000,000 in animals bought in America during the war. Its net loss on animals sold was $22,000,000, and on animals that died, $6,000,000. The best of the animals on hand after the armistice were retained for use by the permanent Army.

CHAPTER XVI

BUILDINGS AND LANDS

ONE of the major industrial activities conducted in the United States during the war was the construction of buildings for the Army. The Army's physical plant, as it existed on the day war was declared, was entirely inadequate for the forces to be mobilized—so inadequate as to be of almost no use at all. Even the old headquarters of the War Department in Washington, which formerly had housed practically all the administrative offices, were none too large to accommodate merely the office staffs of the Secretary of War and his principal assistants, so great was the expansion of the central administration; and as for the tens of thousands of officers, clerks, stenographers, messengers, and other *personnel* employed by the great producing and operating bureaus, they occupied literally miles of flimsy, unsightly "war buildings," which spread out like a defacing rash over the fair open spaces of the capital city.

An even greater expansion of plant was to be observed throughout the country. The plant set up for the Army mobilized against Germany was a practically new creation, specialized for exactly the sort of war in which we were engaged. It was a war in which land transportation had to be linked to ocean transportation, and therefore the plant included vast facilities for the embarkation of troops and a string of mighty export terminals, or bases, strung out along the coast in order to make difficult any blockade of our overseas supply line. It was a war essentially industrial in type, with unusual emphasis laid upon the development of special industrial products, such as powder and explosives; and therefore the plant included dozens of new mills and factories, several of them industrial centers so large as to be virtually small cities in themselves, with housing and modern municipal conveniences for their employees. It was a war in which new and hitherto unknown forms of combat had sprung into existence, and therefore the plant included equipped fields for the training of soldiers in such arts as flying and the employment of poisons as weapons. Above all, it was a war which called upon the ultimate resources of American man power; and, as it turned out, the plant had to be adequate to house, school, amuse, care for, and maintain at least two million men, with all that that implies in barracks, drill grounds, parks for vehicles, water and sewer systems, lighting systems, roads, hospitals, and (in the maintenance line) depots and warehouses for supplies.

It was all fresh creation, new construction. The building industry of the United States—and it is one of the largest and strongest of our industries—had never before been called upon to provide such expansion in an equal time. It follows that the entire building industry must have been engaged in the construction enterprise, that every available man who could drive a nail or lay a brick must have been employed upon government work. If he was not, he should have been; for those in charge of the construction, unable to secure sufficient labor from the entire building industry of the United States, sent ships to Porto Rico and the Bahamas and brought back thousands of workmen to help out. The Construction Division, the war-begotten organization which was in charge of this activity, with 427,000 men on its contractors' pay rolls at the peak of its industriousness, yielded only to the United States Railroad Administration the title of greatest employer of war labor. It engaged in 581 separate construction projects, which called for an expenditure of over $1,100,000,000; and it completed most of them.

Miles of docks, hundreds of acres of covered storage, hundreds of power plants and complete water systems, thousands of miles of roads, railroads, water mains, and sewer lines—the list grows monotonous simply because of the size of its items, which are not to be visualized by stating them in terms of acres and miles. The activity was at its height at the signing of the armistice, when it became incumbent upon the Construction Division to terminate the work.

Four hundred and fifty army construction projects were under way on the day of the armistice. One hundred and thirty-one stood completed. The incomplete projects included some of the largest and costliest ones. But the salvage value of buildings is small unless they can be sold to purchasers able to make use of them as and where they stand. Few war buildings were adapted to civilian use. They were highly specialized for a purely war use, and they were not often located where they could be of economic benefit to the country. A large part of their cost represented the evanescent element of labor, a value entirely destroyed when buildings are wrecked for the sake of salvaging their materials. The war plant, even incomplete, represented an immense investment, but one which would be almost altogether lost if the plant were to be knocked down for salvage. Therefore it was of advantage to the Government to carry on a surprisingly large amount of war construction after the armistice for the sake of getting the use-value from its investment by occupying these installations with the permanent Army.

But there were other reasons for continuing work. Among the largest and costliest of the construction projects were those which provided the ocean terminal bases at Boston, Brooklyn, Philadelphia, Norfolk, Charleston, and New Orleans. These installations were all of durable, fireproof construction; and, with their piers, their great warehouses equipped with labor-saving machinery, trackage, and the like, they were the last word of modern constructional science in developments of this sort. In appropriating the money for these port works, Congress had stipulated that after the war they should be used in the development of American foreign trade. Consequently the Construction Division went ahead after the armistice and finished up these buildings.

The port works alone were enough to account for a large portion of the money expended on construction after the armistice, but in addition other great unfinished projects were carried through. As we have shown, the storage problem became acute only after the armistice, when the wasteful field consumption of supplies ceased and the materials coming from the war factories banked up in this country. Every warehouse and depot project incomplete on the day of the armistice was pressed to completion thereafter in order to provide shelter for valuable and perishable materials. This was another great branch of post-armistice construction. Add to these the continued construction of hospitals (which had to be prepared to receive the thousands of wounded men in France on the day of the armistice), and it becomes evident why thousands of the war builders were kept on the job after the war itself had come to an end.

The fate of every incomplete army construction project on the day of the armistice was submitted to the Operations Division of the General Staff, which looked at the percentage of completion, noted whether the Government owned the ground on which the construction was going forward, studied the availability of the building for commercial use, and determined whether it was needed in the military plans, and then recommended that the construction be abandoned, curtailed, or completed. In general, the projects abandoned were those providing additional facilities for the assembling and training of troops and those providing plants for the production of destructive munitions, such as toxic gas, powder, and loaded shell. Of the 450 projects incomplete on the day of the armistice, 182 were abandoned and 268 carried through.

The completion of so large a quantity of the war construction after the armistice enabled the Construction Division to go through the demobilization of its industry without accumulating large stores of surplus materials. Although in form, at any rate, the Division dealt directly only with contractors who took the various jobs, actually the Division itself procured the lumber, cement, brick, structural steel, roofing, hardware, and the like, for the builders. The demand of the war construction upon the supplies of building materials was so great that nothing less than a centralized stimulation and control of the entire market could have procured the materials in the quantities needed. The Construction Division's Procurement Division located the supplies and then arranged each building contractor's deals for them, even stipulating the producers, quantities, and the prices which must be paid for materials. This last was important, because the war builders worked under a sharply safeguarded cost-plus contract form, and therefore the Government was keenly interested in what the materials cost. In addition to procuring supplies for the contractors, the Procurement Division also purchased equipment for the war buildings—heating, ventilating, and power plants, fire extinguishers, refrigeration equipment, boilers, engines, and machinery of many sorts. Its purchases ran at the rate of $2,000,000 a day in the early autumn of 1918.

After the armistice and after the temporary suspension of effort requested in order to give the Construction Division time in which to take stock of its position, the production of building materials and supplies of which the Government would be able to make no use was rapidly terminated. The Procurement Division was made up of experts in all branches of building construction, and therefore this Division was made over after the armistice into the Construction Division Claims Board for liquidating its war business under the direction of the War Department Claims Board. In six months practically all the terminated contracts had been finally settled by this organization, at an average cancellation cost of 5 per cent of the face value of the contracts.

The termination of supply contracts and of contracts with constructors of buildings not needed by the War Department after the armistice, left the Construction Division with large quantities of supplies on its hands. But these were by no means surplus supplies. The completion of a large quantity of war construction after the armistice saved the Construction Division from having to solve the problem of disposing of much surplus. Supplies accumulated for the terminated jobs were simply diverted to those ordered completed and thus utilized.

But although the Division had no large quantity of building supplies to sell, it was charged, after the armistice, with the duty of disposing of the facilities at the 182 construction projects which were terminated. Many of these projects were large ones, those in this category being for the most part training camps for troops. There was a camp shortage in 1918, and the Construction Division was doing everything in its power to overcome it. We were sending men overseas at the rate of 300,000 a month; and, since it was desirable to give every overseas soldier at least six months' training, that implied camp accommodations for 1,800,000 men in the United States. The actual accommodations provided were for less than 1,370,000 troops. In 1918, after the augmented rate of embarkation became a fact, new training camp projects were consequently inaugurated at frequent intervals. Only a few days before the armistice the Construction Division began the construction of an enormous new camp which was to specialize in the training of infantry. All the national guard camps (sixteen of them) and most of the special-purpose camps, whether completely built or not, were condemned after the armistice for salvage. Most of these were veritable cities, some of them large enough to accommodate 40,000 men each, comfortably—with the adverb accented, for the comfort was based on such substantial (and costly) installations as water and sanitation systems, electric lighting, pavements, sidewalks, and even stores, theatres, and gymnasiums. It was the task of the Construction Division to dispose of these cities to such members of the public as cared to buy.

A city, however, is something more than an accumulation of buildings and other tangible facilities. Quite as much as upon foundations of rock, a city rests upon logic—the logic of its location. Naturally the Government built its camps upon cheap land, therefore upon land not in demand by the population, therefore upon land not so located as to make it a logical place for a city. And so, although it was thought at first that perhaps some of these camps might prove to be the nuclei of permanent civilian communities, that notion soon had to be abandoned for the reason that few civilian movements arose to occupy permanently the former war buildings. An attempt was made, and still is being made, to use the former Nitro Powder Plant as a permanent civilian industrial city, and one or two training camps in the South have been held together by their purchasers with the idea of establishing communities on their sites. The others, however, in which the Government had sunk hundreds of millions of dollars, were sold out to the wreckers, who bought them for the sake of salvaging the building materials.

Now, there is nothing quite so second-hand as second-hand building materials. Boards are full of nail holes and sometimes covered with faded paint or disfiguring marks. Bricks are soiled, chipped, and worn, and conglomerated with stonelike mortar. Hardware and metallic fixtures are corroded and rusty. Such materials are not only wreckage and junk, but not even valuable junk. The chief cost in the construction of a training camp was the labor which laid the brick, installed the underground piping, smoothed, squared, and nailed up the lumber, and soldered the joints in the plumbing. All that labor value was lost when camps were salvaged for their materials.

Yet this was not the only loss which the Government was forced to sustain. Practically all the camps were originally located on leased ground; and this fact implied that in razing the camps the Government was bound to restore the land to its original condition, or, in lieu of that, to pay to the owners the costs of restoration. These questions of property damage greatly complicated the demobilization of the training camps, because the amounts of damage were so hard to ascertain. Concrete roads had been laid across what were originally pastures; fertile corn lands were crisscrossed with clay ridges thrown up above the water and sewer trenches. On the other hand, some of the camp improvements had drained former swamps and reclaimed them for cultivation, and such benefits would offset damages in other places. It was out of the question for the Government to attempt to settle these thousands of cases individually, because of the time it would take; and therefore it was stipulated that the purchasers of the camps must assume all liabilities for property damage and hold the Government harmless from claims that might later be pressed in the Court of Claims. Naturally the purchasers made allowances for these damages in their bids, and wide allowances, too, since the extent of the damages was largely conjecture. This consideration further depressed the prices paid by the purchasers.

The result was that the salvage of abandoned army camps brought back to the Government only a small fraction of the money put into them. Actually in scores of instances it would have been cheaper for the Government to abandon the improvements to the landowners in return for quit-claims for the property damage. Public policy, however, prohibited such a short-cut method. Some of the leased sites had been donated to the Government before the armistice at the nominal rental of $1.00 a year or some other slight sum; but afterwards the chambers of commerce and other civic agencies which had made these concessions, for the sake of securing camps near their communities, refused to renew the arrangements, and the War Department was forced to pay regular rentals. Here was a consideration to force the sale of the camps on any terms possible. The chief lesson learned from the war construction enterprise was that the Government should buy and not lease a site when the value of the improvements is to exceed the value of the site itself. Only by holding such property for permanent use or gradual sale can the Government get value received for its investment.

In general, the salvage recovery from camps and other installations sold after the armistice amounted to about 15 per cent of the money invested in the original building materials. All labor values were lost. All wastage of materials in construction and demolition was loss. Many materials such as cement and concrete, road material, roofing, wood-stave piping, sewer piping, and so on, were a complete loss. The attention of the reader is invited to some typical shrinkages in value.

Project	*Original Cost*	*Salvage Recovery*
Camp Beauregard	$4,300,000	$ 43,000
Camp Bowie	3,400,000	110,000
Camp Hancock	6,000,000	75,000
Camp Logan	3,300,000	137,000
Camp Wadsworth	4,000,000	95,000
Camp Wheeler	3,200,000	144,000

Note, however, that in disposing of these camps, the Government retained practically all the storage and hospital facilities.

During the year following the armistice the Construction Division disposed of fourteen national guard camps, three embarkation camps, sixteen special and regular training camps, four flying fields, four hospitals, and many small groups of buildings. For these the Government received about $4,215,-000. In addition, parts of many other camps were sold; also construction materials of practically every sort.

The most spectacular accomplishment of the Construction Division before the armistice was the building of the cantonments, the primary training camps which housed the soldiers summoned into the military service by the Selective Service Law. These were much more substantial installations than the national guard camps, the salvaging of six of which was noted in the tabular statement above. The national guard camps provided only tentage for the shelter of troops, whereas the cantonments housed their inhabitants in stanch wooden barrack buildings. A cantonment cost from two to three times as much as a national guard camp. Yet, on three months' notice, at the beginning of which not even the sites had yet been selected and acquired, the Construction Division prepared sixteen cantonments ready to receive the first inductives called to the colors.

The cantonments originally were all built upon leased ground. It was evident that, if the Government were forced to vacate the ground to the owners, the cantonments, salvaged for their building materials, would bring no greater recovery percentage of their cost than did the tentage camps. The Government's loss, in such an event, on each cantonment would be twice or three times what it proved to be on the national guard camps. Before the end of the war was in sight the Construction Division had anticipated demobilization by presenting a plan to the Secretary of War for the purchase of the sites of the cantonments. Purchase would accomplish several desirable ends. As long as the cantonments were in use it would save the payment of rents. After the war was over, if the cantonments were retained by the Army, it would give the cantonments their full use-value, which was every penny they had cost. If, on the other hand, the decision was to dispose of them after the advent of peace, then ownership of the sites would permit the Government (1) to market the materials gradually and avoid beating down prices by glutting the market; or (2) to sell buildings intact, with the land on which they stood; or (3) to sell entire cantonments as they stood, together with title to the lands. Any one of these methods of disposition would bring a far greater salvage return than the forced sale of the materials and the payment of property damages.

In March, 1919, the Assistant Secretary of War directed that the leased sites of fourteen of the cantonments—namely, Camps Custer, Devens, Dix, Dodge, Gordon, Grant, Lee, Jackson, Meade, Pike, Sherman, Taylor, Travis, and Upton—be acquired by purchase. The investment in these cantonments was approximately $155,000,000. By continuing to use the cantonments, the War Department could get full value received for the money expended. By salvaging them after the manner of disposing of the national guard camps, the Government might recover $4,000,000 at the outside estimate. By selling the materials gradually or the buildings intact with lands, the recovery could be expected to run as high as $48,000,000. The business logic of the proposition was irresistible.

The purchase of this vast quantity of land was undertaken by the Construction Division. After the commanding officers at the cantonments had indicated what boundaries should be included, the Division sent out its field forces—on April 21, 1919. First to go to work were engineers and surveyors to fix accurate boundaries and secure complete metes-and-bounds descriptions of the properties. Contracts were drawn with various responsible title companies to make search of the land titles and to guarantee them with title insurance. Next followed acquisition officers who closed sale contracts with the private owners. The sale contracts were finally signed in behalf of the Government by competent officers. With the acquisition officers traveled disbursing officers of the Finance Service who stood ready to pay spot cash for the lands the moment the sale contracts were signed. So rapidly was this work carried on that in two months the Government had acquired ownership to more than half the area on which the fourteen cantonments stood. A year later about 55,000 acres had passed in fee simple to the United States at a price of $6,762,000. Considerable property was yet unacquired; but, although it had been estimated that the sites would cost ultimately $9,657,000, the indications then were that the Government would secure them for not more than $8,115,000.

It was found to be impossible, however, to secure all the property so simply and easily. Some owners would not sell at reasonable prices; other owners could not be found; still others were under legal disabilities which prevented them from selling. In such instances the recourse of the Government was condemnation of the lands. Proceedings were instituted eventually to condemn some 22,000 acres for government use. The condemnation proceedings were conducted by the Department of Justice, which found this work to be one of great magnitude.

One of the interesting war developments in the United States was the change in the attitude of the War Department toward real estate. Before the war the various bureaus and other agencies of the War Department acquired their own real estate by lease or purchase as they needed it and as they could secure authority to procure it. The war itself resulted in an intense demand for real estate by the War Department as sites for its war buildings or as quarters to be occupied under lease. Real estate, therefore, came to be regarded as a commodity in the supply of the Army; just as much a commodity as food or ammunition. And, as the procurement of other commodities was eventually administered and controlled by a centralized agency, so the centralized procurement of real estate was placed in the hands of a new organization called the Real Estate Service.

The Real Estate Service acted as the Army's real estate agent. The various bureaus still originated the projects for the acquisition of property, and then the Real Estate Service acquired the property as agent for the bureaus. The Service was composed of experts who saw to it that deeds and leases were correctly drawn and that the Government made good bargains.

The armistice, if anything, meant increased effort for the Real Estate Section, since the problem of the storage of surplus supplies was to be solved only by the acquisition of space. It was also necessary to dispense with high-priced locations, essential as they had been during the actual hostilities, and to substitute more economical facilities. Many of the War Department's war factories had been built on leased sites, and it was necessary to purchase these sites wherever it was expedient for the Department to retain the factory as a preparedness asset or where it was good business to buy the land in order to sell the factory advantageously.

Although few obstacles had been thrown in the way of the War Department in purchasing property, it was discovered after the armistice that, because of existing and obsolete laws, it was most difficult to sell any. Up to the declaration of war the law which controlled this function provided that war department lands useless for military purposes should be sold *by the Secretary of the Interior*. When this law was enacted (1884) most of the lands occupied by the Army had come from the public domain, and it was logical to turn them back to that source when the War Department was through with them. In May, 1917, Congress authorized the War Department itself to sell national guard target ranges. In July, 1918, Congress authorized the President to sell, *through the head of any Executive Department*, lands acquired after the declaration of war against Germany to be the sites of war factories. In July, 1919, Congress authorized the sale under identical conditions of lands acquired for storage purposes. These, however, were the only exceptions granted to the original rule. In fact, when the War Department went about the purchase of the fourteen cantonment sites for the possible purpose of selling these lands later and thus getting better prices for the buildings on them, it did so with the knowledge that it would take a special act of Congress to authorize such a sale.

Congress, without warning, attached a rider to the appropriation bill which was approved on July 11, 1919, forbidding the expenditure of any more money at all in the purchase of real estate by the Army except at the national guard camps or at the cantonments in use before November 11, 1918, and also except where the purchase of sites of industrial plants was necessary to protect the Government's interests. The Secretary of War ruled that the fourteen cantonments then being purchased were exempt from this inhibition, but the law abruptly put an end to projects of the Real Estate Service to buy some 300,000 acres at a cost of $8,000,000. At that time the Service was buying 115,000 acres of land at Columbus, Georgia, to serve as an infantry school of arms, 120,000 acres at Fayetteville, North Carolina, to be an artillery range, and several other large acreages for various military purposes. The project to acquire Camp Humphreys, the Engineers' camp in Virginia near the city of Washington, about 4,000 acres, was allowed to go through.

On the first day of the armistice the War Department was a party to leases obligating it to pay $13,000,000 in rentals annually. By the end of December, 1919, the Real Estate Service had made a large net reduction in the number of leases, and the annual rent bill had dropped to approximately $5,000,000, although in that interval the Service had acquired by lease hundreds of millions of square feet of new storage space.

Photo from Construction Division

WEST INDIAN LABORERS EMBARKING FOR HOME

Photo from Construction Division

VIEW OF CAMP SHERMAN

Photo from Quartermaster Department

IN AN ARMY RETAIL STORE

Photo from Quartermaster Department

CUSTOMERS AT OPENING OF ARMY RETAIL STORE

CHAPTER XVII

SELLING THE SURPLUS

IN our earlier chapters, frequent and more or less extended references have been made to the disposition of surplus property acquired by the various branches of the Army during the World War. In so far as these references have been to surpluses with the American Expeditionary Forces, we have aimed to make the statements complete; but the references to sales of the surplus military property accumulated within the United States have been only incidental, inserted merely to make plain to the reader the extent of the tasks of the various production bureaus after the armistice. This may have seemed haphazard and confusing treatment of what was one of the most interesting and important phases of the demobilization of war industry. We are therefore taking occasion in this chapter to consider this phase—the disposal of the domestic surpluses of war materials—as a whole and in such detail as may be expedient.

That same tendency toward centralization which succeeded in placing under one direction the procurement of all war supplies and, after the armistice, the liquidation of the Government's business engagements, also brought about a unified control of the sale of the surplus materials. Shortly after the armistice there was set up in the Division of Purchase, Storage, and Traffic a Sales Branch under an officer called the Director of Sales. Just as, after the formation of the "overhead" business organization known as the Division of Purchase, Storage, and Traffic, the various production bureaus still continued to procure most of their own supplies, but now under the control and authority of the Director of Purchase, Storage, and Traffic, so after the armistice these same bureaus sold and otherwise disposed of the surpluses they had acquired, but under the supervision of the Director of Sales. With the exception of a few sales made directly with various foreign governments and companies (property valued at $63,450,000 going in these transactions), the Sales Branch itself engaged in no selling, but merely directed the selling activities of the operating bureaus.

It is impossible here even to give an estimate of the value of the surplus materials left on the hands of the War Department after the termination of the war industry, for the reason that the War Department itself has never been able to arrive at an estimate. The subject has been so vast, so intricate, and so complicated by the changing of *personnel* and the evolution of organization, that it has seemed to be a hopeless task to attempt an inventory of the surplus property sold and for sale. We can, however, gain some idea of the quantities of it. It is estimated that the armistice found the Army with a surplus of war supplies on hand of a value of $2,000,000,000. This investment represented goods actually produced by American industry up to November 11, 1918, in the maintenance of a force of 4,000,000 men and in anticipation of a force of nearly 5,000,000 in 1919. But this, mind you, was surplus within the United States. On the same date—the day of the armistice—the A. E. F., through importations from the United States and through its own foreign purchases, had built up a surplus of supplies worth $1,330,000,000 over and above what it would return to the war reserves at home and outside of what it would consume while resting on European soil during demobilization. Thus we have the figure $3,330,000,000 as representing the value of the surplus supplies, munitions, on hand when the active fighting ceased.

But this is only the beginning of the complete inventory; this was merely the surplus existing on November 11, 1918. War industry, under the policy of terminating it by graduating a declining production, still had weeks and months to go on producing goods, for most of which there was no war use. This dwindling manufacture by thousands of factories with millions of employees added to the surpluses materials worth many hundreds of millions. And still the tale is not told. War industry had been fostered by huge federal investments in buildings and machinery. These facilities, too, existed as surplus when the industry ended. This great accumulation was largely augmented by the machinery and other manufacturing facilities taken over by the Government in the settlement with the war contractors. The Government had purchased heavily of raw materials of various sorts, quantities of which remained as surplus after the armistice. In liquidating the war industry it added further to its stores of raw materials and took over, besides, a great mass of semi-finished materials in all stages of completion. When upon this heap we pile a great part of all the war building construction, and on that the additional surpluses automatically created when polity in Congress and in the executive offices made cut after cut in the size of the permanent Army, then we are approximating the total of the surplus.

This was all wealth, the true substance of the nation, its resources fabricated by its labor for the special purposes of war; and, with the war over, with little or no demand or use for these special materials, they could be disposed of only at a shocking sacrifice. Again, we cannot estimate the extent of the shrinkage, but we can indicate it. Up to March 1, 1920, the War Department had disposed of surplus property which had cost it $2,600,000,000. For this it had received $1,633,000,000. The recovery, therefore, was 64 per cent of the cost; the loss, 36 per cent. The shrinkage in values is one of the wastes which any nation must contemplate and accept when it sets forth to wage war on the modern scale. The nation can get value received for the cost of its munitions only by using them in war.

The largest of American companies, the United States Steel Corporation, in 1918, its busiest year, did a gross business of $1,745,000,000. The value of the surplus munitions produced before the armistice was nearly twice as great as that. The Steel Corporation, however, produced only a few dozen or few score sorts of products. The sorts of goods and materials to be disposed of by the Sales Branch were in number about 250,000, and this range embraced goods known in many branches of trade. The Steel Corporation and other great companies usually sell to a relatively small group of customers, who take the products in wholesale quantities. The market which the Sales Branch entered consisted of the entire United States, with 110,000,000 possible buyers; for part of the problem was to dispose of surplus materials by retail sale to the public. All in all, this may be regarded as the greatest merchandizing enterprise ever undertaken in America.

The 250,000 catalogue items in the sales list were divided roughly into seven commodity groups, as follows: (1) railway and building materials and contractors' equipment; (2) manufacturing plants and plant sites; (3) machine tools; (4) vehicles and airplanes, including spare engines and parts; (5) quartermaster stores; (6) ordnance and technical equipment, including office equipment; and (7) raw materials, scrap metal, and waste materials.

It was recognized at the outset that to throw on the market vast quantities of supplies and materials in all these seven categories was to court disaster to the industrial situation. Business and industry immediately after the armistice were in a ticklish position. They faced the complete transition from the war to the peace basis, an uncharted region through which it seemed likely that they could go safely only under the wisest of guidance. If, in addition to its inevitable troubles of reconstruction, industry were to have to face cutthroat competition with the surpluses of the very goods its own mills had created during the war, it was evident that the difficulties of the transition might be doubled.

To safeguard business as much as possible and still dispose of the surplus materials, the War Department adopted certain general principles or policies. The first of these was that the general Government, through its several departments and in the public work which the departments were doing, should utilize all the surplus war materials they could absorb. The second and more important was to sell all general commodities to the public through the medium of the industries which had produced these commodities and thus to avoid disastrous breaks in market prices—even, sometimes, to sustain prices.

There was widespread disapproval of this latter policy. The public for months had been stung and irritated by prices which many regarded as the exactions of profiteers; and now at last, with huge stocks of supplies on hand which had to be sold or lost, the people anticipated a dumping which would smash down prices and bring about the discomfiture of those who had seemingly victimized them. But this was not to be. The Government adopted the view that it was better to have the high (but normally declining) prices and to keep the wheels of industry turning than to risk a collapse of prices that might bring with it general unemployment and business stagnation.

Later on, when it had become evident that business was making a safe passage through the reconstruction period, large stocks of clothing and food supplies were sold directly to consumers at prices considerably below the market averages.

Particularly in raw materials the policy of sale through, or in coöperation with, the industry affected by the sale worked as the Government had expected it to work. The War Department found itself after the armistice with a surplus of 125,000,000 board feet of soft lumber over and above what it would need in completing the various unterminated construction projects. This was lumber enough to build 5,000 houses. To have dumped this on the market would have paralyzed a large part of the lumbering industry until the market had absorbed the army lumber. Accordingly the War Department entered into a contract with the authorized representatives of the lumber industry whereby it was agreed that the lumber should be marketed gradually and at prices fixed by agreement between the Government and the industry. Under this arrangement the surplus was all sold without disturbance to the industry and at prices which brought a good return to the Government.

In the spring of 1919 the Government had on hand a surplus of something more than 100,000,000 pounds of copper. The copper industry was in a serious plight. The producers had on hand a surplus of 1,000,000,000 pounds, but still they were keeping the mines, smelters, and refineries running to prevent unemployment and in the expectation that the resumption of normal business would soon create a demand for copper. Any dumping of the war department surplus most certainly would have closed the mines. Instead of that, the Government sold the entire surplus back to the producers. The industry continued in operation, and the Government received an average of seventeen cents a pound for its copper, a fair recovery.

The War Department's surplus of 161,000,000 pounds of sulphur was sold through the industry. At the armistice the Government had on hand some 600,000 tons of nitrate of soda imported from Chile for the powder factories. About half of this was retained as a war reserve. The Department of Agriculture disposed of 125,000 tons of it to farmers for use as fertilizer. About 142,000 tons was sold for the War Department at market prices by the nitrate importers who had supplied the commodity to the Government in the first place. A stock of 59,000 tons of nitrate in Chile, the property of the American Government, was brought to the United States and sold by the importers on the same terms. Approximately 730,000 bales of cotton linters in the war department surplus are being used by the commercial powder industry on such terms as will return to the Government from one-third to one-half the original cost of the linters. A surplus of 66,000,000 pounds of ammonium nitrate was sold at prices which reimbursed the War Department to the extent of about one-third its war-time cost.

It should be borne in mind that all these sales were actually consummated by the production bureaus in whose hands the supplies remained as surplus after the armistice, the Sales Branch merely coördinating the sales and approving the terms. It will be impracticable here to go into the details of the salvage and sales activities of all the bureaus, but enough can be told to illustrate the ingenuity and business enterprise employed in disposing of the great war surpluses. As the occasion demanded, the government salesmen had to be merchants, barterers, auctioneers, and even partners with commercial organizations.

The production bureaus were organized for their salvage operations precisely as they had been for manufacturing the supplies and, later, for liquidating the business arrangements with the contractors. Those which had created manufacturing districts before the armistice, afterwards established district salvage boards to take over and dispose of the surpluses accumulated by the district claims boards in their settlements with the contractors. These district salvage boards, in turn, were subsidiary to the main bureau salvage boards, which, in turn, reported to the Sales Branch of the Division of Purchase, Storage, and Traffic. The surpluses of ordnance materials, for instance, were handled by the Ordnance Salvage Board through its district salvage boards, and the same system obtained in the Air Service and under the Director of Purchase. The other bureaus disposed of their surpluses through central salvage boards in Washington.

Perhaps the chief challenge to the ingenuity of the government salesman was that offered by the ordnance surpluses, for these were probably the most highly specialized of all military supplies; yet it was often the task of the Ordnance Salvage Board to find civilian needs to which these supplies could be adapted. Great commercial successes have sometimes been scored by those able to develop new uses, and therefore new markets, for the goods they manufactured. In like fashion the ordnance salvers, by taking thought, could sometimes convert what had been regarded as junk into merchandise for which there was a brisk demand at good prices.

These activities took the salesmen far afield. They disposed of lumber to the Panama Canal operators, sold nitrate to the Government of Holland, converted the great ammonium nitrate plant at Perryville into a hospital operated by the Public Health Service for the benefit of disabled ex-service men, transferred tin to the Navy Department, and demonstrated to the Department of Agriculture that the containers in which it had been intended to ship trench mortar shell could serve equally well as containers of dehydrated vegetables. They disposed of rope to the Department of Agriculture. They sold a thousand revolvers to the police force of Washington. To the federal road-builders they turned over trucks and smokeless powder and trinitrotoluol to be used as blasting explosive.

One of the largest single undertakings in ordnance salvage was the disposal of manufacturing plants either built outright or equipped with machinery by the Government. There were some 300 of these, and the Government's investment in them was practically $525,000,000. The array included cannon and gun-carriage plants, shell-loading plants, powder works, chemical and acid plants, toluol plants, small-arms factories, ammunition factories, nitrate-fixation plants, and numerous shell-making plants. In the liquidation of the ordnance industry large additional quantities of ordnance production machinery, both new and used, fell into the hands of the Government. All of it, beyond the selections retained in the military reserves, had to be sold. During the first year after the armistice the sales of ordnance plants and machinery brought in a return of over $70,000,000. (Manufacturing facilities worth double that amount had either been stored or installed at the various arsenals, or else had been turned over to other departments of the Government.) In the spring of 1920 half the vast accumulation of ordnance plants and machinery had been disposed of.

The most spectacular sale accomplished in this branch of ordnance salvage was that of the smokeless powder plant at Nitro, West Virginia. This plant was a self-contained town, with three square miles of land in its site, with houses for 20,000 people, theatres, schools, churches, stores, electric lights, paved streets, gas, a telephone system, water, and other modern improvements. The Director of Sales himself conducted the negotiations whereby the entire establishment was sold *en bloc* to a development corporation, which planned to resell the establishment piecemeal to manufacturers and thus create a permanent industrial city at Nitro. The corporation paid a flat price to the Government for the Nitro plant and in addition admitted the Government as a partner in the profits. Several companies have already occupied factory buildings there. The Ordnance Salvage Board maintained representatives at Nitro to approve the resales as they were made.

The Ordnance Department took over from the producers after the armistice large quantities of steel in process of being made into artillery shell. A great deal of this steel consisted of finished and semi-finished parts for shell. No matter how much labor had been expended on these shell parts, their only value commercially was as melting stock. The users of steel evidently expected to be able to pick up the Government's surplus stock of it after the armistice for a song: the highest bids for the first offerings of it on the market were only about $12 a ton. The ordnance salvers cannily decided not to sell at such prices and, except for some trifling, but advantageous, sales, did nothing about it until the summer of 1919. By that time the commercial revival began to make itself felt in the demand for steel, the prices of which were further enhanced by an impending strike in the steel industry. Then it was that the wisdom of holding on to the steel stocks became evident. The sale of shell steel was handled directly by the Ordnance Salvage Board, which, after the prices rose, dealt only with heavy purchasers. The average price paid to the Government for this steel was about $30 a ton. The Salvage Board handled about 1,000,000 tons of it.

There were also large surpluses of nonferrous metals,—copper, zinc, lead, tin, antimony, and nickel,—the stocks including nearly 20,000 ounces of platinum, which sold, it may be noted, for an average price of $105 an ounce—just about what it had cost. The copper, as we have seen, went back to the producers at a fair price. The Board sold 65,000,000 pounds of zinc at an average of eight cents a pound. The surplus of brass amounted to 135,000,000 pounds, and this has been selling at good prices. During the year following the armistice the salvers disposed of nonferrous metals worth $40,000,000.

The salvers had to use their ingenuity in order to dispose of the surplus cupro-nickel advantageously. Cupro-nickel is an alloy of copper and nickel which is used in making jackets for small-arms bullets, but the metal has no commercial use. The Government was able to secure not a single bid for any of its large surplus of cupro-nickel. The alloy is too tough for ordinary metal-working machinery. The ordnance salvers first proposed that this metal be used at the Mint in making five-cent pieces, but the surplus of it was so large that it would have taken many years to consume it all in this use. The experimenters then took hold and found that, by melting cupro-nickel and further alloying it with zinc, they could produce German silver, a commodity for which there is extensive industrial use. This fact was demonstrated to the market, and the first result was a bid for 5,000,000 pounds of cupro-nickel at a favorable price.

An even more conspicuous example of resourcefulness on the part of the ordnance salvage forces was the sale of the so-called cartridge cloth. The Ordnance Department was an extensive war consumer of textiles of many kinds. Silk, cotton, wool, felt, and linen are used in numerous forms in the production of ordnance supplies. The quantities acquired during the war may be estimated from the fact that the surpluses left after the armistice brought on sale close to $25,000,000. In the surplus of textile goods was a considerable yardage of what was called cartridge cloth; and it must be said that at the outset none of the excess ordnance supplies seemed to be so hopeless as a salvaging proposition, so certain to account for a large loss of investment, as this stock of cartridge cloth.

The cartridge cloth was used during the war to make bags to be filled with the smokeless powder used as the propelling charges for guns of the larger calibers. The cloth was made of silk, for the reason that silk alone among fabrics burns perfectly and leaves no ash to smut the barrel of a gun. Cotton, in contrast, or any other fabric, is likely to leave charred pieces of itself smouldering in the breech of a gun after a shot; and these smouldering pieces may touch off the new powder charge prematurely and kill or maim the men serving the gun. Moreover, silk alone does not cause a flash at the muzzle of the gun when the shot is fired. Such flashes at night betray the gun's position to the enemy.

But though cartridge cloth was made of pure silk, what a silk it was! Naturally, to keep down its cost, it was woven of the cheapest silk materials possible to obtain. It was made of what were practically the by-products of silk-weaving—noils and waste silk. Noils are cut cocoons, immature cocoons, and combings from the outsides of cocoons. The woof of cartridge cloth was made from silk noils and the warp from waste silk. All raw silk is filled with a natural gum, which in commercial processes is boiled out before the silk is woven. Since this gum did not impair the fabric for use in guns (the gum gave perfect combustion and left no ash), it was left in the raw material in order to keep down the cost of the fabric. In order to facilitate the manufacture of cloth from noils, the noils were carded, combed, and spun in oil, oil not being objectionable in the cloth. The result was a greasy, dark colored, rough cloth, looking like oily gunny sacking, a fabric about as unalluring as any that could be imagined. And it cost the Government on the average seventy-two cents a yard. At the time of the armistice the Ordnance Department had on hand about 22,000,000 yards of it. Most of this quantity was set aside as a war reserve. The rest was offered for sale. The best offer for it was twelve and one-half cents a yard. The Government, therefore, faced a considerable loss.

The ordnance salvers were not content to swallow this loss. The Salvage Board obtained $20,000 with which to experiment with the silk. An expert silk maker in the Sales Branch then tried boiling out the gum and oil and otherwise processing the fabric, after which he bleached, dyed, printed, and napped it. The result was a beautiful fabric, suitable for outer garments for both men and women, and for millinery, drapery, and upholstery. Beautiful color effects were obtained with it by certain silk-finishing companies. With this demonstration before the trade, the Salvage Board again asked for bids, and this time received a number of them, offering prices ranging from thirty-one cents a yard to forty. This still was not enough for the salvage salesmen, who went out and negotiated a contract with two companies—the Bush Terminal Company of New York and the McLane Silk Company of Turners Falls, Massachusetts—which netted the Government eighty-five and a half cents a yard, plus half the profits received from the sale of the fabric. A considerable quantity of the silk was sold under this arrangement.

The expenses of the Ordnance Salvage Board were less than 6 per cent of the money received from sales and transfers. This sales cost compares favorably with similar costs in the mercantile world.

The fact that a large part of the money spent by the Air Service during the war was represented after the armistice by finished airplanes and airplane engines precluded any considerable recoupment of the war expenditures from sales of surplus materials afterwards, since, at present, planes and engines have small commercial utility. Aviation engines are too light and too powerful for ordinary tasks, and no real market for airplanes has yet existed in the United States. Consequently, the sales of air service surplus were virtually limited to commodities having commercial use, such as tires, photographic equipment, linen fabric, fur used in making aviators' clothing, and the like. Some of these surplus commodities, however, went at good prices. One New York concern bought 372,500 Chinese dogskins for approximately $700,000. Nearly 5,000,000 board feet of surplus mahogany, used in making propellers, sold for $150 a thousand feet. Great quantities of small tools from the airplane factories, millions of yards of cotton fabric, and nearly 4,000,000 pounds of long-staple cotton sold at good prices. The Government realized $700,000 from the sale of 20,000,000 feet of spruce, fir, and other soft woods used in the manufacture of airplanes. One large sale of airplanes and engines was recorded. For $380,000 the Nebraska Aircraft Corporation of Lincoln, Nebraska, bought 280 Standard J-1 training planes without engines and 280 Hispano-Suiza engines to drive them.

To sell its surplus in the United States the Air Service set up field disposal agencies at Boston, New York, Buffalo, Chicago, Detroit, and Dayton. The property declared surplus was valued at approximately $115,000,000. Up to the present (July, 1921) goods to the value of $97,000,000 have been sold from this surplus, and there is an unsold residue valued at $18,000,000. The average recovery has been 62 per cent of the cost.

The disposition of the property acquired by the United States Spruce Production Corporation in the forests of the Pacific Northwest was delayed by the congressional investigation of the affairs of that official organization. The cost value of all salvageable property was calculated at approximately $19,000,000, of which $7,000,000 represented the cost of three railroads for hauling logs. The rest of the investment was represented by sawmills, roads, hotels and barracks for woodsmen, hoisting engines, drying kilns, and nearly 100,000 other items, among which were 22,000,000 feet of lumber produced and on hand. The lumber of commercial grades was promptly sold, and the Air Service arranged to take over the 3,088,000 feet of airplane lumber stock, for a consideration of approximately $1,000,000. The sale of the remaining property has gone on slowly, and the recovery has been low in ratio to the original cost.

The sale of surplus engineering materials brought to the Government the unusually high average recoupment of 87 per cent of the cost of manufacturing the supplies. The reason is that the largest and most valuable part of the surplus consisted of railroad construction materials and rolling stock. The railroads of the world, and particularly those of Europe, had been neglected during the war, and their rejuvenation had become a necessity even paramount to that of reconstructing general industry. Such governments as those of France and Poland were glad of the chance to secure American locomotives, cars, and cranes at the cost of their manufacture. The largest single sale of engineer supplies was made to the French Government, which paid approximately $63,000,000 for 485 freight locomotives and nearly 20,000 freight cars. By the spring of 1920 surplus engineering supplies which had cost $128,000,000 had been sold for about $110,000,000. Large quantities of excavating machinery and other contractors' equipment were transferred to the Bureau of Public Roads.

Surplus chemical warfare materials, on the other hand, proved to have low salvage value. After the armistice the Chemical Warfare Service found itself with some 1,000 carloads of surplus materials on its hands. These materials had cost $11,000,000. Of the surplus, obsolete gas masks and other accumulations valuable to no one and therefore unsalable, accounted for $2,000,000. The rest consisted principally of raw materials and machinery. Certain of its raw chemicals the Service was able to dispose of to the artificial dye industry at a profit. The outside gas-making plants attached to the Edgewood Arsenal were sold by auction to manufacturers of chemicals.

Though the sales of surplus factories, machinery, raw materials, and scrap and junk were of intense interest and concern to industry and business generally, the great masses of people in this country knew little or nothing about them. The wage earners, the millions drawing salaries of moderate range, were not beneficiaries—not immediate beneficiaries, at any rate—of the bargains the Government was offering. The trade journals were filled with advertising and reading matter about the sales of the war surpluses, but the newspapers seldom had anything to say about them. No doubt there were hundreds of thousands of Americans who, immediately after the armistice, reading about the excess stores which were overflowing the Government's enormous warehouses, expected to benefit personally and at once by the situation. It was the opportunity of a lifetime to pick up a new stock of kitchen utensils for a song, or a lawn mower, or a new Dodge car at a knock-down price, or, at least, new supplies of underclothing and other garments, or of food at figures which would make the corner grocer squirm. But as the weeks and months went by and none of these opportunities ever presented themselves, it became obvious to any thinking person that the Government itself must be in league with the profiteers and must be holding out its stocks in order to let the gouging go on without hindrance.

Those who jumped to such a conclusion were not aware of the restrictions which their own representatives, the men in Congress, had thrown about the sale of government property. Just as the law forbade (with certain exceptions and qualifications already noted in this volume) the government executives to buy supplies except from the best bidder in a competition for the business, so it forbade them to sell supplies except to the best bidder. The buyers therefore had to compete with each other for the surplus stocks, either in auction sales or by sealed bids submitted after goods had been duly described and advertised. And since the Government had its own sales expenses to consider and therefore could not hold auctions to dispose of single cans of tomatoes or advertise for bids for individual hams, the ultimate consumer, unless he were prepared to purchase by the carload, was as much out of it as if the supplies were stored on the moon.

Not until July 29, 1919, did Congress come to the relief of the ultimate consumer by passing an act authorizing the War Department to sell food, clothing, and household supplies at retail. Within ten days the Surplus Property Division (of the Division of Purchase, Storage, and Traffic, which had charge of all food, clothing, and general supplies) inaugurated a plan of direct selling by parcel post. Price lists and order blanks were sent to the 58,000 post offices of the United States, and the postmasters were instructed to receive orders and cash and send consolidated requisitions and payments to the Surplus Property Division. This plan was not a success, thanks principally to the postmasters' unfamiliarity with such work; and a few weeks later it was abandoned altogether in favor of the army retail stores. Through these stores the masses of consumers at last came into direct touch with the surplus war supplies.

The store system was established on September 25, 1919. At the stores a consumer might buy food and other supplies over the counter in such quantities as he chose; or, if he lived too far away to visit the store, he might order from it goods to be delivered by parcel post, postage prepaid and goods insured at government expense. At first the Army established twenty-five stores, and these did so well that additional stores and branches were added, until by the late winter of 1919-1920 there were seventy-seven places where consumers might go and buy, at reduced prices, the goods which their tax payments and bond purchases had enabled the Government to procure. The stores were operated under the supervision of the fourteen zone supply officers.

In selling directly to the consumer, the War Department adopted the policy of pricing goods at four-fifths of the prevalent retail market prices. Since the cost of living had begun to decline in late 1919 and the early part of 1920, this policy meant a loss to the Government, which had paid war prices for the supplies; but it was not a large loss. On the average, the retail sales brought back nearly 80 per cent of the original cost of the goods sold. The sales expenses came to about 10 per cent of the money received.

The War Department did everything in its power to make the stores attractive to the public. It stocked them with a wide range of articles and advertised them heavily. A press bureau was established in Washington, and the newspapers devoted acres of space to the publicity. In spite of the propaganda, however, the response of the public was not so unrestrained as the outcry against the costs of necessaries might have led one to expect. (To be sure, the Government, naturally, could not set up its stores in the high-rent districts—the districts most convenient to the retail customers.) The army retail stores did business at the rate of approximately $5,000,000 a month—not much for 110,000,000 potential customers. As the sales went on it became evident that, although the protest against high prices was practically universal, only the thrifty minority was willing to step across the line of convenience and custom in order to secure lower ones. The rest preferred to grumble and follow their lines of least resistance.

Yet it is probably true that the retail stores benefited all, since the continued sale of great quantities of surplus military supplies at reduced prices doubtless had an effect in bringing down commercial prices. Although only some 350 items in the Army's supply list were applicable to retail selling, this range, after all, was considerable. In the subsistence list it ran from Apples, Evaporated, to Vinegar, and in general supplies from Arctics, Cloth Top, to Whips, Artillery. The Surplus Property Division even sold a few motorcycles at the stores.

Far overshadowing the retail sales in quantities of goods moved were the sales to jobbers, dealers, and speculators, by informal bids on advertised lists of supplies. The sales headquarters in Washington and the zone offices became busy markets for months after the armistice as the War Department got rid of the surplus supplies procured by the Director of Purchase. As stated, there were regular commodity days—textiles were sold on Mondays, raw materials on Tuesdays, and so on. At the Monday sales the Surplus Property Division had taken in, by February 20, 1920, nearly $66,000,000 paid for clothing and equipage alone. These sales benefited the general public in that they usually resulted in the goods being sold at retail by salvage companies or by regular mercantile houses at reduced prices.

The fluctuations of markets sometimes made it possible for the Government to sell surplus to bidders at a profit. For instance, a ton or more of camphor, acquired originally for the Medical Department, brought a profit of 84 per cent, due to a post-armistice increase in the price of camphor. Medical supplies generally, although they were sold principally to public institutions, brought a 99-per-cent recovery of their war cost. General supplies—including hardware, kitchen utensils, brushes and brooms, rope, paper, office furniture, musical instruments, and athletic goods—sold at prices which brought back to the Government more than 72 per cent of their war cost.

Apparently useless supplies—useless to civilians, that is—were purchased by bidders who had found unique uses for them. The nonbreakable eyepieces of gas masks were found to manufacture well into motorists' goggles. The anti-dim paste used to keep the gas-mask eyepieces from fogging from the wearers' breath had a practical use upon the windshields of automobiles during rainstorms. Trench fans were bought and used as aprons for cannery workers.

Surplus leather was sold in auctions held in Philadelphia, Chicago, San Francisco, Boston, and elsewhere; and the cash recoveries generally were large, ranging from 71 per cent to 100 per cent of the war cost, and even, in instances, returning a profit. Harness did not sell well, because much of it was made of russet leather, which does not attract the commercial buyer, or else because the harnesses were of special designs not used by teamsters.

The demands of other departments of the Government for surplus army motor trucks were so great that only a few were sold as surplus, and those few were neither new nor in good condition. Automobile tires, however, were placed on sale in the retail stores.

The total sale of surplus materials acquired by the Division of Purchase, Storage, and Traffic amounted to $357,000,000 between the date of the armistice and January 31, 1920. The recovery was 77.57 per cent of the original cost.

CHAPTER XVIII

THE FOREIGN LIQUIDATION

ALTHOUGH as these words are written it is more than two and a half years since the armistice of November 11, 1918, was signed, it is still impossible to give a clean-cut and definitive statement of the accomplishments of the industrial demobilization. It may never be possible to do so. Although in the main it was possible to terminate the war contracts with supplementary agreements fixing the Government's liability to the penny, the consolidation of these agreements would not give the full cost of the termination. A few claimants are stubborn and insist upon the ultimate legal redress guaranteed them by the terms of their contracts. The administration in Washington has changed, and some few of the claims once settled—as it was believed, finally—are being reopened. And then, on the credit side of the war ledger there is the same indefiniteness. Surpluses of war supplies are indeterminate—expanding or contracting as policies change, as the military establishment finds need of materials once declared surplus, as war reserves deteriorate. Thus it is impossible to draw a line and say that all transactions on the one side should be entered in the war account and all on the other in the account of the permanent Army.

But in one important branch of our war industry there was a complete, definite liquidation. The red line was drawn and the balance struck. This was the branch in which the Allies and other foreign nations were participants, as either buyers or sellers. The promptness with which this transaction was consummated, and the completeness of it—down to the last dollar due, down to the last pound of materials exchanged—mark it as one of the outstanding accomplishments in the whole industrial record of the war. Its benefits to the countries affected are not to be read entirely in the footings of the columns of debits and offsets: rather, they are political and economic—the prestige of the United States enhanced, international good will sustained, irritation and ill feeling, which might easily have been aroused among the late Allies and their associates in the settlement of their business arrangements, avoided.

It is evident that these war transactions fell into two classes: one class in which the Allies dealt (through the American Government) with American industry for the production of supplies; the other in which the United States was the customer, and the industries of the Allies (and to a slight extent the industries of certain neutral nations) the source of supply. And, as the business of terminating the arrangements was thus a double-barreled proposition, the War Department found it convenient to attack it with two agencies: the so-called Cuthell Board (which, officially speaking, was the "Special Representative of the Secretary of War" and his assistants) and the United States Liquidation Commission.

Mr. Chester W. Cuthell was the Special Representative of the Secretary of War. His Board consisted of lawyers and accountants whom he chose and appointed. The duties of Mr. Cuthell and his Board were to terminate and settle up the war business of the Allies in the United States under those arrangements in which the War Department had been a participant, whether as agent, producer, or partner. The Board was therefore essentially the agency for liquidating the international business on this side of the Atlantic. The United States Liquidation Commission, on the other hand, was the agency created to liquidate America's war industry abroad; and this was much the greater of the two tasks. The United States Liquidation Commission was charged, also, with an added duty: that of disposing of all American surplus military property on foreign soil.

We must think of both these activities in international demobilization as going on simultaneously, as they did. The two agencies were created almost at the same time: Mr. Cuthell was appointed on January 22, 1919, and the United States Liquidation Commission was created on the following February 11. Also it was necessary that they both work in the closest contact and coöperation with each other, since the arrangements of both would have to come together in the final settlements, the American claims against the Allies, as substantiated by the Board, going to offset the Allied claims against us, as acknowledged by the Liquidation Commission. This liaison and harmony existed. The coöperation, too, extended to the adoption of certain broad policies which were to be followed by both in liquidating the business. One of these, and perhaps the most important one, was that, in the negotiations that were to follow, no nation should expect to profit at the expense of any of the others. The settlements should be made on the basis of actual cost. A second policy was that international agreements and understandings, even though they had never been committed formally to writing, were to have the binding force of formal contracts. In other words, the business would be settled as among partners and friends, no one of whom wished to take advantage of the others.

Upon both liquidating agencies bore the need for haste in terminating the business. Armies were demobilizing, *personnel* familiar with the subjects in negotiation melting away. If the discussions were to be long protracted they would take on the aspect of contentions, with evidence and affidavits to be secured, inventories and audits taken, hearings conducted, examination and cross-examination of witnesses, causes perhaps finally going into international tribunals or before commissions of arbitration. Nothing but ill feeling could result from such an outcome. The international business relations had become enormously intricate during the war. It was obviously an impractical thing to go into details, as a creditor might attack the schedules of a bankrupt corporation. Such procedure would drag along for years. It was to the advantage of every party to the transactions, the parties being sovereign nations having regard for their international contacts, to give and take in rough bargaining, accepting estimates and lump sums rather than insisting upon items and particulars, and finally to agree to totals which at the best would be only approximations. The important thing was to get the business over with justice done to all.

That was the spirit in which both boards worked.

Mr. Cuthell, upon his appointment, found in the Division of Purchase, Storage, and Traffic a consolidated and condensed record of every claim held by the War Department against the governments associated with us in the war. This showed him the field. He discovered, however, that none of the war missions maintained by the Allies in the United States was vested with power to adjust and settle these claims, many of which were disputed. Therefore, while his hastily gathered force of experts was preparing the claims for presentation, Mr. Cuthell himself (in April, 1919) was sent to Europe to ask the foreign governments concerned to create liquidating agencies competent to deal with the United States and, further, to retain in their respective services, until the liquidation should be effected, the officers familiar with the American transactions.

It should be noted here that this was a wide departure from international precedent. Ordinarily, financial claims between nations are settled by the slow and cumbersome processes of diplomatic interchange, or else by arbitration. To have allowed the war claims to go into this channel would possibly have meant the end of the amity between the Allies and the United States. Our liquidation agencies proposed direct dealing through business plenipotentiaries, with restrictions even less exacting than would be drawn by two private corporations.

In Paris Mr. Cuthell found representatives of Italy prepared to discuss the American claims against Italy. Soon after the conferences started, however, President Wilson made public at the Peace Conference his attitude toward the Italian occupation of the Adriatic port of Fiume; and the Italian delegation, including those ready to negotiate a business settlement with us, withdrew from Paris.

Mr. Cuthell thereupon went to London to negotiate with the British. The British Government appointed and empowered a special commission, headed by Lord Inverforth, then the British Minister of Munitions, and including several eminent representatives of the British Government, among them Mr. W. T. Layton, a man of unusual ability and the one who took the actual lead for the British in the subsequent negotiations, to deal with the American claims. Meanwhile Mr. Cuthell's principal assistants had arrived from the United States, bringing with them the now formulated statements analyzing the British war business in America and setting forth what our negotiators regarded as the proper charges for the British to pay in settlement. These assistants were Mr. Ralph W. Gwinn, who was to present the Liberty engine case; Mr. Miller D. Steever, in charge of the airplane lumber claim; and Mr. F. C. Weems, who had prepared the smokeless powder and cotton linters cases. The conferences began immediately, and such was the progress made that within ten days a complete agreement was reached, and the British war business in the United States was definitely terminated. The so-called Cuthell-Inverforth Agreement, which embodied the terms of settlement, was dated May 10, 1919.

The agreement, reached so speedily and with such complete mutual accord, terminated a vast business within the United States. From the United States as dealer, Great Britain had procured smokeless powder, picric acid, airplane lumber, and Liberty engines. As a partner of the United States, Great Britain participated in the pool of cotton linters which cornered the entire American supply for the benefit of the powder mills. England was also a partner with us in the project to build a chain of chemical factories in America to produce acetone, used in making dope for airplane wings. These factories never came into production, and the project was closed out with a loss of over $6,000,000, half of which loss the British were bound to share. We participated with England in the purchase of Australasian wool. The terms under which the wool contract was closed out were noted in a previous chapter of this volume.

The celerity with which these complicated war transactions

were terminated was a distinct triumph in international negotiation. The British, when they entered the conferences, probably had no idea that they were to be rushed through to any such speedy conclusion. The conferences, in fact, began as if they were to drag along for an extended time. On the first day Mr. Gwinn gave a careful and clear exposition of the Liberty engine case, setting forth in detail just what we had done and to what extent the British ought to participate in the costs. Although, whenever any of his figures were challenged, the American delegation proceeded then and there to make adjustments apparently to the satisfaction of the British commissioners, yet when Mr. Gwinn had concluded, the Americans were unable to gain from the British any expression of opinion as to whether the total would be accepted, at least tentatively, as the British obligation. It was evident that the British expected to prepare and, later on, press an argument against the American statement. If this procedure were to be followed throughout the negotiations, it would be many weeks before the conferees could reach any final agreement.

This outcome of the first day's negotiation was a disappointment to the Americans, but they determined to try again next day. The next morning Mr. Steever took up the airplane lumber case, and talked for nearly four hours. He went into a description of the picturesque phases of the northwestern lumbering enterprise—the felling of the spruce trees, the steel cables on which the great trunks slid down the mountain sides, the railroads built into hitherto inaccessible wildernesses. But punctuating his rhetoric were the hard figures of costs, expenditures, losses, deliveries, and values. The British had shared in this whole enterprise in the Pacific Northwest, the development of which had never reached the stage of turning out the airplane lumber at low prices. As Mr. Steever talked he invited interruption and objection, and the British delegates availed themselves of the invitation. The various objections were resolved as the case was unfolded. At the conclusion Mr. Cuthell asked for any further objections to the statement. But the British had exhausted their challenges during the presentation of the claim. The only objection raised was to British participation in the cost of certain dry kilns in which the export airplane lumber was not treated. This item was promptly subtracted from the claim's total, and then Mr. Cuthell briefly urged that the column's footing be accepted tentatively as the British obligation. If not to the surprise of the Americans, certainly to their extreme gratification, the British commission agreed.

That was the real victory, for it set the precedent for the entire settlement. Each day the Americans presented a new case; and each evening when the American representatives left the Hotel Metropole in London, where the conferences were held, a tentative agreement in that case had been reached. Finally all the claims were settled tentatively, except the Liberty engine claim. Once more the Americans pressed to have the original statement accepted, and it was. It was understood, however, that all figures were to be subject to verification by a British audit of the books of the War Department in Washington.

On the tenth day the Americans brought to the Metropole a tentative written agreement, embodying all the sub-settlements agreed upon. Mr. Cuthell then pointed out the considerable cost of a British audit of our books, the possibilities of friction arising over the presence of British auditors in our War Department over an extended period, and the likelihood, since all the American estimates were conservative, that the audit would not in any event greatly change the amount of the British obligation and might even increase it; and he suggested that it would be good policy for the British to accept the tentative figure as final and let it go at that. Lord Inverforth promptly agreed. That was cricket, as the English say.

The agreement fixed the cash liability of the British Government for its unpaid American war bills and its obligations arising from the termination of its American contracts and engagements at $35,464,823.10. Of this the Liberty engine item was the largest item—approximately $14,000,000. The British paid over $13,000,000 to satisfy all claims of the

United States arising from the British purchases of airplane spruce, fir, and cedar. Its powder contracts accounted for nearly $4,700,000 of the settlement sum, wood distillates (principally acetone) for about $2,900,000, and its 2-per-cent share in the linters pool for the rest.

Practically all the settlements made by the Cuthell Board were carried as offsets to the American liabilities under the general foreign liquidation accomplished by the United States Liquidation Commission; but the British preferred to make their settlements separate transactions. Accordingly, on August 2, 1919, a representative of the British Treasury delivered to the War Department a check in payment of the British obligation under the terms of the Cuthell-Inverforth Agreement. This, however, was not a complete termination for Great Britain. That Government admitted full liability under numerous other, but small, claims which the War Department had not yet had time to prepare in detail. As invoices were subsequently presented to the British Government, these claims were promptly paid. The minor cases came to approximately $7,000,000.

Progress almost equally swift was made by the Cuthell Board in securing a settlement of the American claims against France. At first there was no official French agency empowered to make such a settlement. Mr. Cuthell and his assistants proceeded immediately to Paris after making the British agreement and importuned the French Government to designate a representative competent to conclude a settlement. There they were joined by Messrs. Charles B. Shelton, William Fisher, John H. Ray, Jr., and Harry A. Fisher, who brought with them from Washington the formulated statements of various American claims against the French. After several days' delay Premier Clemenceau appointed the French Liquidation Commission, headed by M. Édouard de Billy, who had been with the French High Commission in Washington during the war and was therefore familiar with the French contracts in the United States. To France the War Department had sold picric acid, cotton linters, smokeless powder, airplane lumber, and Liberty engines. The French liability in these cases was finally fixed at $95,968,561.87, and a formal agreement admitting the liability was signed on May 29, 1919. There were other considerable claims against France, the statements of which had not yet been prepared. Later (September 9, 1919) Mr. Cuthell came to an agreement with M. Casenave, minister plenipotentiary of France in the United States, whereby the French admitted an additional liability of $64,910,352.92. Of this sum, $38,000,000 represented ocean freight charges upon war supplies bought by France in the United States and carried to France in American army cargo transports.

Two additional settlements with France, one terminating the French contract with J. G. White & Company for raw materials for airplane manufacture and the other terminating the French contract with the General Vehicle Company for the production of Gnome rotary airplane engines, increased the French liability by $2,117,785.34. These settlements were made in France by Mr. Monte Appel, chief assistant to Mr. Cuthell. The total liability arising from the American war business of France was therefore $162,996,700.13. This sum went into the general settlement agreement made with the French by the United States Liquidation Commission.

Soon after the French settlement was a fact, the Italian Government appointed a commission to treat with the Cuthell Board. The Italian agreement, dated August 13, 1919, admitted an obligation on the part of Italy in the sum of $5,200,000, representing Italian war purchases of picric acid, smokeless powder, airplane lumber, linters, and trinitrotoluol, this agreement not including an admitted obligation of approximately $395,000 for Liberty engines, clothing, and other small items not yet invoiced. Against this obligation Italy presented a claim for $4,053,073 for the overseas transportation of American troops on Italian ships. The Italian Government paid the difference, namely, $1,146,927 to the War Department on September 26, 1919, and also paid the minor claims as they were presented.

Minor claims against the governments of Belgium, Brazil,

Canada, Cuba, and Czecho-Slovakia, to the total of $4,709,-330.89, were presented by the Cuthell Board and paid by the governments concerned.

While the Cuthell Board was engaged in rendering the bills to the Allies for supplies purchased by them in America and collecting the money on those bills,—and here let it be said that the collections were greater in aggregate amount than the total sum involved in all the claims for or against the United States prosecuted or resisted by the nation's official diplomacy from the beginning of our national existence up to the outbreak of the war in Europe; international transactions which included the Louisiana Purchase, the purchase of Alaska, and the purchase of the Canal Zone,—all the while that Mr. Cuthell and his associates were collecting money for Uncle Sam, the United States Liquidation Commission was busy adjusting the fit of the shoe on the old gentleman's other foot. In other words, the Commission was paying the war bills owed by the United States to the Allies. This was a business equally great and even more important.

There was some question whether the President, with all his war powers, could legally empower boards and commissions to conclude international settlements involving the passing of money, since such power resided only in the State Department, the acts of which had to be ratified by Congress before they were binding upon the United States. The Cuthell Board and the United States Liquidation Commission were actually created in January and February, 1919; but to remove any doubt as to the binding force of their settlements, Congress, on March 2, 1919, passed an act empowering the Secretary of War to settle, through any agency he might set up, all international war claims in which the War Department was involved.

The Secretary of War appointed Mr. Edwin B. Parker chairman of the United States Liquidation Commission. As members he appointed Brigadier General Charles G. Dawes, Mr. Homer H. Johnson, and Hon. Henry F. Hollis. During the active part of the war Judge Parker had held the important post of priorities commissioner of the War Industries Board. General Dawes, in private life a Chicago banker, had been General Purchasing Agent of the A. E. F. In 1920 he sprang into national prominence when, as a witness before a congressional investigating committee, in vigorous and unconventional style he defended the material transactions of the A. E. F. and denounced those critics who, in searching for waste and lavish expenditure, evidently overlooked the fact that the prime purpose of the A. E. F. was to defeat a dangerous enemy on the field of battle. His striking utterances on that occasion did more than reams of printed propaganda to reconcile the American public to the inevitable wastes of the war. President Harding soon afterwards appointed "Hell and Maria" Dawes, as he had come to be known, federal budget commissioner, thus placing him in charge of the most important attempt at economy in national expenditures which the United States had ever made. Mr. Johnson was an able and well-known lawyer of Cleveland. Mr. Hollis was a former United States senator from New Hampshire.

When the Liquidation Commission reached France and organized for work about March 1, 1919, it found the ground well prepared for it. Mr. Edward R. Stettinius, the well-known New York financier, had been sent to France in July, 1918, as a special representative of the Secretary of War to act as a sort of surveyor-general over the war industry resulting from the foreign orders placed by the American Expeditionary Forces. Mr. Stettinius found that a considerable part of the munitions being procured abroad was being produced and delivered under informal and more or less vague agreements and understandings. Before the armistice Mr. Stettinius had done his best to reduce some of the more important of these understandings to the form of written, definite contracts. Promptly after the armistice he took steps to cancel all further production for the Americans and then began the negotiations leading to the settlements. Mr. Stettinius resigned in January, 1919, and the United States Liquidation Commission inherited these various negotiations in the stages at which Mr. Stettinius left them.

Although, as we have said, the characteristic note of our industrial demobilization abroad was outright cancellation of contracts and the payment of indemnities, the policy was not maintained consistently. There were several important exceptions, and one of these was the method adopted in terminating the British manufacture of artillery and shell for the A. E. F. The numerous orders, contracts, and agreements placed and made by the A. E. F. for the delivery of British artillery and ammunition were consolidated, on October 19, 1918, by Mr. Stettinius in conference with Mr. Winston Churchill, then the British Minister of Munitions, into a single formal agreement. In terminating this contract after the armistice Mr. Stettinius assumed that it would be better to accept completed guns and ammunition, even though these might be surplus above the future requirements of the Army, than to pay heavy cancellation indemnities and receive nothing in return. Artillery does not deteriorate rapidly, either materially or in design. The negotiations opened by Mr. Stettinius with the British Government looking to this end were picked up by the Liquidation Commission, which, in March, 1919, reached an agreement with the British that, in lieu of paying any cancellation damages, the United States would accept a limited quantity of *matériel* completed after the armistice under the American contract.

America accordingly accepted the post-armistice delivery of 498 British-made guns, ranging in model from 60-pounders to 8-inch howitzers, and 420,000 rounds of ammunition for them. For this *matériel* the American Government paid £6,637,598.

A most interesting negotiation conducted by the Liquidation Commission for the United States was that which wound up the tripartite international project for the construction of 36-ton tanks, better known as the Anglo-American Mark VIII tanks. France was originally a party to this transaction only to the extent of agreeing to provide a site for the assembling plant in France. England and the United States were equal partners in the enterprise, England supplying hulls and guns and America the power and traction. The French, however, were to be permitted to buy tanks at the partnership price; but the French at first did not ask for any, asserting that their own light tank production was sufficient for them.

The plant was built at Châteauroux, Neuvy-Pailloux. About the time the project was getting well under way, heavier tanks began to demonstrate their effectiveness in the field; and then France insisted that, because her armies held the most front-line mileage, the most of the Anglo-American tanks to be built at the Châteauroux plant should be allotted to her. Reluctantly the British agreed that the first 1,200 tanks should be divided equally between France and the United States and that France should receive all of the next 300.

Then the war ended. About 24,000,000 francs had been invested at Châteauroux. The British had spent £3,000,000 in the manufacture of components and the Americans a like sum, expressed in dollars. France had not put in a centime; yet she had expected to receive nine-sixteenths of the first year's output. The question was, what share of the heavy loss should France stand? The French arrangement with the Tank Commission was tantamount to a contract, with the British-American partnership standing in the light of contractor. It was evident, then, that the French were morally bound to pay cancellation charges—to stand part of the loss, in other words. The British and American negotiators at London thought it would be about right if France would pay back the 24,000,000 francs expended by the British and Americans at Châteauroux, and the British and Americans would throw in the tank plant itself as an inducement.

Then the question arose, how would this 24,000,000 francs be divided? Both England and America had lost heavily in the big-tank enterprise—each had, in fact, agreed to let these losses balance each other; neither was to bill the other for anything in the settlement—and here seemed to be the chance to get some of the money back. Naturally, the Americans assumed that the French reimbursement would be divided equally, since both America and England had contributed equally to the cost of the Châteauroux plant. But no, the British contended; since they had surrendered their share of the first year's production of tanks, the lion's share of the reimbursement should go to them. There was logic in this, but, without deciding the point, both sides repaired to Paris to present their joint tank claim to the French; and then it appeared that the British and Americans had been dividing some French chickens before they were hatched. Through M. Louis Loucheur, the Minister of Munitions, the French Government metaphorically lifted its eyebrows in surprise that its associates could present such a claim. To be sure, the French expected to take the Anglo-American heavy tanks, but so did the Americans and British expect to receive light tanks from the French industry. These were merely understandings, not formal contracts; and the French, to do their share, had made large expenditures in developing the light-tank manufacture for the benefit of all. Needless to say, the French Government had lost heavily in terminating its tank industry. These national losses should set off each other. . . .

The British and American representatives retired to ponder this rejoinder. It seemed to have merit; yet the fact remained that somehow or other France was evidently going to emerge from the tank discussion with the Châteauroux plant in her possession. The delegates returned and argued with such force that the French Government agreed to pay 20,000,000 francs in settlement, taking over the Châteauroux plant.* Since the salvage value of this plant was estimated at 5,000,000 francs, the sum of 15,000,000 francs was considered as the indemnity paid by France. England then asked for five-sixths of the total payment, but the American argument scaled this down to 70 per cent. America thus received 6,000,000 francs out of the settlement.

The bargaining Yankees, however, were yet to have the final word in the tank deal. With the settlement complete, sealed

* The French Government later converted the plant into a railroad car repair shop.

and delivered, the British had on their hands 105 sets of tank parts with only junk value, although it had cost the British £5,000 a set to manufacture them. The Americans offered £1,000 a set for these parts, and the British snapped at the offer. This fine bargain enabled us later, at low cost, to assemble these parts with the American-built components and thus place in the war reserves 100 of the largest and most formidable tanks ever built.

Another, a minor, tank transaction should be noted. The British Army had supplied, during the action, sixty-four tanks of various sorts to the 301st Tank Battalion of the A. E. F. Fifty of these, some of them more or less damaged, had been returned to the British after the armistice, and the remaining fourteen were shipped to the United States. For the purchase of the fourteen and for the war use of the other fifty, the Liquidation Commission agreed to pay the British Government the sum of £189,233 2s 11d.

Outside the claims for payment for materials actually delivered, the British pressed upon the Liquidation Commission collateral claims of several sorts. One of these was for interest upon money invested by the British in stocks of goods destined for American consumption. Our people protested successfully against paying interest upon such investments, but admitted the point that we should pay interest after the goods had been delivered and we had been billed, allowing a reasonable interest-free period for vouchering and checking. Investigation showed that both armies had been dilatory in paying their bills to each other, and that the average time of delaying payment had been five months and a quarter. The British bills against America exceeded the American bills against England by some £51,000,000. One month and a half was allowed as a reasonable interest-free period after billing. Accordingly the commission agreed to pay 5-per-cent interest on the British billing excess, a sum which amounted to £797,854 11s 2d, and this America paid.*

* This sum was much more than offset in our favor by the decline in sterling exchange during the time bills were unpaid.

It was impossible for the Liquidation Commission to make a lump settlement of all the minor bills, accounts, and claims of Great Britain against America, because of the difficulties in securing full statements of the indebtedness. It was roughly estimated, however, that these claims would aggregate £10,000,000.

One obscure and involved problem for the Commission to solve related to the so-called British "hidden losses" on steel products sold to the United States during the war. The British treatment and control of its war prices differed radically in method from ours. The War Industries Board, it will be remembered, fixed prices high enough to stimulate production and then held the industries to those prices, no matter to whom they sold. The British plan was an opposite one. With steel, for instance, the British Government simply monopolized the raw materials and sold them to the producers at prices that represented a loss to the Government. In effect, it was a subsidy. To the British public it made no difference whether it paid this subsidy or an equal amount in the increased cost of artillery, ammunition, and other munitions made of steel. But when it came to a settlement between England and the United States, the British Government insisted that the United States was not fairly entitled to the "manufacturers' issues" price for the raw steel that went into the British-made munitions supplied to America. The British, therefore, after the main settlements, presented a supplementary claim to compensate for the hidden loss, and this claim amounted approximately to £3,770,000.

In principle, the Commission was willing to admit the force of the British contention. It asked the British, however, to prepare a more definite statement, showing (1) the average British governmental loss on all steel supplied to manufacturers for the year preceding the armistice, (2) the amount of such steel that went into products sold to America, and, finally, (3) the hidden loss on all steel furnished to America as thus estimated. When the revised statement was presented, it was found to contain items of hidden loss which America could not possibly allow. The British war subsidies went all through their war industry. For instance, in order to stimulate production, the British Government had paid subsidies to the makers of silica brick, used in building steel furnaces. The British asked us to stand a part of this subsidy, inasmuch as some of the shell supplied to us had been produced from furnaces built of subsidized brick. The Commission retorted by asking why Great Britain did not also ask us to share the subsidy on the bread the British steel workers had eaten while they were working on the American artillery and shell orders. In other words, we were willing to pay hidden losses so long as they were not too remotely connected with the American contracts. The Commission also raised the shrewd question, why, since the British were asking us to pay for hidden losses, they did not admit us to the benefits of their "hidden profits"—*viz.*, the profit taxes collected from the British steel manufacturers.

In the autumn of 1920 General G. W. Burr, the Director of Purchase, Storage, and Traffic after the armistice and a member of the War Department Claims Board, went to England to close up all the outstanding claims existing between the United States and Great Britain as a result of the war. The outcome of his negotiations was the Burr-Niemeyer Agreement, which tied up all loose ends and brought about a final termination of the war business between the two nations. All pending claims were brought into one lump-sum settlement, under the terms of which the United States paid to Great Britain the sum of £2,946,511 2s 8d. This sum settled all the miscellaneous and minor claims noted above; settled, too, the debt owed by the United States to the British for the maintenance of our Siberian Expedition; and settled all other claims, including the hidden-loss claim and a British claim for reimbursement for various "overhead" inspection and storage charges. The settlement figure was much under what the British had originally claimed. In this settlement the hidden-loss and "overhead" claims were paired in a single item which accounted for approximately £1,500,000 of the total paid by the United States. The Burr-Niemeyer Agreement was dated November 23, 1920.

One general claim set up by the British Government against the United States the Liquidation Commission rejected. After we had paid to Great Britain the bill rendered for the transportation of our troops and supplies in England, the British Government rendered a supplementary bill for the same services. During the war Great Britain gave guaranties of income to the British railways, and in settling with the railroads the British Government granted to them an increase in military passenger rates, an increase which was retroactive to April 1, 1919. The British asked us to pay our share of the retroactive increase. This was refused on the ground that by the same token we could hold the British to their share of the loss sustained by the American Government in its operation of the American railroads by the United States Railroad Administration, since our roads had hauled great quantities of British supplies. To open up closed settlements because of retroactive agreements would open up a Pandora's box of troubles for both nations.

Thus the international bargaining went on, back and forth, give and take, broad principles of settlement prevailing rather than the minute and individual merits of particular items, both sides accepting estimates and unaudited totals and each relying upon the good faith of the other. Thus this tremendously involved and intricate business was closed up with dispatch and amiability. As a rule the A. E. F. in its purchases had dealt with governments, with which such liquidation methods could be adopted; but there were a few relatively small contracts made directly with private individuals in England, France, Italy, Portugal, Spain, and Switzerland. These contracts were canceled outright in the full knowledge that we should have to pay indemnities. In the settlement of such contracts the United States Liquidation Commission acted for the A. E. F. much as the War Department Claims Board did for the producing bureaus at home—as a supervisory body, approving the settlements made by the various services of the A. E. F. and paying off the contractors. In all, indemnities were paid for the cancellation of some 450 contracts in Europe. In making these settlements, the United States benefited greatly by the depreciated rates of exchange against the currencies of several of these nations, since all indemnities were paid by the United States in the currency of the countries in which the claims arose. Expressed in dollars at par, it cost the United States $3,568,653.23 to cancel the miscellaneous European contracts, but the reduced exchange rates effected a considerable saving under that figure.

It is much easier to detect the failings and peculiarities of aliens than it is to recognize our own shortcomings; and if in these pages we have exulted somewhat over the successes of our delegates in checkmating the designs of our European associates, this is not to be taken as any boast that we ourselves were too disinterested and altruistic to overlook the main chance for ourselves. The truth is that, although all the belligerents were in the field primarily to win a victory of arms, not one of them entirely lost contact with the counting room. This was clearly shown in the American arrangements for the supply of French artillery.

The numerical expansion of the A. E. F. in the spring and summer of 1918 resulted in a greatly increased demand by the A. E. F. for French artillery and ammunition. America supplied schedules of the raw materials which she could furnish, and the French made estimates of the numbers of guns they could deliver monthly to the A. E. F. But this was all understanding and mutual agreement—no formal contract was drawn. When Mr. Stettinius reached Paris in the summer of 1918, he immediately began to press to get this agreement down in black and white, so that America might know exactly what her obligations were. At that time, of course, there was no thought that the war would end within the year. About the 1st of November, however, it became evident that an armistice was drawing near, and immediately the Americans grew lukewarm on the subject of a formal contract. The reason was evident. Under the terms of a formal contract, America's termination obligations would be questions of fact; with the affair left as an unwritten agreement, our obligations would be questions of equity, to be negotiated, and we were likely to emerge from such negotiations in better case financially than we should be if held by the set and rigid conditions of a formal contract.

Nevertheless, the United States did not seek to evade its just obligations under the French ordnance agreement. France had spent large sums of money in expanding the industry to take care of the expected American consumption, and the money so spent was a proper charge against the United States in any settlement. Immediately after the armistice Mr. Stettinius ordered production stopped on our orders; but this the French, for domestic, social, and economic reasons, were unable to do; and at first they were inclined to insist that we should accept and pay for a large quantity of artillery produced during a gradual termination of the industry. Mr. Stettinius successfully maintained the position that this post-armistice production was undertaken purely in pursuance of an internal policy of the French Government and that by no stretch of logic could it be entered as a proper war charge against the United States. Mr. Stettinius then went on to conduct the settlement negotiations, and these were about complete when the Liquidation Commission arrived to inherit the transaction and to draw the final settlement contract.

As in the settlement of the British artillery contract, the American negotiators accepted guns and ammunition produced after the armistice by the French; and they did it in complete consistency with the position and policy defined in the preceding paragraph. The armistice found great numbers of French guns in process of manufacture for the A. E. F. The United States was obligated to accept and pay for this unfinished material. After the inventory of it had been taken, the Liquidation Commission suggested that in lieu of the unfinished parts the United States accept their value in full completions and that the production of all other guns be canceled without charge to the United States. This alternative, allowing, as it did, a measure of post-armistice production in the French mills, the French Government quickly accepted and, in carrying out the terms of the subsequent settlement contract, delivered to the United States 944 75-millimeter gun units, 700 155-millimeter howitzer units, and 198 155-millimeter gun units, all with limbers and with additional parts as spares. For these the United States paid 117,501,887.45 francs.

The French agreed to a similar plan in canceling the construction of airplanes and engines for the United States. This construction had been undertaken under a formal contract, signed by General Pershing. The contract contained no cancellation clause, but the French Government had provided for cancellation in its subcontracts with the French producers. Under the terms of the contract large numbers of airplane cellules (airplanes without engines), engines, and other aëronautical supplies were in production on the day of the armistice. In lieu of unfinished parts, the French agreed to deliver their equivalent (in value) in finished equipment. Under a preliminary agreement the United States acknowledged a cancellation debt of 167,667,761 francs. Of this, about 23,000,000 francs represented cancellation charges and the rest money to be paid for completed materials, the schedule of which included 3,568 cellules and 3,979 engines. This preliminary agreement, however, was modified later by the French Liberty engine settlement negotiated by the Cuthell Board. Under this settlement France agreed to accept and pay for Liberty engines still to be delivered, to the value of $19,530,000, and in addition to pay nearly $2,000,000 in cancellation indemnities.

This, then, was the situation. We were bound to accept and pay for a large number of French airplanes and engines which we did not need. The French were bound to accept and pay for a large number of Liberty engines which they did not need. We could, however, use some of the French planes and engines, and the French wanted 500 Liberty engines. Therefore we agreed to deliver the 500 engines and to accept French materials up to their value, and then to offset the excess number of Liberties provided for in the engine settlement agreement against the excess of French air materials named in the French aircraft settlement contract. This left a surplus of Liberty engines with the A. E. F., but these were delivered to the British to fulfill our obligations under the British Liberty engine settlement; and a few of the engines were sold to Poland.

The settlement with France for our use of her railroads during the war was so complicated that it would not be profitable to go into the details here. The intricacy of the problem was due to the fact that, while 2,000,000 Americans in France had used the French railroads for every transportation need,—and our forces fought farther from their expeditionary bases than did any other army in France,—we, in turn, had supplied to the French railroads locomotives, cars, crews, repairing, coal, track construction, and many other items. The Liquidation Commission itself did not attempt to go into these details, but turned the whole transaction over to a special section headed by Colonel F. A. Delano, the Deputy Director General of Transportation for the A. E. F., who had formerly been president of the Wabash Railroad and a member of the Federal Reserve Board. The upshot of the settlement was that we acknowledged a debt to France of 434,985,399.73 francs after all our claims had been set off against the French claim.

The United States Liquidation Commission agreed to pay to the French Government the sum of 3,000,000 francs for port dues assessed against our vessels for their use of French ports during the war.

When these and other subsidiary questions of settlement had been decided and the proper credits established by agreement in each instance, the United States Liquidation Commission took up the task of a general blanket settlement of the business relations between France and the United States during the war. This was a long and involved work; but, since the major items in the settlement had already been determined, there was little difficulty in securing an agreement. The General Settlement was dated November 25, 1919. It embraced all transactions between the two nations from April 6, 1917, to August 20, 1919, except (1) France's purchases of our surplus military property, (2) the railroad transportation and the port dues settlements noted above, and (3) France's claim arising from the overseas transportation of American troops in French transports. The sum total of the other claims showed that the United States owed France 1,488,619,027.52 francs and that France owed the United States $177,149,866.86. The rate of exchange and form of payment were left to future negotiations by the United States Treasury; but, assuming that francs were worth ten to the dollar, the net balance in favor of the United States was about $28,000,000.

We are not yet ready, however, to determine the net financial result of the international war business relations in which America was a participant. There was still the money to be realized from the sale of our surplus military property abroad. It will be remembered that one of the two functions of the United States Liquidation Commission was to dispose of the expeditionary property. Out of the sales transactions arose the largest single credit to the account of the United States on the international ledger: the proceeds from the bulk sale of A. E. F. installations and supplies to the French Government.

The arguments sustaining the wisdom of a bulk sale of the expeditionary property have already been sufficiently rehearsed in this volume. The first step on our part leading to the negotiations was to take an inventory of the entire property. The difficulty encountered then may be deduced from the fact that the French and the British, whose surpluses were not inordinately greater than ours, never even attempted such an inventory of their own property. The A. E. F. was a going concern, continually drawing from the stocks on hand, and its *personnel* was shifting and diminishing. Nevertheless, by a strong force of men, under the direction of Colonel J. H. Graham, Engineer Corps, in six weeks of day and night work, such an inventory was taken, the property being divided into eighteen categories, as follows: 1. Clothing and textiles; 2. Subsistence supplies; 3. Kitchen utensils and household furnishings; 4. Machinery, metals, tools, and hardware; 5. Building materials; 6. Forest products; 7. Railway and dock equipment; 8. Transport equipment (trucks, motor cars, motorcycles, wagons, horses and mules, etc.); 9. Hospital supplies, toilet supplies, and chemicals; 10. Photographic, measuring, and musical instruments; 11. Electrical equipment; 12. Oils, gasoline, and paints; 13. Ordnance and gas-warfare equipment; 14. Blasting apparatus and supplies; 15. Printing machinery and supplies; 16. Office fixtures, stationery, and supplies; 17. Hides and leather; 18. Aëronautical equipment.

These eighteen categories included only the movable property of the A. E. F. There were still to be considered the fixed installations—the barracks, camps, hospitals, warehouses, docks, railroad yards, buildings of almost every conceivable type. Judge Parker, the chairman of the Commission, cabled to France, before he sailed for Europe, a direction that the installations be inventoried and appraised. This work was first undertaken by Colonel Graham, who later, after he took charge of the inventory of movables, was succeeded by Brigadier General Edgar Jadwin, whose subsequent appraisal was known as the Jadwin Report. It showed the war cost of construction to have been $165,661,000, the normal cost $81,543,000, and the armistice value $39,256,000. As a matter of fact, any sum obtainable for the installations was clear gain, since the salvage value of the structures would not have paid the cost of dismantling (assuming that this work would have required the labor of 40,000 men for seven months), the ground rentals, and the costs of restoring the sites to their original condition.

Then arose the determination of the "utilization value" of the movable stocks. This was estimated by taking the war cost of production, plus the cost of freighting the goods to France, and subtracting various estimated allowances—for natural deterioration, for expected losses from fire, theft, and other causes, for the saving to the United States in costs of merchandizing, labor, storage, insurance, interest on investment, and other overhead expense obviated by a possible bulk sale, for the fact that the stocks were widely scattered and had to be collected to be of use. The Commission consolidated these sub-

Photo by Howard E. Coffin

WRECK OF COAL MINE AT LENS

Photo by Signal Corps

MOTOR TRANSPORT SALVAGE IN FRANCE

From a photograph taken in France

INTERALLIED PURCHASERS

Left to right: Louis Loucheur, French Minister of Munitions; Winston Churchill, British Minister of Munitions; David Lloyd-George, Prime Minister of England; and Bernard M. Baruch, Chairman of the War Industries Board.

tractions into a lump deduction of 25 per cent of the estimated value. Thus determined, the utilization value of both installations and movables was set at $562,230,800; and this was the figure carried by the Commission into the negotiations with the French.

The French Government designated M. Paul Morel, the French Undersecretary of Finance for the Liquidation of War Stocks, to represent it in the negotiations with the Commission. On April 7, 1919, it was agreed in principle that France would buy the American *installations*, at any rate, at a price still to be fixed, the French assuming all charges and claims against the installations. The French were not so sure about the movables. M. Morel first proposed that the French Government pick out what it wanted and negotiate a price for the selection. But this would have skimmed the cream of the American property and left the A. E. F. with large quantities of unsalable materials which in all likelihood would eventually have become fuel for bonfires. This proposal was therefore rejected, and the French representatives were urged as a duty to buy all the movables in bulk, since the French people could use practically all the supplies. M. Morel, after consultation with his principals, eventually agreed to buy all the stocks at a price to be fixed.

Came the question then of the price. M. Morel's first bid was 1,500,000,000 francs. Reckoning the value of francs then at ten to the dollar, that was an offer of $150,000,000, an offer firmly rejected. This was followed by other offers which our representatives could not entertain. The negotiations, which had begun early in April, continued throughout the spring and the fore part of the summer. M. André Tardieu and other eminent Frenchmen entered the conferences in July. On July 24 a tentative agreement was reached, and its terms were practically those of the bulk-sale contract, which was dated August 1, 1919.

France paid $400,000,000 for the property, the United States accepting in payment interest-bearing 10-year French bonds. Not all the property listed in the original inventory was involved in the sale. America made certain exceptions: (1) all animals (these were sold separately for a total of $29,016,-506.59); (2) supplies previously sold out of the surplus stocks to France herself and other buyers to the value of $77,265,-597.83; (3) military equipment returned to the United States, valued at $15,000,000; (4) supplies needed for the maintenance of the remnant of the A. E. F., worth $4,000,000; and (5) supplies worth $10,000,000 turned over to the American Red Cross as a gift. Thus, the utilization value of the original inventory was scaled down by these subtractions to approximately $427,000,000, and for this quantity the French Government paid $400,000,000—a fair return. It should be noted that in paying this price the French Government also canceled its claim for the payment of customs duties on the goods, and a conservative estimate placed the aggregate amount of these unpaid duties at $150,000,000. An even greater benefit to us was the fact that by the terms of the settlement France assumed all land claims which might otherwise have been pressed upon the United States by French nationals for years to come.

The bulk sale to France was the largest single transaction in the disposition of the A. E. F. surplus; but there were many other sales, some of them large. Goods went in these transactions to the governments of the Allies (France herself, outside the general sale, being a purchaser to the extent of $95,000,-000), to individuals, companies, and syndicates in western Europe, to relief societies, to coöperative societies in the Balkans (these, being the economic organization of whole peoples, were not affected by political changes and sometimes seemed to have greater stability than the new governments themselves), to the governments of the so-called "liberated nations," and to other purchasers. Although the United States Liquidation Commission made every effort to keep each transaction on the dollar basis, it was not always possible to do so, and payments were accepted in pounds sterling, in francs, in marks, and in other European currency, sometimes much depreciated. Yet, translating foreign money into terms of the dollar at average rates of exchange, and adding in the $400,000,000 received from France, we reach a total of approximately $800,000,000 received by the United States for the entire quantity of American military property left in Europe after the return of the expedition. It is roughly estimated that the property thus sold cost the United States $1,328,000,000. The salvage return, therefore, was practically 60 per cent of the cost. The miscellaneous sales transactions have practically all been closed, and the receipts have been covered into the Treasury. The French $400,000,000 is represented by bonds maturing in 1929.

The two blanket transactions with France—the bulk sale of buildings and supplies and the general settlement of claims—were of great value to the United States in relieving this nation of the responsibility of having to deal with individual French claimants. In taking over all the A. E. F. installations the French Government agreed to hold the United States harmless from all claims for property damage and restoration. In the general settlement the French Government assumed responsibility for all other claims of French nationals against the United States and agreed to settle with the claimants. If, however, the claims paid by France exceed 12,000,000 francs, America is bound to pay the excess up to 6,000,000 francs. Except for this arrangement, the American Government would have had to maintain in France for years an organization for dealing with French individuals' claims.

We are now in position to see in close approximation the financial result to the United States of the international war business. On the credit side we have the Cuthell settlements, amounting to $48,716,080.99 in all—this figure, however, not including the Cuthell Board's settlement with the French, the debt of France on her American war contracts being carried over into the general settlement effected by the United States Liquidation Commission. We have, as a further credit, the 6,000,000 francs which were the American share of the French payment in the liquidation of the Anglo-American heavy tank project. Finally, the general settlement of the Liquidation

Commission with the French Government brought to the Treasury the further sum of $28,000,000. To all these credits must be added the $800,000,000 received from the sale of the A. E. F. property. The sum of all the American credits (counting ten francs as a dollar) is approximately $877,000,000.

From this credit, however, we must subtract, first, £17,726,685 13s 13d as the American obligation embodied in the termination contracts made with the British Government by the Liquidation Commission, and £2,946,511 2s 8d as our debt to England under the Burr-Niemeyer Agreement. We must subtract also the $3,568,653.23 paid by the A. E. F. in cancellation charges to individual European contractors. A final subtraction is the 437,985,399.73 francs paid by the Liquidation Commission for port dues and for the transportation of the A. E. F. on French railroads. Translating pounds sterling and francs into dollars at average exchange rates, the total debit of the United States is found to have been about $120,000,000. The net balance, therefore, in favor of the United States as a result of the international war industrial transactions was the sum, approximately, of $757,000,000.

CHAPTER XIX

THE BALANCE SHEET

WHAT did the war cost America? It may be that an accurate answer to that question will never be given. Certainly it cannot be given now, when the stocks of surplus materials are still being sold and the final settlements of the more difficult claims are still being made. Still, we can arrive at a fair approximation of what the war cost the War Department alone. In doing so we must deal with billions of dollars in our columns, and therefore errors and differences of a few millions, or even of a few hundred millions, have no important effect upon the totals. Even if all costs and credits could be figured out to the penny, the result would not be much unlike the estimates which follow.

As a starting point we can take the appropriations for the Army made by Congress, since all the war costs of the War Department must be included within those appropriations. And we find that for the Army Congress appropriated in all, for every war purpose, the sum of $24,373,274,223.67. But not all these appropriations were expended. Some were made late in the war, and none of the money authorized by these acts to be spent was even obligated before the armistice terminated all proposed new projects. Congress hastened to repeal the untouched appropriations, and the various repeal acts canceled authorizations to the amount of $7,703,448,569.36. Therefore, the net amount made available to the War Department by the war appropriations was $16,669,825,654.31.

This figure still does not represent the gross war cost of maintaining the War Department, but it is close to it. Since final expenditures and reimbursements have not yet been determined, but are still growing, as claims are paid and surplus property is sold, it is necessary that we accept a date somewhere and examine the ledger on that day, and from this examination we may be able to estimate closely the final figures. The date chosen here is April 17, 1920,—a day far enough this side of the armistice to bring the figures fairly close to their ultimate and conclusive form. By that day the Army was almost completely demobilized, the liquidation of the Army's foreign affairs was virtually complete, the demobilization of the domestic war industry was approaching the end, and the greater part of the surplus war supplies had been sold.

On April 17, 1920, then, we find that the actual expenditures of the War Department had reached the total of $16,276,288,337.19. This was within $400,000,000 of the net war appropriations, the difference, of course, being in the Treasury as unexpended balances available to those paying the final war bills of the War Department. Yet this expenditure cannot be labeled the cash cost of the war to the Army. We must first make several large deductions for money derived from sales of materials and, especially, for the property on hand set aside for the permanent Army and for the military readiness of the United States.

The foreign liquidation, as we have seen, recovered into the Treasury approximately $757,000,000. On April 17, 1920, the sales of military property in the United States had brought in the sum of $641,261,000. Transfers of army property for use by other departments of the Government—a proper credit—involved materials valued at $42,096,000. On the date selected there still remained in the United States surplus, but unsold, army property valued at $600,000,000. The average recovery from the sale of surplus within the United States was about 75 per cent of the cost. Assuming that this ratio would hold throughout the entire liquidation, we can anticipate a cash recovery of $450,000,000 from the surplus still existing on April 17, 1920.*

These reimbursements, however, even in the aggregate, con-

* Due to the slump in business and prices in 1921, this estimate is probably too high.

stitute a minor credit when compared with the value of the equipment left by the war enterprise to be the inheritance of the permanent establishment and to be insurance of the continued safety of the United States in a world not yet willing to lay down its arms. The property of the War Department at the beginning of the war with Germany was estimated to be worth $500,000,000. At the end of the demobilization the property of the War Department was worth, at a rough estimate, $6,000,000,000. It is evident, therefore, that this increment in value—$5,500,000,000—represents present useful property, and that it must be subtracted from the expenditures in order to arrive at the net cost of the war itself. This valuation of property on hand, incidentally, does not include the value of real estate and buildings acquired during the war and retained in use afterwards, since it has never been fully determined as yet which of these installations will be kept.

The deductions, then, on account of sales and on account of property retained, amount to $7,390,000,000, and this is the gross credit on the war page of the army ledger. To find the net cost of the war proper, we must subtract this from the gross expenditures, and we must do this roughly; because with transactions so large, indefinite, and complicated, it becomes absurd to reduce the figures to cents or even to thousands of dollars. The rough subtraction gives us the figure $8,885,000,000, which is not many millions away from the actual net cost. This, of course, represents cost to the War Department alone. It does not include the Navy's costs, nor those of the United States Shipping Board, nor of the United States Railroad Administration, nor any costs of other great and expensive war enterprises which properly must be added in to give the full score of the cost of the war to the United States.

This net cost, this sum of $8,885,000,000, represents what the Government paid in transporting the 4,000,000 men of the Army, in feeding them, clothing them, and providing them with all other sorts of expendable supplies which they actually consumed, and in paying the troops their wages. The supply cost, of course, includes the cost of the industrial liquidation after the armistice and the losses from the shrinkages and wastes of war. The whole bill comes out at about $2,200 a man.

This, too, is but the direct cash cost, the cost in money. The intangible costs, which are never brought into a tabulation of this kind, are, after all, the true costs of war. They include the 50,000 American soldiers killed in battle in Europe. They include also the 200,000 Americans who were wounded in the fighting—some of them still, two and a half years after the armistice, in hospitals and thousands of them facing life with permanently impaired bodies. These usually unreckoned costs, too, include the 57,000 who died of disease or accident while in the service.

But beyond these losses of life there were other profound penalties which the people paid and are still paying. These, too, must be set down to the account of war in any complete reckoning. One of them was the greatly increased cost of almost everything necessary to sustain life and render it pleasant, including particularly an increase of rentals, bringing with it, as a natural consequence, the overcrowding of living quarters, to the detriment of the health of those existing in such conditions. The high costs of living are aggravated by the special war taxes laid everywhere, taxes which, in one form or another, must be imposed for many years to come in order to pay for the losses of the war.

There were, moreover, spiritual losses—an incredible moral slump from the national exaltation of the war to the bickering and bitterness of the demobilization. Governments fell as the war-ridden peoples of the earth blindly and brutishly vented their spleen and irritation for the hardships they had experienced upon those who chanced to be in power. Erstwhile statesmanship lapsed into a narrow, advantage-seeking partizanship that regarded not, it sometimes seemed in this country, even the fate of the world. The United States turned its back upon the League of Nations, which was the most ambitious attempt ever made by the nations of the earth to substitute a rule of reason for the rule of force.

But if we recite these and other intangible and indirect costs that might be named, then we are equally justified in looking for the benefits derived from our participation in the war; and we find these benefits to be great ones. First of all, we gained the victory; and that alone, and especially so because the cause of America was righteous, was worth all it cost in blood and money and burdens shouldered for the future. We gained, moreover, a state of preparedness for war that would have been impossible of attainment under any other circumstances. In the reserves of supplies we have equipment ready to arm 1,000,000 men as rapidly as they can take the field. In the reserves of machinery we have a potential war industry capable of maintaining such an army until industry generally can take up the manufacture of munitions. Not again during the existence of the present generation should we, if the emergency came, have to experience the uncertainties and delays of 1917 in the production of supplies. We have within our war reserves the machinery and the materials for producing all the more difficult sorts of munitions, and we have, moreover, preserved records of how to produce them.

Then, again, the health of the nation has presumably gained a benefit from the experience. Hundreds of thousands of young men were removed from sedentary occupations and placed in the vigorous, ordered, athletic regimen of camp life. Several months of this, on the average, did not fail to have its effect, and the medical records of the Army showed a marked increase in the average weight of soldiers during the war. Akin to this consideration is the fact that men were picked up from farms, villages, and city neighborhoods and transported to distant parts of the earth. This travel broadened thousands of them, quickened their ambition, and strengthened their life purposes. Moreover, the men of the Army were thoroughly mixed in the ranks and services. The boy from Maine fraternized with the one from Arizona, and Illinois and Virginia sent their sons to be comrades. Sectional, national, and even racial lines disappeared in the ranks. This extensive regional interacquaintanceship is to-day a national asset. The infiltration of 4,000,-

000 men who secured these individual benefits into the civilian life of America is calculated to elevate the physical, mental, and moral tone of the whole nation and to improve America's homogeneity.

Other benefits might be named. The principle of selective military service has been established by the precedent set in the World War. As long as that experience is remembered there will be no danger that America would ever return, in any serious emergency, to the unscientific volunteer system that takes the brave and the enterprising and leaves behind the indolent and timorous. Above all, we must count as gain from the war the confirmation it gave us in our faith in our ability to continue our existence as a nation. The experience demonstrated that our national resources include not only valor in arms in boundless quantity, but also the ability to organize effectively a nation as great as ours for a purpose as complicated as modern war has come to be. The experience in 1917 and 1918 gave us a firm foundation for national self-confidence.

These are all benefits and gains which may properly be set off against the intangible costs of the war. Among the benefits secured, however, is not yet one which we might, in 1917 and 1918, have expected to find there. The American host which crossed to France went, almost to a man, uplifted and made heroic by the feeling that it was an army of crusaders fighting to end wars forever. No mere instinct of self-preservation, no simple prospect of a victory over a strange, foreign enemy in gray uniforms, could have inspired the morale of the American Expeditionary Forces, nor yet that of the forces in training in the United States, nor that of American industry in its eager, headlong devotion to the national undertaking. This was to be Armageddon, the last of wars, the war to make safe the unwarlike peoples of the world; and no cynical dictum that man is still too near his neolithic savagery to rely on anything other than might in his international contentions, no Chauvinistic picture of new migrations of Asiatic hordes, can change the fundamental fact that America went to war in the belief that its chiefest object was to end war forever. Until we have made some national attempt to secure that benefit, the page will not balance.

INDEX

PRINTED IN THE UNITED STATES OF AMERICA